The 'New Right' Enlightenment

To Tim

You may find chapter 12
of particular interest.

Happy Birthday

Z. & Shiley

February 1995 .

The 'New Right' Enlightenment

The Spectre that Haunts the Left

Essays by Young Writers Mustered by
Arthur Seldon

John Burton	Tim Janman
Mark A. Smith	Chris Tame
Marilyn Daljord	Matthew Lynn
Nigel Ashford	Stephen Davies
Peter Saunders	Andrew Melnyk
Janet Parrett	Martin J. Anderson
Graham Dawson	Chandran Kukathas
Peter Clarke	Robert Miller
Brian Micklethwait	David Green
Christopher Knight	Marc Henri Glendening

Heralded by F. A. Hayek

First published in 1985

by

Economic and Literary Books
PO Box 193, Sevenoaks,
Kent TN15 0JW

British Library Cataloguing in Publication Data

The 'New Right' enlightenment:
the spectre that haunts the Left.
1. Great Britain — Economic policy — 1945 —
I. Seldon, Arthur
330.941'0858   HC 256.6

ISBN 0-948115-01-7
ISBN 0-948115-02-5   Pbk

Printed in England by

GORON PRO-PRINT CO LTD

6 Marlborough Road, Churchill Industrial Estate, Lancing, W. Sussex

Filmset 'Berthold' 10 on 11pt Century

CONTENTS

SOCIALISM, LIBERALISM AND THE YOUNG

FREDERICK HAYEK, *Nobel Laureate, Companion of Honour*

In my lifetime I have witnessed a remarkable reverse in the attitude of young people to the conflicting appeals of socialism and liberalism.

From my early days in the 1920s until very recently young people were strongly attracted to the 'left' in politics, philosophy and economics — from collectivist communism to socialist 'planning'.

Throughout the 1930s, when I came to the London School of Economics, the uncritical approval of Soviet communism, the state economy of the 1939-45 war, the euphoria of post-war low inflation, and as long as Keynesian full employment continued into the 1960s and 1970s, the young tended to look to the state and showed relatively little interest in the market.

My *Road to Serfdom* in 1944, which I dedicated to socialists in all parties, attracted more criticism from older people than agreement from the young. *The Constitution of Liberty* in 1960 did not do much to reverse the trend. As late as the early 1970s it seemed to me that hardly anyone was listening to the argument for liberalism. But in the last 5 or 10 years I have seen a change I never thought would come — mostly in the USA but also in Britain, in the Scandinavian countries, in the Netherlands, in the Far East, and even in France where I thought it least likely.

Now young people are anxious to learn the forgotten truths of the classical economists. They are increasingly studying liberalism in the universities. And they want to hear how the classical principles can be applied to the contemporary anxieties of their day.

I therefore welcome this book arranged by Arthur Seldon of essays by young economists, political scientists and philosophers. And I am not surprised to hear that many of them began their intellectual lives on the Left. I understand they have lost the faith in the state that induced them to embrace socialism. These essays could have been written, with variations according to national conditions, by young people in many other countries. I think I know how they feel, since I was also for a time misled by socialism in my early days.

The socialist argument continues despite its many defeats — on the impossibility of economic calculation under collectivism, the fallacious claims for the use of markets under socialism, the incompatibility of liberty and state direction of the economy, and many others. The argument is being won by the new liberals of the late 20th century. But many people still do not understand it. And most on the Left continue to resist it.

I have been in the habit of saying that if the politicians do not ruin the world in the next 15 years there is hope for liberty. For some time I have been writing a book, *The Fatal Conceit*, to show the deceit that the teachers of socialism have practised for a century. If more young people come to see the pretences of socialism and understand the liberal thinking and ideas the critics call 'the New Right', which this books calls *The New Enlightenment*, there is yet hope for Western civilisation and mankind.

F.A.H.

'CLASH AT DARK SATANIC MILL'

The Bewildered Left   the Assertive 'New Right'

THE SPECTRE THAT HAUNTS THE LEFT

ARTHUR SELDON

I rejoice in the ease with which I assembled these young people to write on what, despite the 'New Right' in the title, they and I see as a modern refinement, sharpening and application of classical Scottish and English liberalism: the New Enlightenment.

When I first learned of liberalism nearly half a century ago at the London School of Economics from Frederick Hayek, Lionel Robbins and Arnold Plant, Frank Paish, George Schwartz and Ronald Coase, I was intellectually excited by finding a superior alternative to the socialism I had briefly imbibed from a Fabian teacher at school. Since then I have had a satisfying life of research, thinking, writing and applying liberalism to the distribution of property (in a report for the Liberal Party in 1938 as a raw graduate), after the war to shopkeeping, licensing, pensions, hire purchase, advertising and the welfare state, in the last ten years to unemployment, local government, democracy, tax rejection, capitalism and socialism. 'Mustering' these authors and assembling their essays has been one of the most rewarding tasks I have undertaken.

Since 1956 I have applied this thinking at the Institute of Economic Affairs, the main intellectual rallying ground of the liberal counter-revolution against the state. Historians, rightly or wrongly, are recording it also as the source of the radical economic liberalism that took Mrs Thatcher's Conservatives to electoral triumph in 1979 and 1983. But ideas are not a party monopoly: liberalism cannot be cornered. And the best hope for it lies in competition between the new liberal Conservatives and a second political grouping or coalition, which some see as possibly emerging with the advent of the new Social Democratic Party if it loses its lingering collectivist tendencies.

The 'New Right' appears in the title because that is how this new/old British school of thought is known to the general public, who are intrigued or puzzled by it. But 'New Right' is the derogatory description used by critics who dismiss the new liberalism as reactionary because it rejects the post-war all-Party consensus based on Fabianism, Beveridgism and Keynesianism: the notions that the state could, and would, run industry efficiently, ensure security and welfare for all, and cure unemployment and inflation.

In this book the 'New Right' as a title is condemned by most of the essayists as a pejorative description of modern classical liberalism — the New Enlightenment that most of them, explicitly or implicity, portray. It is neither new nor right (-wing).

The essayists differ in their social origins, education, work, Party sympathies, and in how they see 'the New Right', but, with two deliberate exceptions, they unite in rejecting the state as the source of the good life. In its place they see individual dignity, liberty and sovereignty better assured in the market. The two exceptions, chosen as independent critics, are a University academic, who sees 'the new Right' as half right (and half wrong), and an observer writing a doctoral thesis on its impact in education, a subject as good as any to indicate how the influence of the 'New Right' is exerted for good or ill.

*   *   *

I chose the writers as young people with whom I have worked as colleagues at the Institute of Economic Affairs, or as authors of IEA Papers or *Economic Affairs* articles, or whose thinking I know from their writings or speeches. I considered that, although young, or *because* they are young, they were independent in spirit, fresh in their thinking, and self-confident in their adherence to aspects of classical philosophic liberalism. In some, their assertion of liberalism may derive from earlier attraction to socialism, in others from finding themselves expected to support statist policies as Conservatives.

The importance of this book is that it shows the way the wind is blowing. I present it as an account of what more young people will be thinking, and older people in all political Parties applying to policy, in the three decades ahead. The British have seen the state as all-powerful for nearly half a century, and now they are restive. Academics in all schools of thought and politicians in all Parties who ignore the evidence of their eyes, and continue to tell the British they are incompetent to run their lives and must have them run by political activists and bureaucrats, will be unceremoniously ignored in the 1990s.

The state will be rejected overseas as well as in Britain because it is not equipped to run a modern complex economy. The peoples of Eastern Europe vividly understand, even if they cannot denounce, the blundering incompetence of the state, and they will follow the peoples of Western Europe and North America.

It will become easier to reject the state as rising living standards (despite, not because of, state influence in the economy) enable more people down the income scale to escape to the market, even for the two most intimately personal services that politicians and bureaucrats will strenuously struggle to keep under their control — education and health. The essential populism of the market — and therefore its massive potential popularity as the protector against both the insolents of public office and monopolists among private suppliers — is still dawning only gradually.

The escape to which the common people are forced to resort until they are allowed a choice between the state and the market — tax evasion — will steadily spread, and the state will be unable to suppress it.

Not least the scientific revolution, even more rapid now than at any time since and during the industrial revolution, in which we see new labour-saving techniques appear almost daily, will accelerate escape to the market because it will ease the establishment of new services that will be more responsive to individual preferences than the state can provide, again not least in education and medicine. Politicians will not be able to decree the pace of economic reform. If they inhibit change, they can do so for a time only by coercion.

In terms of political parties it seems to me the future for several decades lies between the New Conservatives and the new Social Democrats who are emerging as the real liberals in the Alliance by reacting against the over-centralised state economy and understanding the market as the means to create decentralised institutions. They will also increasingly see that it is the only mechanism revealed by history by which man can submerge his myopic interests as a producer to his long-term, elemental interests as a consumer, and therefore as the *only* way to avoid the feudalism, mercantilism, socialism, corporatism, and syndicalism that have caused society to seize up and break down.

*   *   *

The title of this introduction and the sub-title of the book is borrowed from the opening line of Stephen Davies' essay, which echoes the opening sentence of Karl Marx' and Friedrich Engels' *Communist Manifesto* of 1848: 'A spectre is haunting Europe — the spectre of communism'. The difference is that the spectre of 1848 has plagued the world; the New Enlightenment will destroy the spectre of 1848.

We have had a century of increasing power wielded by government in the person of politicians and bureaucrats who have claimed to represent the people but have yielded to organised pressure groups. They have invaded and usurped the authority of individuals in industry, commerce, agriculture, scholarship, art, health, housing, even in the intimate life of the family. 'Politics is for People' is the title

[xiii]

of a book by Mrs Shirley Williams. *Politics is for political people.* But political people are no longer uncritically accepted as providers of the good life.

What is known philosophically as socialism, technically-economically as collectivism, politically as the Left has had a long run of 150 years or more, but its high moral tone and unexceptional aspirations no longer suffice to conceal the tyrannies it has produced everywhere that subject mankind to indignity, penury, and conflict. Socialism is a disease of adolescence. I was lucky to escape it early. Many have harboured it much longer. Some have died uncured. But it is now being rumbled by the young.

These essays comprise a message of good cheer to men and women of all ages. For the disintegration of collectivism as an economic system will free mankind to turn to the liberalism of the 'New Right' Enlightenment that offers new/old solutions for the task of producing adequacy and increasing plenty without trampling on humanity.

'Classical' liberals who understand the market have for decades been derided by the Left which does not. These essays are a counter-attack from the young. I hope sympathisers and critics alike will read them with the intention of understanding the argument and assessing it so that we may all approach nearer to the truth.

September 1985   *Arthur Seldon*
Godden Green, Kent

Acknowledgements

I have to thank Marjorie Seldon, author of the first E & L book *Poppies and Roses*, for discussing aspects of our second book as it developed, Professor Frederick Hayek, belatedly acknowledged as the father of contemporary liberalism, for 'heralding' the essays, Jeanette Giblin, whose art-work for *Poppies and Roses* drew universal admiration, for designing the cover, Martin Anderson for reading the early drafts for literary infelicities, Richard Willson for the telling cartoon, Ruth Croxford for patiently keeping track of drafts, correspondence, biographical notes and photographs with her accustomed aplomb, not least, Goron Pro-print for their sensitive service.

I thank all 20 essayists for contributing their thoughts and several for bearing with my editing and suggestions.

A.S.

I

HISTORICAL

DAVID GREEN

David Green begins the book with an historical survey of the changing attitudes of the British to the state as protector, provider and liberator.

He was born in 1951 in Thetford in rural Norfolk. His father was a village schoolteacher.

He was educated at a local authority boarding school in Norfolk.

He studied Political Science and Sociology at the University of Newcastle upon Tyne from 1970 to 1973. He then did postgraduate research at Newcastle, which earned him a doctorate in 1980.

As a student much of his energy was absorbed by the community action movement. He served as Secretary and Chairman of Student Community Action Newcastle, which organised community service as well as operating as a pressure group. He was Secretary of the advice centre financed by Shelter in Newcastle's then notorious West End. For nine years from 1972 to 1981 he was a Labour Party activist and for six years from 1975 to 1981 sat on Newcastle City Council as a Labour Councillor, acting as Chairman/Vice Chairman of a number of committees or sub-committees.

*Since 1981 he has written three books (*Power and Party in an English City, *Allen & Unwin, 1981;* Mutual Aid or Welfare State *(with L. Cromwell), Allen & Unwin, 1984; and* Working-Class Patients and the Medical Establishment, *Maurice Temple Smith, forthcoming, 1986). He is now working on a book on the New Right commissioned by Wheatsheaf Books. He has also written for a wide range of journals.*

In his essay David Green writes of the transition of the British allegiance/culture from liberalism to socialism and now back. He explains this trend by the reaction against the view of the state, taught by Fabian socialism, that it could be regarded as the beneficient source of the good life in favour of the view that it has failed both as a protector of the weak and provider of desirable services. He argues that the 'New Right' now draws strength from the view of the classical attitude that the citizen requires protection against the state.

[2]

1

FROM SOCIALISM TO THE NEW LIBERALISM

DAVID GREEN

Interest in what is called 'the New Right' is growing. Indeed, some would say that the market perspective is the dominant standpoint of the day. This belief is not unfounded, but it is not shared by large sections of the middle-class salariat. Here the post-war left-wing orthodoxy continues to hold sway. There are thus two interesting questions. First, why is there a growing interest in the ideas of the New Right? And second, why, in spite of this revival of interest, is there such strong resistance to New-Right thought among the intelligentsia?

Why the growing interest in the New Right?

Why is interest in market ideas growing, and in particular, why are elements of the traditional Left turning to the New Right?

One of the main reasons that many people have identified themselves with the Left in general, and the Labour Party in particular, has been their desire to champion the underdog, to 'do their bit' for fair play and decency. Also important, particularly among intellectuals, has been the belief that socialism was the best, perhaps the only, way to achieve liberty. This belief is, ironically, articulated by Mr Tony Benn. He writes, for instance, in *Parliament, People and Power*, (1982):

> One of the general functions of a socialist economic policy
> would be to liberate our initiative, our capacity to develop,
> and to allow us to remake our lives for ourselves. This dream
> of real freedom is what inspires socialists all over the world.

Some socialist academics use similar arguments. Dr Steven Lukes of the University of Oxford describes 'individualism' as having to do with the dignity of the individual, self-direction, a 'private existence within a public world', and self development. But he contends that 'the only way to realise the values of individualism is through a humane form of socialism' (*Individualism*, 1973). And he claims:

[3]

Whatever the threats to equality and liberty that are posed by the state's control over production and distribution — and whatever the threats to liberty involved in taking equality seriously — it is quite unwarranted to oppose socialist planning and redistribution in the name of those values.

The transition from liberalism to socialism . . . and back

The view of socialists like Benn and Lukes contrasts sharply with the classical liberal view. Classical liberals have tended to see the state not as a force for good but as a potential oppressor which ought to have its responsibilities limited to the protection of its citizens from external threats of violence or internal criminality. The protector state should, in the classical view, maintain a private sphere of free action for each citizen by maintaining individual rights *against the state*, as well as against other citizens. Above all, it should protect the weak from the strong by maintaining a framework of just laws.

Towards the end of the last century this view of liberty came to be called 'negative' liberty, and a 'positive' conception was preferred by some writers such as T. H. Green and L. T. Hobhouse. In their view tha state should become a liberator, using its powers to assist the poor more vigorously and to see 'fair play' in the market-place. Alongside this conception of the state as a liberator lay a third view — that the state should be a provider, to supply each citizen's basic needs. I shall argue that when intellectuals were being converted in droves from liberalism — with its suspicion of the state — to socialism — with its optimistic faith in the potential of the state for good — it was the conception of the state as a *liberator* that inspired them. Many socialists never favoured either Fabian paternalism or Marxist authoritarianism. But imperceptibly these doctrines took hold of left-wing thought and, particularly since World War Two, socialism has ceased to value the liberation of the individual, preferring in its stead full-blooded collectivism.

Why is there an increased interest in liberty today? The chief reason is the intellectual conversion of the group of socialists who have always believed socialism to be primarily about liberty. The provider state is now seen by them to have failed to enhance liberty. Many have consequently turned to its liberal opposite for guidance about where to go next. Some are turning to the liberalism of Adam Smith and Herbert Spencer, with the state seen primarily as a protector; and others are turning to the positive liberalism of T. H. Green and L. T. Hobhouse. This conversion is reflected in the growing interest in 'market socialism' as well as the 'social market'.

Why was classical liberalism pre-occupied with the rights of the individual against the state rather than with the potential of the state to do good?

The state as protector

The 17th century saw the triumph of individualist principles over the authoritarianism of the church and state, and its history explains why the liberalism of the day was so fiercely opposed to central power. A major grievance in the economic sphere was the royal practice of granting monopolies to favoured individuals or groups in a wide range of products and services. The extent to which monopolies affected the lives of ordinary men and women is revealed in this passage from the Marxist Christopher Hill's *The Century of Revolution* (1970):

> It is difficult for us to picture . . . the life of a man living in a house built with monopoly bricks, with windows (if any) of monopoly glass; heated by monopoly coal . . . burning in a grate made of monopoly iron . . . He slept on monopoly feathers, did his hair with monopoly brushes and monopoly combs. He washed himself with monopoly soap, his clothes in monopoly starch . . . His clothes were held up by monopoly belts, monopoly buttons, monopoly pins. They were dyed with monopoly dyes. He ate monopoly butter, monopoly currants, monopoly red herrings . . . monopoly salt, monopoly pepper, monopoly vinegar. Out of . . . pewter mugs made from monopoly tin he drank monopoly beer made from monopoly hops, kept in monopoly barrels or monopoly bottles, sold in monopoly-licensed ale-houses. He smoked monopoly tobacco in monopoly pipes, played with monopoly dice or monopoly cards, or on monopoly lute-strings. He wrote with monopoly pens, on monopoly writing-paper; read (through monopoly spectacles, by the light of monopoly candles) monopoly printed books . . . .

In 1621 there were around 700 monopolies. Not all affected necessaries. But, as Hill comments, 'monopolies added to the price of just those semi-luxuries which were beginning to come within the reach of yeomen and artisans whose standard of living was rising'.

Royal power was also used oppressively in religious affairs. During the Eleven Years' Tyranny from 1629 until 1640 Archbishop Laud attempted to impose uniformity of worship on Christians. Then opposition to the power of the government began to be effective. The Long Parliament abolished royal monopolies and supported religious tolerance, and in 1649 Cromwell's Commonwealth was established amidst high hopes. But it resulted only in new threats to liberty, this time at the hands of the Major-Generals: they displayed scant respect

[5]

for parliamentary sovereignty and sought to influence parliamentary elections. The Commonwealth was followed in 1660 by the Restoration, when new conflicts between the Crown and Parliament ensued, culminating in the Glorious Revolution of 1688 with the accession of William and Mary.

The 17th century then saw a long battle against central power. Men fought against the compulsory billeting of soldiers in private homes, against arbitrary taxation, censorship by church or state, religious persecution, church courts, the monarch's ability to use force through the possession of his own army, and against royal monopolies. As a result the English idea of liberty came to be concerned above all with the rights of the individual *against the central authority*.

The rights of the individual were won by establishing *absolute* rights against the state, especially absolute rights in property. And until well into the 19th century this idea was shared by the poorest sections of English society. William Cobbett, for example, the great radical spokesman for the poor, opposed on traditional individualist grounds the repression which characterised the years during and just after the Napoleonic wars of 1793 to 1815. Arguing against the Combination Acts which repressed trade unions, he described labour as the only property of the poor and demanded the same rights for labour as for other property:

> The principle upon which all property exists is this: that a man has a right to do with it that which he pleases. That is, he has a right to sell it, or keep it. That he has a right to refuse to part with it at all; or, if he choose to sell it, to insist upon any price that he chooses to demand: if this be not the case, a man has no property (*Political Register*, 1818)

How did this view come to be abandoned? During the early years of the 19th century men who favoured 'negative' liberty were stalwart defenders of the poor. Certainly they did not regard extensions of state power as of any service to poor people. But as industrialisation spread so the threats to the health and well-being of individual workers grew. The traditional concern to limit the powers of the state seemed inappropriate to many who otherwise held liberal views. It appeared to be the only instrument available for rectifying certain evils, and the risk of destroying freedom was discounted.

The state as liberator

Such thinking had a considerable effect on practical public policy throughout the century, but it was not until the 1880s that it was fully articulated as a distinct standpoint. T. H. Green, writing in 1881,

[6]

questioned the extent to which freedom of contract should be tolerated. He argued that:

> freedom of contract, freedom in all the forms of doing what one will with one's own, is valuable only as a means to an end. That end is ... freedom in the positive sense: in other words, the liberation of the powers of all men equally for contributions to a common good.

Property rights, he contended, should be limited by this principle. No-one, he continued:

> has a right to do what he will with his own in such a way as to contravene this end. It is only through the guarantee which society gives him that he has property at all, or, strictly speaking, any right to his possessions. This guarantee is founded on a sense of common interest. Every one has an interest in securing to every one else the free use and enjoyment and disposal of his possessions, so long as that freedom on the part of one does not interfere with a like freedom on the part of others, because such freedom contributes to that equal development of the faculties of all which is the highest good for all. This is the true and the only justification of right of property.

On these grounds Green supported state intervention in the markets for labour, education and housing. Restrictions may have to be placed on labour contracts 'to prevent labour from being sold under conditions which make it impossible for the person selling it ever to become a free contributor to social good in any form'. This, he said, 'is most plainly the case when a man bargains to work under conditions fatal to health'. The purchase or hire of 'unwholesome buildings' is also 'properly forbidden on the same principle'. And the state is entitled to make education compulsory on the same ground: 'Without a command of certain elementary arts and knowledge, the individual in modern society is as effectually crippled as by the loss of a limb . . ..' He is not free to develop his faculties.

Writing just before the First World War, L. T. Hobhouse approached the issue in a manner similar to Green's. Liberalism, he acknowledged, is often seen as opposed to restraint as such. But, he asserted; 'all social liberty rests upon restraint ... the restraint of one man in one respect is the condition of the freedom of other men in that respect ...' (*Liberalism*, 1911). He favoured the use of the power of the state, but only where

> the object of compulsion is to secure the most favourable external conditions of inward growth and happiness so far as

[7]

these conditions depend on combined action and uniform observance . . . . There is no true opposition between liberty as such and control as such, for every liberty rests on corresponding acts of control.

So Hobhouse favoured state-imposed restraint as long as it increased the chances of an individual for self-direction and self-realisation. Or, in the words of his contemporary, J. A. Hobson:

each enlargement of the authority . . . of the state must justify itself as an enlargement of personal liberty, interfering with individuals only in order to set free new and larger opportunities . . . (*The Crisis of Liberalism*, 1909)

The state as provider: Fabian socialism

During the 1880s and 1890s collectivist ideas began to grow in influence. For collectivists the whole individualist approach was wrong; neither negative freedom from arbitrary political power nor positive freedom to realise personal talents offered a satisfactory way forward. Individualism was seen as selfishness in disguise. Men, it was said, had a choice between selfishness and co-operation: on the one hand there was competition, with its naked pursuit of profit; and on the other, there was co-operation, with its common purpose and fraternalism. Unlike 'positive' liberals, collectivists rarely talked of removing constraints in order to release individual potential. They emphasised the elimination of 'wasteful' competition and the achievement of common purpose through 'democratic' co-operation. The state machine was to be used to improve the well-being of the people. This was the socialism of the Webbs, Shaw and the early Fabians. They placed only one limitation on the use of the powers of compulsion available to the state: they must be approved by the popular assembly, Parliament, which was held to be accountable to and representative of the people.

Closely allied to this 'democratic' collectivism was a second set of ideas, 'authoritarian' collectivism. It differed from its democratic cousin in one sense: there was no nonsense about being accountable to the population. No limits were placed on the use of state power. Any action was good if it was approved by the state as in the real interest of the nation, race, class . . . . In both Fascism and Soviet Communism the idea that there should be any limit on the actions of the state was derided. Lenin wrote, for instance, that:

We recognise nothing private. Our morality is entirely subordinate to the interests of the class struggle of the proletariat.

[8]

And Giovanni Gentile, the Fascist, wrote in the 1920s:

And so, nothing private, and no limits to state action.

The liberal socialist tradition

These distinctions were well understood by the liberal socialists of the early part of this century. Hobhouse distinguished between three kinds of socialism: mechanical socialism (which I have called authoritarian collectivism); official socialism (called here democratic collectivism); and liberal socialism (in which, in the terminology of this essay, the state is seen as a liberator).

Mechanical socialism, according the Hobhouse, had three attributes:

1. It was based on a false interpretation of history: it attributed the phenomena of social life and development solely to the 'economic factor'. Here Hobhouse was referring to crude Marxism.
2. It supposed a class war, resting on a clear-cut distinction of classes which, asserted Hobhouse, 'does not exist'.
3. It proceeded by the construction of a utopia which makes insufficient provision for liberty, movement and growth. The fancied clearness of its utopian vision was, Hobhouse said, illusory, because its objects were ideas, not facts.

Official socialism, maintained Hobhouse, had two main attributes:

1. It began with a contempt for ideals of liberty based on a confusion between liberty and competition; and it proceeded to a measure of contempt for average humanity in general.
2. It saw mankind as a helpless and feeble race which it was its duty to treat kindly. True kindness must be combined with firmness and the life of the average man must therefore be organised for his own good.

Hobhouse preferred liberal socialism. It had two properties:

1. It must be democratic: it must come from below and not from above.
2. 'It must give the average man free play in the personal life for which he really cares.' It must make for the development and the suppression of personality. Its aim should be to secure 'the conditions of self maintenance for the normal healthy citizen' (*Liberalism*).

Bertrand Russell also clearly saw a distinction between liberal, socialism and collectivism. 'There ought to be', he wrote in *Political Ideals* (1916):

[9]

a constant endeavour to leave the more positive aspects of government in the hands of voluntary organisations, the purpose of the State being merely to exact efficiency and to secure an amicable settlement of disputes, whether within or without its own borders. And with this ought to be combined the greatest possible toleration of exceptions and the least possible insistence upon uniform system.

In education, for instance, he was in favour of the state making education compulsory, but he drew the line there:

The state is justified in insisting that children shall be educated, but it is not justified in forcing their education to proceed on a uniform plan and to be directed to the production of a dead level of glib uniformity. Education, and the life of the mind generally, is a matter in which individual initiative is the chief thing needed; the function of the state should begin and end with insistence on *some* kind of education, and, if possible, a kind which promotes mental individualism, not a kind which happens to conform to the prejudices of government officials.

As the 20th century wore on, the distinctions drawn by Russell and Hobhouse came to be forgotten, and the Labour Party fell more and more under the sway of collectivists blind to the defects of central direction.

Who opposes the new liberalism and why?

Socialist thought developed in three ways. Many traditional supporters of the Left believed that freedom — 'real' freedom — was their goal. But as concrete experience of statism grew, the results appeared more and more disappointing. For some on the Left this evidence of failure was enough. Their chosen aims — in housing, health, education, and social services — had been clear and their chosen method, the state machine, had failed to deliver planned gains. They drew no artificial boundaries around their search for alternatives.

Others attributed the poor results to a failure to go far enough. If only full-blooded socialism were tried, they believed, the results would come. Some could accept that there had been failures of individuals, leadership, or in the details of public policy; but the goals and chosen means were held to be essentially right.

Still others tried what appeared to them to be a middle course. Socialism, in this view, need not be abandoned, only *centralised* socialism, The solution lay in the adoption of *de*centralised socialism.

Decentralisation appeared, and continues to appear to many today,

[10]

to be an attractive alternative. But in the main it represents a kind of escapism, for it seeks not to abandon compulsory collectivism but to replace the compulsory collectivism of the central power with the compulsion of the locality, whether local authority or region.

Decentralisation as escapism

In his *Face the Future* (1981) Dr David Owen keenly advocates decentralised socialism as an alternative to bureaucratic socialism. For him the question of decentralisation 'forms the real divide in the politics of the Left'. He finds inspiration from the institutions for mutual aid forged by manual workers during the last century, chiefly the co-ops, the friendly societies, and the early trade unions. To signify that such thinking has a proper, time-hallowed role in the labour movement, he cites a distinction drawn in an early Fabian pamphlet of 1886:

> In other parts of the civilised world . . . Socialist opinion has taken shape in two distinct schools, Collectivist and Anarchist. English Socialism is not yet Anarchist or Collectivist . . . There is a mass of Socialistic feeling not yet conscious of itself as Socialism. But when the unconscious Socialists of England discover their position, they will probably fall into two parties: a Collectivist party supporting a strong central administration, and a counter-balancing Anarchist party defending individual initiative against that administration.

Owen believes (or believed in 1981) that there is a need for a socialist philosophy which 'asserts the radical democratic libertarian tradition of decentralised socialism, which revives the concept of fellowship and community within a participatory democratic society'. By decentralisation he means the devolution of central government powers to regions and localities and local worker participation in industry as opposed to nationalisation.

It is unclear how much devolution is intended, but Owen apparently wishes central government to retain very considerable powers of compulsion. He wants to reduce geographical inequality, presumably by government taking resources from people in some areas to give to other people in other areas.

Mrs Shirley Williams leaves less room for doubt about the extent of her commitment to devolution. She acknowledges the public dissatisfaction with being over-taxed and over-governed and offers more participation and decentralisation as the solution. She has in mind the devolution of some of the powers of central government to regional authorities and to local communities. But her commitment to decentralisation is severely qualified. She favours it only 'whenever it is compatible with social justice' (*Politics is for People*, 1981), and this qualification appears to mean that she is in favour of the compulsory equalisation of material differences between localities.

In practice, therefore, the decentralisers within the SDP — along with like-minded Labour Party members — have tended to opt not for decentralised socialism through autonomous, *self-organised* groups or other voluntary institutions but for adminstrative decentralisation to agents of central and local *government*. The essential distinction is that *this brand of decentralised socialism retains its collectivist character*. The method of arriving at decisions is to be by majority voting among elected representatives. Funding is to be by compulsory taxes, with no citizen free to withold his support from decisions with which he disagrees.

To sum up: decentralised socialism continues to be far removed from the liberal socialism of Hobhouse and Russell. The recent return of enthusiasm for decentralisation represents a willingness to embrace liberty which is only half-hearted. The chief reason for this uneasy compromise is a simple mistake. Advocates of decentralisation believe themselves to be in favour of change which will enhance liberty, but they have failed to appreciate the extent to which their thinking remains *collectivist*.

Egoism and altruism

Why is there a continuing reluctance by many on the Left to take seriously the new liberalism of the New Right, particularly among sections of the salaried middle class? There are many explanations, but two factors stand out. Ironically, they are opposites: selfishness and altruism.

Many of those who favour the current degrees of state provision are the very officials who man the bureaucracies. And it is the middle-class salariat rather than the public-sector blue-collar workers whose selfishness sets them apart. Local government social workers and residential home staff, organised in the trade union NALGO, have taken strike action to maximise their take from the hapless taxpayer. And, more recently, schoolteachers have struck in the hope that the sudden inconvenience and the breaking of their contracts of employment will coerce the Government into raising taxes from the general population so that teachers may enjoy a better lifestyle. It is no coincidence that the voices most strident in their demands for the 'protection of public services' are those of the middle-class government salariat. But their words are hollow, their true aims purely selfish.

Yet not all who resist the new liberal thought are out for

[12]

themselves. There are many for whom the dictates of conscience were, and remain, the prime cause of their socialism. For this group the intellectual force of the new liberalism is strong, but there remains an emotional barrier of guilt (or even shame) to be crossed. Without paternalistic socialism would not the poor experience more hardship? Would there not be less fair play, more injustice? I encountered this anxiety myself whilst serving as a Labour councillor in Newcastle upon Tyne for over five years. It is a powerful sentiment, but it is based on an intellectual error.

There is no automatic association between the provider state and altruism. Altruism lies in the hearts and minds of individuals and it can co-exist with very many kinds of institutions. This is not to argue that institutions count for nothing. Institutions are vital to the creation and maintenance of altruism, and some institutions encourage it more than others. The provider state, ironically, tends to *destroy* the personal sense of duty on which altruism rests. Historically it undermined the spontaneous institutions for mutual aid and charitable assistance evolved over the centuries; and, having undermined them, it encouraged individuals to look to government to help the needy rather than to their own organised endeavours. Historically, altruism flourished alongside classical liberalism. The 19th century high point of *laissez-faire* was also the high point of charitable endeavour. There is no reason why liberty and altruism cannot flourish in tandem again.

Perhaps the strongest allure of socialism for would-be altruists is that it offers a view of the good life. But to take a view about how life should be lived, and about what institutions one would like to see, is quite compatible with support for either the protector state or the liberator state. It would be perfectly consistent for someone to prefer, say, the liberator state to the provider state and within the liberator state to work privately for the development of non-profit institutions. In industrial production the historical omens for workers' co-operatives are not good, although there are some grounds for optimism. In the welfare sphere there are strong grounds for optimism that self-organised mutual aid can supply services both more sensitive to individual needs and more efficient than the provider state (*Mutual Aid or Welfare State; Working-Class Patients and the Medical Establishment*). In a liberator state the individual may personally work for whatever vision of the good life he or she chooses. And without the state to help huge corporations extend their power and wealth at the general expense, and without the crippling rates of personal taxation of the present day, the ensuing wide distribution of income and wealth would enable the individual citizen, by combining his efforts with only a few associates, more easily to put together the resources necessary to back his judgement against the

[13]

wishes either of the government of the day or of any other powerful vested interest.

Socialist dislike of big corporations could also co-exist alongside support for a liberator state. The slogan of the liberal socialist might be, not 'production for use not profit', but 'success only through service'. Companies or workers' co-operatives which grew big through satisfying consumers without resort to force or fraud or anti-competitive connivance with other producers would be entitled to be left alone. But artificial contrivances to restrict competition with the intention of growing wealthy without offering service to others would be outlawed.

Conclusions

So far I have used the term 'New Right' without questioning it. This course was unavoidable because it is the term that has caught on as the popular description of the new liberalism that has made its mark in recent times. But the use of the term is misleading because the old left-right dichotomy is defunct. It implies too sharp a distinction between two self-contained political standpoints. Today this contrast no longer reflects reality. The vital issue in modern politics is the role of the state, and there are more than two alternatives. To suggest, as this essay has done, that there are *three* principal options — the state as provider, protector and liberator — is no less a simplification, but it more nearly reflects political reality than does the ancient two-part left-right divide.

After a long absence from the political agenda liberty is now back in the forefront. But its supporters are already dividing into different camps. There is a group of full-blooded libertarian anarchists who dislike even the protector state. They prefer mutual protection associations in place of the police, and private arbitration instead of law courts. Far more numerous are proponents of the protector state so disliked by anarchists. Equally important is — to paraphrase the 1886 Fabian pamphlet — the mass of libertarian feeling not yet conscious of itself as liberalism. Under banners such as 'market socialism' or the 'social market' many on the left are increasingly edging away from collectivism, with its provider state, and towards the liberal socialism of Bertrand Russell and L. T. Hobhouse, in which the role of the state is that of liberator.

All these groups are very sharply to be distinguished from the collectivists, who increasingly form a rump. They are those who, whether through wilful blindness to the evidence of history, romantic attachment to working-class, envy, organised selfishness, the hatred exemplified in the class-war mentality, Fabian paternalism, the misguided association of altruism with collectivism, or simple inertia,

[14]

adhere to the discredited shibboleths of collectivism. They have yet to understand that liberty is back on the political agenda because of their intellectual defeat by 'the New Right'.

II

FIRST PRINCIPLES

STEPHEN DAVIES

*Part II comprises a group of 6 essays that discuss the main principles
of the New Right. The first opens with a direct challenge to the Left,
Old, New and Nondescript, by adapting Karl Marx's 1848 opening
words of* The Communist Manifesto: *'A spectre is haunting Europe —
the spectre of Communism'. Stephen Davies retorts in 1985: 'Today a
spectre is haunting the political "Left"* . . . *the socialist Left is in retreat
before a new political movement'.*

*Stephen Davies was born in 1955, the son of a metallurgist and
a nurse. He was educated at state primary schools and a grammar
school in Wales and state grammar schools in Scotland. He graduated
from St Andrews University in 1979 with a first class honours MA in
Medieval and Modern History; in 1984 he was awarded the degree of
Ph.D. His two posts so far have been part-time Tutor in Modern
History at St Andrews and, since 1979, Lecturer in the Department of
English and History at Manchester Polytechnic.*

*He writes of his movement away from his parents' and
grandparents' sympathies with Left-wing causes — socialism, trade
unionism — to his present position as a neo-liberal or libertarian.*

*He describes the five roots of the New Right 'revolution of our time':
the theoretical failure of socialism to explain the contemporary world;
the practical failure of socialism wherever it is practised; the failure in
particular in Britain of the Middle Way that vainly tried to combine
socialism with market capitalism (further analysed by John Burton in
essay No. 8); the dissatisfaction with the conventional divisions
between traditional (old) socialist Left and (old) conservative Right;
and, underlying the intellectual revolution, the growing hostility to the
state, seen increasingly not as the solution to problems, the common
error of the old Left and the old Right, but as their cause.*

*He concludes that New Right thinking and policies could be adopted
or adapted by the Social Democrat-Liberal Alliance or even Labour as
well as by the Conservatives.*

2

THE SPECTRE HAUNTING THE LEFT

STEPHEN DAVIES

Today a spectre is haunting the political 'Left'. Throughout Western Europe and North America the traditional, socialist Left is in retreat before a new political movement. In the war of ideas socialism is losing ground and is increasingly lacking in confidence and intellectual vigour. This confession is often made by 'left wing' observers who comment upon the new-found confidence of the 'Right' and the vibrant intellectual activity found in that part of the political spectrum. Remarks such as 'all the new ideas are now coming from the Right' are commonplace. The continuing vitality of feminist and ecological/decentralist analyses only emphasises the bareness of the mainstream socialist movement. The new intellectual movement which has increasingly gained the initiative is most usually called the 'New Right'. (Whether this is an appropriate or accurate designation is doubted in several essays.) Growing awareness amongst 'Left' intellectuals and activists of the 'New Right's' success has led to a flurry of analytical articles and accounts. These, with a few exceptions, reveal more about their authors and the problems facing the 'Left' than they do about their putative subject. (Examples are Nicholas Bosanquet, *After the New Right*, Heinemann, 1982; David Selbourne, *Against Socialist Illusion*, Macmillan, 1984; James Curran, *The Future of the Left*, Polity Press, 1984.)

On reading these works one is forced to conclude that the 'Left' is having severe difficulty in coming to terms with the 'New Right' and in developing an adequate critique of it. In a recent review of two critical works Professor David Beetham (*New Socialist*, February 1984) made precisely this point. Much 'New Right' thought and argument goes virtually unchallenged: there has been no attempt, to give one example, at any fundamental critique of the work of Hayek. Much of the socialist response simply dismisses 'New Right' arguments without any effort at reasoned rebuttal, or misunderstands the nature of these arguments. In detailed policy proposals there is a general lack of new, original socialist alternatives to the proposals of organisations and thinkers supposedly identified with the 'New Right'.

[19]

Most frequently, accounts of new developments in political and social thought which are written from a generally 'Left' perspective simply do not understand the nature of the so-called 'New Right' and hence are unable to come to grips with its arguments. There is a widespread assumption that this movement is reactionary, defends privilege and hierarchy, and is racist, authoritarian and repressive. None of this is true.

The Left is confounded by 'the New Right'

This misunderstanding of the 'New Right' and the failure to come to terms with it have several sources. Sometimes deliberate malice and the desire to smear political opponents by associating them with generally reprobated attitudes is the cause. More often, it reflects a mixture of ignorance and arrogance. The second is easier to see: no attempt is made to rebut many arguments because they are seen as plainly absurd. Surely, the unspoken assumption runs, no reasonable man can believe such things? This attitude reflects the way in which socialist arguments are taken for granted in much intellectual debate and never examined or defended. The ignorance of many commentators is also plain. In a recent work on the history of liberalism (*The Rise and Decline of Western Liberalism*) Professor Anthony Arblaster discusses the revival of neo-liberal economics in a fashion which not only is superficial but simply misunderstands the argument. This failure is in marked contrast to the earlier part of his work which, while hostile to liberalism, is also learned, perceptive and judicious. It is an attitude which is widespread. It leads to a conflation of several distinct intellectual tendencies with the assumption that all share the same beliefs and attitudes.' Thus Professor Arblaster assumes that neo-liberal economists all share the militant anti-communism of the 'cold-war liberals' such as Mrs Jeanne Kirkpatrick.

Three distinct movements are commonly conflated in this way.

First, there is the revival of fundamentalist religious thought, particularly in the United States, in the form of the 'Moral Majority', a movement hostile to personal liberty and particularly opposed to feminism, full freedom of speech and the press, and to social acceptance of homosexuality. There is also a strong tendency towards racism.

Secondly, there is a genuine conservative and right-wing movement which emphasises the importance of values such as hierarchy, authority and tradition and the paramount importance of the nation state as the 'natural' political form. This movement, as yet small, is broadly neutral in its attitude towards the economic order of capitalism, defending it on utilitarian grounds of its efficiency but also advocating a strong interventionist state. In Britain this body of opinion is represented by figures such as Roger Scruton (as in *The Meaning of Conservatism*) and the body of intellectuals associated with *The Salisbury Review*.

Thirdly, there is a movement best described as 'neo-liberal' or, in American terminology, 'libertarian'. It is this which is dominant amongst so-called 'New Right' intellectuals, particularly in Britain.

Obviously it is dangerous to draw hard and fast divisions of this sort — there will always be individuals who straddle categories. But it is even more dangerous to put often fundamentally opposed ideas together and assume that if a person holds one he automatically holds the others as well. Thus Hayek is regularly described as 'conservative' (despite his explicit rejection of this label) and assumed to have views which he rejects.

This conflation derives not only from ignorance but also from the fatal weakness of modern socialist thought — its 'economism'. The assumption that the fundamental divisions in politics are all economic leads to a simplistic, one-dimensional view of politics. In this approach people are graded according to their attitudes towards capitalism — with opponents on the left, and supporters on the right. This sub-division leads to some strange results, with Bolsheviks and anarcho-communists both on the 'left', conservatives, liberals and anarcho-individuals all on the 'right', despite their many and fundamental differences. The idea that beliefs come like grapes in clearly-defined bunches, one marked 'right', the other 'left', is a stubborn hindrance to clear and accurate analysis. Those who know only my views on economics assume that I am very 'right-wing', others who know only my attitudes towards social policy, nuclear weapons and moral issues believe me to be far out on the 'left'. The few who know both sides frequently tell me that I am inconsistent!

Six themes in 'the New Right'

What then is the 'New Right' which so exercises socialists today? Should it perhaps have another name? The dominant tendency amongst people opposed to socialism and collectivism of all kinds is best described as neo-liberal or libertarian. (A good introduction to these names and groups is Professor Geoffrey Sampson's *An End to Allegiance*.) Out of the manifold groups, organisations and individuals in these intellectual currents, six broad themes and arguments can be seen. The most fundamental is individualism — the belief that the individual human being is primary, rather than some collectivity such as society, class, state or nation. The ideal social order is one which allows the maximum scope for individual development and achievement. Morality is seen as being based upon a personal responsibility for one's actions. The individual is commonly seen as

[21]

sovereign, possessed of rights which cannot be restricted or impaired except where their exercise would harm or violate other people's rights. The individualism of the 'New Right' is sometimes derived from a concept of natural law and self-ownership, very often from Kant's notion of people as ends not means, less frequently from religious premises such as the individuality of the soul and the personal nature of any individual's relationship with God.

Second in importance, but most clearly apparent, is anti-statism. Tom Paine's remark that 'Government is at best a necessary evil, at worst an intolerable one' sums up the attitudes of most libertarians. The anti-statism of some 'New Rightists' extends to philosophical anarchism, a fundamental rejection of the legitimacy of states. Most are minimal statists, prepared to tolerate governments but no more. In the economic sphere this view implies support for a policy of 'free market' capitalism, which is defended not only on utilitarian but also on moral grounds. It does not mean uncritical support for the existing economic order — far from it. In the sphere of morality, anti-statism means rejection of attempts to impose moral standards upon individual adults by force. This coercion is seen as both misguided and morally wrong, since it violates the principle of personal responsibility. Actions which are coerced cannot be moral; only those which result from the free choice of the actor qualify. In international politics, anti-statism means hostility to war, militarism and nationalism. The general belief is that government action, in whatever sphere, causes and exacerbates problems rather than solving them. The optimum path is free co-operation through contract and the market mechanism.

The third main element of libertarian 'New Right' thought, which follows clearly from the above is voluntarism. This concept means that voluntary private and local effort is more effective in every way than public (state) action and that society should wherever possible be based upon free, voluntary co-operation for moral as well as practical reasons. It is a way of thinking opposed to the authoritarian principle that people must be coerced into co-operation because they do not know what is best for themselves and that society depends upon certain persons or classes having the power to give orders and be obeyed.

Fourthly, the individualism of this body of thought also leads to hostility to all forms of collectivist doctrines which assert that groups have identities independent of the individuals who compose them and that there are inherent differences between groups which justify different social standing or legal positions. Thus the neo-liberal 'New Right' is hostile to racial, religious and sexual prejudice.

Fifthly, there is fierce hostility to privilege, in the sense of special powers or dispensations acquired by groups and individuals, not by virtue of competition or agreement but rather through the manipulation of political power and thus by force. This approach clearly leads to opposition to the special legal status of trade unions in modern Britain. But, contrary to assumptions made by 'left-wing' commentators, it also entails being against the perks enjoyed by middle-class professions and the owners of capital, as with limited liability. Much 'New Right' objection to the welfare state derives from the way in which in practice it works substantially to the benefit of the better off.

Finally, most libertarian 'New Right' thought is pervaded by two values: rationalism and optimism. Behind much of it lies firm confidence in the power and potential of human reason. This may seem a strange comment, given the hostility of Hayek and many other liberals to utopianism and planning. Yet this paradox is only apparent: Hayek is opposed to the *misuse* of reason and to *mistaken* ideas of its potential. More generally, the 'New Right' is favourable towards science and technology and deeply hostile to the present revival of superstition and irrationality — as in the growth of mystical cults and interest in matters like astrology. Confidence in human reason and in the market as a 'discovery device' — whereby new stratagems and techniques are discovered and tested — mean that most libertarian 'New Right' thinkers have an almost Whiggish confidence in ultimate progress. This attitude is most marked amongst American authors but can be seen among Europeans as well. In particular, there is confidence in the ability of applied intelligence, the market, and technology jointly to produce solutions to social problems. The extreme opposition to technological advance of some in the environmentalist movement are rejected.

Strengths and weaknesses

Is it possible to make an assessment of this body of ideas, its strengths and weaknesses?

There are three main weaknesses. Leaving aside fundamental objections to its basic premises, on, for example, the status of individuals as independent entities, there are clear flaws in the present output of this school of thought. It suffers from the common weakness of all present-day political philosophies in being strongly economistic and excessively concerned with economic issues as opposed to social questions. The overwhelming majority of published works are concerned with aspects of economic philosophy or policy. Subjects such as the social impact of science, aesthetics, relations between the sexes and cultural politics are generally ignored. In particular, the New Right has not yet developed an adequate philosophy and theory of history and historical change. The 19th century philosophy of inevitable progress has been killed by the events of the 20th century, but no liberal replacement has yet evolved. This gap leaves the field clear for Marxism, given the widespread desire for some kind of macro-theory to give order to the past.

Another major weakness of much neo-liberal thought is the absence of a specifically moral dimension. This deficiency is particularly noticeable in many economic works where arguments are proposed and defended upon purely utilitarian grounds. Moral arguments are rejected as being incompatible with the *Wertfrei* status of economics and political science as studies that are not concerned with moral values. Consequently, the moral pass is sold to the opponents of the free society who can claim that their ideal is morally superior; the only available counter-argument is then to attack the practicality of their proposals. This position is not inspiring. Moreover, it leaves the movement open to the charge of being amoral, of ignoring the 'higher' moral issues by hiding behind the tomes of 'dismal science'. There are major exceptions to this rule, thinkers who start from a moral premise, such as the late Ayn Rand or the libertarian psychiatrists Peter Breggin and Thomas Szasz. Yet such figures will remain in a minority so long as the New Right movement is dominated by economics, with its traditional 'value-free' approach.

The third main flaw in many works, is a degree of conservatism, a pronounced tendency to look back to a supposed Golden Age, whether in Victorian Britain or elsewhere. Study of the past can be helpful and informative, but while it may provide suggestions on future action, it is nevertheless hopelessly inadequate as a guide to what is to come. Any intellectual and political movement which sees itself as resisting the 'tendency of history' is bound to fail because of the pessimism and negative outlook which this approach encourages. Fortunately, this last proclivity, hitherto common among opponents of collectivism, is diminishing rapidly.

The strengths of the New Right movement curiously complement its weaknesses. With the dying pessimism arising from almost a century of minority status amongst intellectuals, the movement is increasingly orientated towards the future and confident of its judgement. This sense of confidence lends a feeling of excitement and tremendous future potential to many of its writings. More and more, it is the 'New Right' not the 'Left' who are the utopians, possessed of a vision of how things might be which transcends current reality. By contrast, the 'Left' is disturbed and lacks confidence, and not primarily because of narrow party-political setbacks. The sense of 'Angst' has deeper roots in the perceived failure of socialism in practise and the growing fear that it is incompatible with the 'liberal' ideals of personal freedom.

[24]

Secondly, despite its current economism, the libertarian movement has the potential to move away from this approach. The philosophy of the movement has far broader applications than to narrowly defined economic issues. With the battles in the theories and applications of economics more or less won, the bulk of intellectual activity can move to other subjects. Here the contrast with the 'Left' is marked. Since Marx, socialism has been an economistic doctrine, based upon an analysis of society and history which gives a central place to economic developments and class conflicts. This interpretation of history makes it very difficult for socialists to move away from an economics-based argument without committing various heresies. As the inadequacies of the classical socialist arguments and analyses become more clear, new philosophies and ideas are introduced to fill the vacuum. But this process leads to contradictions, tensions and unresolved dilemmas. The best example is feminism, which has been taken up in a big way by the 'Left' but which cuts across the traditional socialist categories and analyses. The result is growing tension between feminism and socialism, parties from both sides concluding that the time has come for a trial separation, if not a divorce. The potential non-economism of the so-called 'New Right' means that it is not tied to one main form of analysis. It is more open and able to take on board recent development in widely separated intellectual activities, such as biology, psychology and history to give just three examples.

This potentially all-embracing nature of the New Right is its main strength. In intellectual terms what is emerging is a new paradigm — an all-embracing theory covering all aspects of intellectual life. Most Tame in essay No. 20). Such an intellectual revolution in social and political thought seems to happen about once every hundred years. political thought seems to happen about once every hundred years. Certainly, the last such revolution took place in the 1880s and 1890s with the 'rise of collectivism' and the downfall of classical liberalism.

The neo-liberal revolution

But why should such a revolution be happening now and why should it take the form it has? The main movement on the intellectual front is best described as neo-liberal or libertarian. A frequent objection is that this amounts to no more than a revival of 19th century notions. There is undoubtedly much similarity between the ideas circulating today and those urged a hundred years ago by groups such as the Liberty and Property Defence League (below). But the new liberal concepts often show clearly the impact of the intervening years. Thus, the whole discussion of 'public goods' has been transformed by technological developments and the rise of the economics of 'public

[25]

choice'. Nor is current intellectual activity simply a resuscitation of old ideas. Rather, the old generation of thinkers in organisations such as the LPDL (Liberty and Property Defence League) are now being rediscovered as a *consequence* of current developments.

The intellectual revolution of our time has five main roots:

— first, the intellectual crisis of socialism, its growing failure to explain the nature and direction of contemporary events;

— secondly, the increasing evident failure by its own criteria of socialism in practice, which means that it can no longer be held up as an ideal or goal: failure in one country could be blamed on peculiar conditions, but when the same features — loss of liberty, repression, poverty and economic disorder — recur wherever the system is tried, excuses become more difficult;

— thirdly, the failure in practice, particularly in Britain, of the so-called 'Middle Way' of the mixed economy: its showcase society, Sweden, is seen now as a dreadful warning rather than an example as the totalitarian features of the Swedish system become ever more prominent;

— fourthly, the general dissatisfaction with the existing, competing ideologies of conservative 'Right' and socialist 'Left';

— fifthly, the growing hostility to the State, seen more and more as the cause of problems rather than their solution.

This movement of ideas is also affecting the 'Left' as the revival of anarchist and decentralist ideas indicates. Thus much current leftist thinking is critical of the state and advocates a decentralised economy and polity. Here the ideas of authors such as Gorz, Bahro and Hodgson are significant.

A personal intellectual exploration

The development of my own personal beliefs follows this pattern quite clearly. By the time I left school I was quite clear in my own mind about what I did not like but not at all sure what my political/philosophical position really was. My father's side of the family has a long tradition of radicalism — my grandmother had been a member of the Labour party and a trade unionist much of her life, a suffragette and a campaigner for various causes including disarmament. By the time she died she was deeply disillusioned with the practice of socialism and unionism, both at home and abroad. Her, deepest contempt was reserved for Harold Wilson. Wilson's example and the events of the 1960s and early 1970s, such as the Russian invasion of Czechoslovakia in 1968, all pushed me away from any commitment to socialism. I was also repelled by the 'Right', both by its support for the Vietnam War and by its repressive attitudes to personal morality. By the age of 17 I had already decided that I had 'Right' views on economics, 'Left' views on social issues. Then two things happened which crystallised my views. The first was my discovery of two authors who not only introduced me into a whole new world of ideas but also clarified my own beliefs. One was the American science-fiction writer Robert A. Heinlein. Of all his books, *The Moon is a Harsh Mistress*, with its picture of an anarcho-capitalist society, had the strongest impact on me. The other author, whom I discovered quite by chance, was Ayn Rand. Her books — especially *The Fountainhead, Atlas Shrugged* and *Capitalism: The Unknown Ideal* — had a shattering impact on me. They illustrated very clearly that there were other options besides the two package deals marked 'left-wing' and 'right-wing'.

The second event was my going to university. Because I had attended a Scottish school I was unable to go to an English university, and so I went to St Andrews. Here I found that the Conservative Association was the national focus of ideas like those I had just discovered. Through the Association I was introduced to other thinkers, notably Hayek. My position at that point was best defined as 'an old-fashioned Liberal'.

After my graduation I began research. Whilst checking a reference to Milton Friedman's *Monetary History of the United States*, I discovered another book lying beside it on the shelf. It was *The Machinery of Freedom* by David Friedman. Having read it, I was finally able to identify my own politics: I was a libertarian. Then, by seeming chance, I came into contact with the Alternative Bookshop, the contents of which introduced me to the existence of a wider movement and reduced my isolation.

There were four themes concurrent throughout the development of my own political philosophy: disillusionment with socialism in practice and with the failure of the mixed economy in modern Britain; impatience with the arbitrary and unnatural division of 'Right' and 'Left'; and a growing feeling that the dominant intellectual traditions had run out of steam and no longer had any credible solutions.

From principles to policy

What are the implications of the broad philosophical position sketched out above for British politics today? Simple answers do not exist. Put five libertarians together and you will find seven opinions. The broad libertarian principles set out above can be aplied to a wide range of issues. A whole series of reforms can be made in fiscal policy:

— the legal tender laws should be repealed and a move made to a system of free banking unregulated by the state with competing currencies;

[27]

— capital gains tax, stamp duty and capital taxes should be abolished;
— a reform made in income tax by abolishing all reliefs except for a personal allowance with a much lower marginal rate;
— the abolition of national insurance, which is now little better than a pay-roll tax;
— all remaining reliefs for corporation tax should be removed while reducing the general rate.

In general economic policy the aim should be threefold: to encourage as wide a distribution of property as possible; to allow a free, unregulated market in labour, capital, goods and services and therefore to reduce the direct role of the state to a minimum and ultimately to reach an economy of high wages and high productivity. In practice, this aim would require the removal of all subsidies whether through the tax breaks, direct grants or regional aid; the removal of the legal immunities of trade unions and also the special legal privileges of the professions; the deregulation of the labour market by the abolition of wages councils and the repeal of employment protection laws which in effect destroy jobs. Protection against breach of contract, unfair dismissal and other forms of overt exploitation should be ensured by easy access to civil redress in a reformed system of the civil law. The limited liability of the people who finance industry should be restricted and ultimately abolished both on moral grounds and because it tends to concentrate capital and to prevent its movement. Companies should consequently be prohibited from owning shares. Restrictive trade practices should be outlawed. In external trade we should move to a policy of free trade, withdrawing from the EEC if necessary. In particular, Britain should withdraw from international arrangements such as the Multi-Fibres Agreement (now due for renewal) which force up labour costs here and prevent development in the Third World, thus maintaining poverty there.

The structure of welfare benefits should be integrated with the tax system by a negative income tax to replace all existing benefits; and mutual-aid ventures should be deliberately encouraged. As far as education is concerned, direct state provision should be stopped and a move towards a system of finance by voucher or capitation fee. Law-and-order requires radical reform; the present complex criminal code can be drastically simplified, based upon the principle that crimes are acts which harm other individuals. This approach would abolish the concept of 'victimless crimes'. There should be a move away from retribution/reformation to restitution wherever possible, so putting the emphasis upon the victims of crime, the personal responsibility of the criminal and the necessity of re-integrating the criminal into society by his making direct financial or other amends.

[28]

Defence policy centred upon the independent nuclear deterrent should be abandoned in favour of one based upon a Swiss-style 'citizens' army. Scrapping the nuclear element can be defended both on moral and practical grounds. The use of nuclear weapons can never be justified and, as Enoch Powell has argued, the British threat to use them has no credibility since it would involve total self-annihilation. Such a defence policy would almost certainly mean adopting a posture of neutrality, similar to that of Switzerland. It is important to stress that this attitude should not imply moral neutrality between the USA and USSR.

Britain should leave the CAP and abandon the unjust, horrendously expensive system of agricultural subsidy, reverting to a policy of free trade and cheap food. As the recently published works of Richard Body MP show, the present system, which has been followed since 1931, has destroyed much of the countryside, misdirected capital on a massive scale, and harmed the interests of consumers, Third-World countries and most British farmers. It has benefited only a few large land-owners and chemical companies.

All the immigration laws passed since 1963 should be repealed along with the two 'Race Relations Acts'. The immigration laws are racist both in concept and operation and violate personal liberty. Moreover, the historical evidence is that immigration has always benefited the receiving nation. The Race Relations laws are unnecessary because many of the offences covered are crimes under existing laws (e.g., incitement to hatred), while the attempt to outlaw prejudice is self-defeating — in the event these laws have worsened race relations.

Reform the constitution

This survey of some of the practial applications is far from complete. It contains nothing about reform of the legal system, local government, police or the constitution, but some general principles are clear. Although many who share my general views would disagree strongly with some of my specific proposals, there would be agreement with the broad thrust. All of the specific proposals can be defended by the basic principles set out earlier. Most of the proposals could be described as 'negative', involving repeal or abolition. In other words, the general drift is drastic reduction in the scope and power of the state and a returning of power to the people. Finally, although many of these proposals would find a welcome in the present Government, the programme as a whole is not necessarily Conservative or even conservative. It may well be that an Alliance or even a Labour Government will put some of it into effect.

Finally, what of the future? Gazing into crystal balls is a risky activity, but two or three long-term trends do seem to emerge from the last 20 years. There is a general move in all parts of the political spectrum away from planning towards the wider use of markets. The newly elected Labour Governments of Australia and New Zealand have been as radical in this respect as Mrs Thatcher, if not more so. Thus the Hawke administration in Australia has moved towards charging for all health care. Here in Britain there is now a movement among some academics on the 'Left' for a less controlled, more market-orientated economy, as anxiously (or seriously) proposed in Geoffrey Hodgson's *The Democratic Economy*.

Perhaps a new economic consensus is emerging. There is an increasing tendency, again affecting all varieties of politics, towards decentralisation, anti-statism and libertarianism. The 'New Right' may be seen in future years as one part of a more general transformation of politics. The new politics that is starting to emerge is more concerned with broadly non-economic issues — in particular with the implications of science for morality, the nature of the community and general development of society. The current debate over the Warnock Report on 'in-vitro' fertilisation may well be a foretaste of the politics of the 21st century.

NIGEL ASHFORD

The second essay in this group reviews three intellectual forces that developed the New Right.

Nigel Ashford was born in 1952, the son of newsagent parents. He was educated at a Roman Catholic Primary School and Bristol Grammar School. He graduated from Exeter University with a BA in 1973, from Warwick University with an MA, and a doctorate in 1979. Since then he has held lectureships in politics at the Paisley College of Technology, Strathclyde University and, from 1984, at North Staffordshire Polytechnic.

He has written for academic and intellectual journals and has had articles translated into German, Swedish and Norwegian.

He has been active in Conservative politics since 1968.

His three intellectual influences in the New Right are neo-conservatism, the economics of public choice and libertarianism. Neo-conservatism identified six forms of 'government failure', which is also explained by the new school of public choice (known in Britain as the economic of politics), as the growth of government not by its benefits but by the self-interested pressure of politicians, bureaucrats and vested interests. And libertarianism supplemented the utilitarian argument of neo-conservatism and public choice with moral argument that capitalism was superior to socialism. Collectivism is morally as well as politically bankrupt.

3

THE POLITICAL AND MORAL BANKRUPTCY OF COLLECTIVISM

NIGEL ASHFORD

I do not think of myself as a member of the New Right, although that is the label usually placed upon the views I hold. I describe myself as a neo-liberal in my moderate moods or a libertarian in my radical ones. By libertarian, I mean someone who believes in a minimum role for the state: the protection of the individual from external and internal force and the provision of courts as a peaceful means of the resolution of conflicts. (Some anarcho-capitalists who believe that the state should be abolished and all its functions, including defence, handled in the market, also call themselves libertarians.) By neo-liberal, I mean someone who believes in the primary value of liberty, but not necessarily to the exclusion of other values, and in the 'utilitarian' assessment of state action based upon its consequences. Libertarians base their opposition to the state on grounds of principle, particularly because of its coercive nature, and neo-liberals on the harmful consequences of state action. On most issues of policy, the two are in agreement.

I have been a member of the Conservative Party since the age of 15, partly because my image of capitalism was created by my hard-working parents who ran their shop for long hours, burdened by heavy taxation and numerous regulations, and partly because communism represented the worst oppression of the individual. I have always been a Conservative and have never been tempted towards another political party, but I am not a Conservative of the Right. To me, the Right is associated with hostility to social minorities, the enforcement of popular morality by the state, capital punishment, racism, support for South Africa, and xenophobic nationalism. When I was at school and an undergraduate, the symbol for these ideas was (sometimes inaccurately) Enoch Powell, who said some sensible things on economics but otherwise seemed reprehensible, and the instrument for the promotion of these ideas within the Conservative Party was the Monday Club. The modern spokesman for these ideas is Roger Scruton and his *Salisbury Review*. My reaction to Scruton's *The*

Meaning of Conservatism was summed up by the first sentence of my review of it: 'It would be fairly difficult to write a book about conservatism with which this reviewer could disagree more than with this recent interpretation of the conservative view in politics'. It was Scruton's view that state and society has precedence over the freedom of the individual that I found so repugnant. This to me is the Right and I maintain an immense suspicion of it.

I was on the 'left' of the party because the Right was a negative reference point. As a student politician I was most involved with Europe and the liberalisation of social laws. I was a child of the 1960s, rejecting the New Left because of its association with Marxism, its intolerance and its susceptibility to violence, but attracted to the social libertarianism of the counter-culture. My attitude on social issues, my casual life-style (my preference for jeans, my dislike of suits and ties), my taste in music are products of the 1960s. My lack of interest in economics was also a significant characteristic of the time. All this seemed to place me on the 'left' in Conservative politics.

Why then by the mid-1980s was I now considered 'New Right'? My views on the issues that I cared most about then have not changed: freedom to choose one's life-style and the unity of Western Europe as a bulwark against Communism and as a large internal free market. What changed was my intellectual development as a political scientist.

Most libertarians are economists, influenced by the Chicago school of Milton Friedman and the Austrian school of Friedrich Hayek. I am a political scientist and my ideas developed as a result of my pursuit of an understanding of the central concept of my discipline, the nature of the state. Three intellectual forces were fundamental to that development: the neo-conservatives, public choice and the libertarians.

I. *Neo-conservatism*

My interest in the neo-conservatives began when I was a post-graduate student at the University of Kansas in the USA in 1973-74. I did some research for a course on American conservatism and rapidly discovered that I was uncomfortable with the traditionalist conservatism of Russell Kirk and William Buckley of the *National Review*. I then came across two American journals that I found intellectually exciting: *Commentary*, edited by Norman Podhoretz, and *Public Interest*, edited by Irving Kristol and Nathan Glazer. *Commentary* articulated the thinking-man's anti-Communism; *Public Interest* provided analysis after analysis of the failures of government intervention in the USA. These two journals provided the main public platform for the intellectual movement, known (incorrectly) as neo-conservatism, of former left-liberals moving to a more conservative stance. Their most enlightening intellectual

[34]

contribution to me was to demonstrate that the negative unintended consequences of government action were more powerful than the beneficial consequences. Government programmes had to be tested not by the worthiness of their aims but the likelihood that they would be achieved and their full costs.

Neo-conservatism arose from the recognition of the failure of government action, particularly that of the Great Society programmes of President Lyndon Johnson of the 1960s, and from the explanation of the causes and consequences of that failure. They identified six causes of failure. First, government action causes unanticipated and unintended consequences which seriously reduces expected benefits, produce adverse consequences elsewhere or even cause the opposite to that intended. One example is the destructive effect of welfare on the family, well documented in a recent book, *Losing Ground*, by Charles Murray. Secondly government refuses to acknowledge the limits of knowledge — that there are many problems that we do not know how to solve. Thirdly, govenment agencies pursue their goals without regard to their conflict with the aims of other government bodies. Fourthly, state intervention frequently weakened traditional problem-ameliorating institutions such as the family, the ethnic group, the churches and the community. Fifthly, a 'New Class' is identified of an educated middle class with a vested interest in the expanding role of the state. The power, status and wealth of this New Class is dependent upon activist government, the promotion of new statist programmes and the protection of old ones. Due to their education, direct interest, professional commitment and access to centres of decision-making, the middle class are highly successful in using government for their own purposes. The sixth cause of failure is a utopianism which refuses to accept the modest nature of man, that he is capable of evil and is strongly (although not exclusively) motivated by self-interest. The key to government failure lies in a naive view of human nature and a belief in the infinite malleability of man.

Neo-conservative concern with government failure is not primarily motivated by questions of efficiency and waste but with how it has undermined confidence in the Western system of representative democracy. The proponents of new policies, whether politicians after votes, bureaucrats after jobs, interest groups after benefits or well-intentioned reformers after 'progress', raise public expectations about the consequences of those actions so that their inevitable failure leads to a decline in confidence and trust in the democratic political system. It is the concern of the neo-conservatives that the political system of representative government is under threat that makes them urge much more caution in the role of the state.

The neo-conservatives completely changed my perception of

[35]

government from problem-solver to mess-creator. Yet there was one aspect of their ideas that I found disturbing, their social conservatism. *Commentary* published a whole series of articles attacking social-liberalism — feminism, homosexuality, etc. — which I felt to be mean-spirited. While strongly respecting Judaeo-Christian values as a major foundation of Western civilisation, I did not share the religious beliefs, whether Jewish or Christian, of the neo-conservatives.

Upon my return to the UK in 1974, some similar ideas to those of the neo-conservatives were being articulated in the 'ungovernability' debate, with slight variations by Professor Anthony King, Samuel Brittan and Professor Richard Rose. In summary, the argument was that the demands on the state were so large that the system was unable to cope with them, and the failure to satisfy those demands undermined confidence in the representative political system, thus creating a situation of governmental 'overload' and ungovernability, with the inability of government to translate policies and laws into desired results.

The role of government has vastly expanded in the post-war period, so that King felt that government had 'come to be regarded, in Britain at least, as a sort of unlimited liability insurance company, in the business of insuring all persons at all times against every conceivable risk. There is now hardly anything in which government can avoid taking an interest'. The expanded role of the state was explained by reference to the behaviour of the politicians, the electorate, interest groups and the bureaucrats. The politicians encourage expectations amongst the voters in order to win elections. They claim the ability to provide growth, employment, and so on, and therefore require the policies to achieve these objectives. The electorate provides the demand for more policies, as voters suffer from the fiscal illusion that these policies can be provided for their benefit at the expense of others and without regard to the costs. The interest groups find it easier to get government to provide what they want than to raise support voluntarily, as Samuel Brittan argues. The bureaucracies (including public employees such as social workers and teachers) have an interest in the expansion of the state that provides them with jobs, salaries, resources and status. This combination of forces provides strong pressures for big government.

At the same time 'as the range of responsibilities of government has increased, so, to a large extent independently, their capacity to exercise their responsibilities has declined' (King). Governments both attempt to do more and are less successful at achieving their objectives. Why? Several explanations have been offered. Lack of resources because of the low rate of growth is Professor Rose's main explanation. In this view the solution lies in the correct economic policies to provide growth, and the restraint of increased public

[36]

expenditure to rise only with the rate of growth. A second explanation is intellectual, that a man fails 'because he did not know nor understand that which he needed to know or understand in order to succeed' (King). This deficiency of knowledge can be met by attempting to expand the knowledge available and to attempt policies for which the knowledge is already available. The third explanation is that as government has become involved in new activities, so the number of groups upon which it is dependent has grown, while the willingness of some groups (such as the trade unions) to carry out the government's wishes has declined. In King's words, 'the number of dependency relationships in which government is involved has increased substantially and the incidence of acts of non-compliance ... has also increased substantially'. King's solution of this problem is to reduce the role of government and/or to ensure that government objectives have the broadest possible support in order to encourage compliance.

The consequences of these developments were that Britain had become harder to govern, that the people had become increasingly dissatisfied with the political system, and citizens were far more willing to disobey the law, either privately through tax evasion or social security fraud, or publicly through refusal to accept industrial relations laws.

These ideas, both American and British, convinced me that the future of liberal democratic societies depended upon the reduction of the role of government.

II. Public choice

By 1978 I was alerted to the tremendous likelihood of government failure. In political debate the solution would be to replace the politicians with a better group of politicians, but the conservative governments of Heath and Nixon were not remarkable for their success. I began to feel that the problems of government failure lay in the very nature of government, and the public choice school helped to provide the explanation.

There has developed a sub-discipline of economics called 'public choice', or sometimes in Britain 'the economics of politics', which applies the traditional concepts of micro-economics to political behaviour. The individual is seen as rational and 'utility maximising', seeking to promote his own interest within the limits set by the institutions of the time. This conception of man is presented not as the whole truth about all men but as the major explanation for the behaviour of most people most of the time. The application of this 'model' of man has proved very fruitful in both explaining and predicting economic behaviour, and the public choice writers believe

[37]

that it can be as enlightening in understanding politics as it can economics. This approach can be used by social scientists of different political persuasions, but the major figures of the public choice school are associated with scepticism about the role of the state and with a preference for the free market. They have constructed a model of the constitutional system that would be accepted by rational individuals: a limited government. And it is contrasted with modern liberal democracies. They argue that government has grown much bigger than people desire because of the rational behaviour of politicians, bureaucrats and interest groups. Their solution is a new constitutional settlement. The foremost founders of public choice, Professors James Buchanan and Gordon Tullock, run the Centre for the Study of Public Choice, an academic journal, *Public Choice*, and they have attracted a large number of scholars, especially young ones, who have pursued their analysis into a wide range of fields.

The first question that Buchanan and Tullock ask is: why would people want government at all? Why don't they favour anarchy? In the state of anarchy, the individual can: (1) produce goods, (2) take other people's goods or (3) defend his own goods. By accepting an institution that seeks to prevent the stealing of goods, and therefore reducing the necessity of defending them, more time and effort can be devoted to the production of further goods. A part of this additional production can pay the costs of government and still leave the individuals better off. The bargain is rational if the state is limited to the protection of individual rights and the provision of public goods (those from which beneficiaries cannot be excluded, such as defence). Decisions that are not unanimous will be accepted, provided rights are protected. But when the state goes beyond the protection of goods to the transfer of resources, the legitimacy of government is questioned, the amount of disobedience grows and the state has to spend more on law and order. This of course is not a description of historical reality but a guide against which to measure the real world, which has grown much beyond the stage of limited government. Public choice explains this growth through the behaviour of politicians, bureaucrats and interest groups.

The behaviour of politicians is assumed to be based on their desire to be re-elected, and one might predict that politicians would therefore provide the policies desired by the voters. Two factors prevent that result: 'log-rolling' and the political business cycle. Log-rolling means that legislator A agrees to vote for something legislator B wants in return for B's vote on something A wants — when, for example, the Minister of Education supports the demands of the Minister of Health in return for the Health Minister's support when education is up for discussion. Tullock gives the example of a bill which would cost £9 (£1 for each of nine taxpayers) and benefit A by

£7. It would be in A's interest to trade four of his votes of £1 each in order to gain a majority and he would still benefit by £2. Thus society would pay £9 for something only worth £7. Log-rolling is likely to lead to higher public expenditure than desired by the taxpayers. This result can be avoided by a rule that decisions must be approved by more than a simple majority such as two-thirds, which substantially increases the cost of log-rolling.

Another way in which political self-interest prevents the achievement of the policies desired by the voters is in political business cycles. The idea that governments tend to increase expenditure in a period leading up to elections, to boost employment and create the image of prosperity, is not new. Professor Bruno Frey of Switzerland has provided a more elaborate model of this behaviour, examined the empirical evidence and concluded that governments resort to such policies when they fear defeat. The interventions of governments are thus frequently destabilising although one of the primary declared justifications for such intervention is to achieve stability. Frey suggests that constitutional changes would be required to overcome this effect, or the removal of economic decisions from government.

Public choice emphasises the role of the bureaucracy in government policy. This aspect was developed by Professor William Niskanen, who identified the self-interest of bureaucracies in 'size-maximisation', or empire-building, because the status, salary, power, and desire for a quiet life are increased with the size of the agency or 'bureau'. Bureaucrats are in a strong position to obtain their objectives because of their strategic location, their control of information, their low costs of organisation and their ability to co-operate with interest groups. Bureaucracies are monopoly suppliers of their services, which places them in a strong position *vis-à-vis* the politicians, who lack an alternative source of supply. Those legislators with responsibility for oversight of the bureaucracies often represent groups with a high demand for the service, so there is oversupply of the government services and a lack of incentives to be efficient. Niskanen argues that

> All bureaux are too large. For given demand and cost conditions, both the budget and output of a monopoly bureau may be up to twice that of a competitive industry facing the same conditions. Bureaucrats produce outputs in excess of those that the voters would demand if they were aware of the costs.

A third source of over-government, in addition to vote-buying and empire-building, is the power of interest groups. Professor Mancur Olson of Maryland University developed his theory of interest-group formation in *The Logic of Collective Action* and applied this theory to

[39]

explain *The Rise and Decline of Nations*. Olson argues that individuals with a common interest will not organise collectively unless there is a rational incentive to participate. Small and homogenous groups, like manufacturers in the same industry or workers in the same firm, will be easier to organise than large and diverse groups, such as taxpayers. In the small group, the individual's participation matters and contributes to benefits for a small number of individuals. These organised groups are distributional coalitions concerned to redistribute income and wealth in their favour through the use of government power. They will have considerable influence over political decisions because they will be the direct beneficiaries. The National Farmers Union, for example, will be willing to spend resources to obtain agricultural subsidies, to support politicians who will favour their interests, and to mobilise as voters on this issue. Such a policy may be against the interests of the large majority of the population as consumers or taxpayers, but they lack the direct incentive to organise against the farmers. The benefits are concentrated among a relative few while the costs are spread over many, but only a little on each. Interest groups therefore do not counter-balance one another, because some groups are more likely to be organised than others.

Stable societies will accumulate many of these groups over time. Their activities will reduce economic efficiency and the standard of living and make political life more divisive, because they concentrate on the distribution of the economic pie rather than the production of a bigger pie. The accumulation of such distributional coalitions increases the role of government, the amount of regulation and the complexity of understanding, which helps to explain the notion that modern democracies have become ungovernable. Olson uses this theory to explain many differences in economic performance. The destruction of these coalitions in the last World War enabled West Germany and Japan to perform their economic miracles. The growth in coalitions hinders growth in modern Britain in contrast to the 19th century. The relative weakness of coalitions in the Newly Industrialised Countries such as Hong Kong contrasts with strong coalitions such as the caste system in India.

The voters in a representative democracy are unable to control the actions of government, in such a way that those which overproduced or underproduced would be removed at the next election. This rigidity arises from four factors. First, the costs of information to ordinary voters of discovering the full costs of a policy are too high. Secondly, the organisational costs of maintaining a coalition in favour of tax reduction or efficiency are also too high. Thirdly, the interest groups can impose costs, such as higher prices through subsidies, on others without alerting ordinary voters. Fourthly, voters suffer from the 'fiscal illusion' that the benefits of government policies can be obtained without cost to themselves. This deception is the result of the Keynesian argument that increased expenditure stimulates the economy, without recognising the cost in inflation.

Public choice therefore persuaded me that the political process was biased in favour of big government and in the interests of the organised few against the interests of the unorganised many. I became convinced by my study of political institutions that political reform, such as constraints on monetary policy and taxation and limits on the power of the legislature, could help. But these biases were inherent in any democratic system and could be rendered less harmful only by minimising the power, scope and size of government.

III. Libertarians

Neo-conservatism and public choice provided a formidable critique of the state and its inability to satisfy the people. But I was aware that the attraction of socialism was not primarily 'utilitarian' — that it would provide more goods and services. This argument had been rebutted, in theory by Ludwig von Mises in the economic calculation debate of the 1930s, and in practice by the performance of the communist economies.

The attraction of socialism to my students was essentially moral, that the distribution of income arising from the market was unjust. Piling up studies by Chicago economists of the numerous failures of government would not convince these students. And neither did I find it emotionally satisfying. Without denigrating the importance of material possessions (usually by those with plenty of them), life is about more than material wants. It is necessary to address the great moral questions of right and wrong. It was the search for moral arguments against the state that led me to Hayek, with his rejection of the concept of social justice, to Ayn Rand, with her celebration of the moral superiority of capitalism, and to Professor Robert Nozick, with his philosophical case for the minimum state.

Hayek has a utilitarian concept of the value of freedom, that freedom contributes to material and intellectual progress, and thus he did not provide the moral arguments for freedom that I was seeking. But he did provide the moral argument against one of the most attractive principles of socialism, that of social justice.

He argued that the concept of 'social justice' is meaningless. Social justice as a principle of state action requires agreement on who deserves what and on the existence of sufficient power in the hands of the state to ensure that the distribution is achieved. The first condition is based on the view that some sort of merit should be the determinant of the distribution of income — but everyone has a

[41]

different view of who deserves what. The value of an action to others is not determined by merit. A good voice and a beautiful face are valued but they are not the result of merit. There is no consensus in a free society about the 'correct' distribution of income. The second condition requires that the state has the power to achieve social justice, to determine who gets what. Whoever controls the state would determine what everyone received, which would lead to a tremendous concentration of power. Income would be determined not by the ability to satisfy consumers in the market but by political influence, and government becomes a scramble between interest groups over the political allocation of income. Hayek believes that justice is procedural, that just rules establish fair procedures and are not directed to a particular end. Just rules would include the stability of possession, transfer by consent, and the keeping of promises. In a free society, the distribution of income that results from these rules is not the concern of government. From this perspective, social justice is a totalitarian concept, because the distribution of income would be determined by some body, the 'party' or the 'majority', and your property is yours only by the whim of the state. This proposition struck me as immoral because my property, my home, my books, are an integral part of my personality, and the state would be empowered to use force to deprive me of my property in order to satisfy their conception of 'social justice'. Social justice as a principle of government is immoral.

My full recognition of the essential morality of capitalism, indeed that capitalism is the only moral system, came with the books of Ayn Rand. Her novels have been read by millions, particularly *Atlas Shrugged* and *The Fountainhead*, which dramatically present the conflict between individualism and collectivism. As a social scientist I was also influenced by her non-fiction work, such as *Capitalism: The Unknown Ideal* and *The New Left: The Anti-Industrial Revolution*. Man's right to pursue life in the light of his own values leads to the importance of the right to justly-acquired property, because it is the right to retain what he produces that enables him to sustain his life. The most unjustified act is the use of force to obtain your goals, because it is the denial of the right of others to pursue their own lives without hindrance. It is for this reason that, for Rand, capitalism is the only political-economic system compatible with morality because it is based on voluntary transactions and respect for property rights: 'Capitalism is not merely the "practical" system, but the only moral system in history'. The essential immorality of the state arises from its disposition to interfere in voluntary relationships between individuals. Although, like most libertarians, I have significant problems with some of Rand's views, such as her concentration on the importance of a few great men and her intolerance of those who deviate from her views, her greatest contribution to my intellectual development was her strong sense of the morality of capitalism because it was based on consent.

If any one phrase can sum up my belief in freedom both in the market and in lifestyle, it is from Robert Nozick's magnificent *Anarchy, State and Utopia*, that 'the socialist society would have to forbid capitalist acts between consenting adults'.

Nozick's claim 'that a minimal state limited to the narrow functions of protection against force, theft, fraud, enforcement of contracts, and so on, is justified, and that the minimal state is inspiring as well as right', accurately sums up my own view. My deepest moral belief is that one should not use force against another person (except in self-defence). Yet nearly all first year students of politics are taught about the central role of coercion to the concept of the state. Max Weber's definition of the state as a claim to a monopoly of the legitimate use of force is only the best known of the many concepts of the state which recognise its essentially coercive nature, and it is this recognition which makes me emotionally attracted to anarchy. Based on individual rights and the coercive nature of the state, Nozick provides a defence of the minimal state against the anarcho-capitalists in Part I of the book.

Most commentators hostile to Nozick concentrate on Part II because it attacks their own belief that there is any justification for more than the minimal state. Nozick attacks a wide range of justifications of the interventionist state, from equality to philanthropy, and most especially the argument based on social justice as presented by his Harvard colleague John Rawls. Nozick criticises 'end-state' theories of distributive justice which identify justice with some particular distribution of goods (rarely clearly articulated), in favour of an entitlement theory of justice, that the distribution is just if the process by which it was obtained was just. Thus, by this definition, a just society could be one of wide differences in wealth. Nozick provides a moral justification for material differences, but only if they are justly acquired, which cannot always be assumed in a collectivist society. This is no defence of the status quo, because much of the inequality in present-day societies is due to coercive acquisition, often by use of the state. This is a radical position from which to criticise all current statist societies, which seek to influence the distribution of income.

The third part of the book is Nozick's exciting concept of competing communities or 'utopias', between which individuals could choose that closest to his own values. This chapter, like the whole book, is imbued with an enthusiastic recognition of the tremendous diversity of human beings as a cause for celebration.

Unless one is a hermit, one must learn to live with others.

Relationships with others can be based on three factors — exchange, love or coercion. Exchange is the primary method under capitalism, based on the voluntary exchange of goods and services to mutual benefit. Socialists complain that exchange relationships view people as simply instruments for the satisfaction of personal wants, rather than as ends in themselves. Socialists want a society based on love, concern for others, so that you satisfy the wants of others out of your own love for them. The market does not exclude relations based on love, provided they are voluntary. But human beings are unable to love all people or to the same extent. We all have a preference for some people over others, due to friendship, family, politics, social values, sexual preferences, nationality, etc. We can actively express our love for only a minority of people in the world. Indeed, it is often those who express their love for 'humanity' who are least able to show concern for the real people around them. Because socialism is unable to create a social system totally based on love, it has to resort frequently to force to achieve its ends. Socialist rejection of exchange forces it to depend on either love or force, and when love proves insufficient, force becomes the basis of society. A free society is one where the individual can choose to base his relationships with others either on love or exchange, and capitalism does not insist on the priority of one or the other. It is only the use of coercion which is denied.

Conclusion

This was how a political scientist, and from a position widely perceived as being on the Conservative 'left', became a libertarian. It was a process that begun with a recognition of the political bankruptcy of collectivism and developed into a recognition of its moral bankruptcy.

None of this means I believe that freedom and the market will solve all our problems or bring a utopia. I am fully aware of the existence of 'market failure' — the imperfections that would exist in a free market — which has provided the intellectual justification for state action. But the neo-conservatives and the Chicago economists provide plenty of evidence of 'government failure'. Much of the failure attributed to the market (like pollution) is due to the failure of government (as in the protection of property rights). When the reality of government failure is measured against the reality of market failure, the former is much worse. I believe that a free society is not a perfect society, but a much better one than any alternative.

I was convinced of the value of freedom and the dangers of state action on utilitarian grounds of prosperity first, and that probably remains the best way to convince someone new to these ideas. I would now favour the market even if it was less productive and efficient, because it is the only moral system based on the voluntary choice of individuals and therefore based on the recognition of the dignity of the individual. No-one has the right to impose his values upon others. The consequence of allowing people to exercise free choice is that they will often choose to do, to buy, to wear, things that some dislike. Your attitude to freedom is not discovered by your attitude to the freedom of others to do the things you like, but when they do the things you dislike. It is the love of freedom that now motivates my political actions, and my discussion of specific policies is designed to demonstrate that the policies that are morally right, because they are based on freedom, are also practically best. I am excited that so many others have come to the same conclusions — and I am sure that many others will too.

ANDREW MELNYK

The next essay in this group takes further the examination of the origins of 'the New Right'.

Andrew Melnyk was born in Twickenham in 1962. His English mother was a teacher, his Russian (Ukranian) father an engineer. He attended a junior (state) school and changed at 10 years to a private preparatory from which he went to St Paul's School as a Foundation Scholar. With an Open Scholarship he went to Corpus Christi College, Oxford, at which he read Greats and graduated with a First this year. He is staying on to take a doctorate in philosophy, with a Claude R. Lambe Fellowship for 1985-6.

He is the Secretary and co-founder of the Hayek Society in Oxford and an occasional contributor to Economic Affairs *and to the* Libertarian Alliance journal, Free Life.

His essay emphasises a difference between the anti-intellectual Old Right, which shirked theory and was reluctant to argue with the Left, and the New Right, which rejoices in confident intellectual battle. Its new confidence derives from the New Right's belief that capitalism is morally as well as economically superior to socialism.

He traces the emergence of the New Right to the Chicago and Austrian schools of economics, the public choice analysis of politics, and the libertarian critique of the state. He sees the New Right as radical libertarianism based on the intellectual sources of classical British liberalism and the English and Scottish philosophers who refined it in the 18th and 19th centuries.

He argues that the Left, Old or New, fails to 'come to grips' with the New Right's radical defence of the free market.

4

THE INTELLECTUALS AND CAPITALISM

ANDREW MELNYK

All the political parties have their fair share of idiots, but traditionally the Conservative Party alone is stigmatised as the stupid party. Why? The reason is not that the charge is justified; I have personally met too many Conservatives of very high intelligence to believe that. The explanation is, I think, that the traditional view contains a grain of truth.

Conservatives and the Conservative Party are not outstandingly stupid, but they show a marked reluctance ever to *argue*. This is something I myself experienced when, before I acquired my present political views, I worked for the Conservative Party as a Young Conservative. The idea that political activists might bother to keep themselves informed about current affairs, seek out arguments and defeat their opponents with reason struck most of those I knew as quite unnecessary. The further idea that, in order to be a Conservative of good conscience, one ought to look into the case for Conservatism, consider opposite points of view and convince at least oneself that the case was strong, was regarded not only as unnecessary but also as absurd.

This conservative attitude often, of course, takes the form of extreme distrust of what is referred to contemptuously as 'theory' — as if *any* political action were possible which did not assume the truth of *some* theory, whether good or bad, of how the social world works. Conservative anti-intellectualism extends even as far as the works of philosophical defenders of conservatism such as Michael Oakeshott, Roger Scruton and J. R. Lucas. I cannot be the only reader who has detected in their writings, and been baffled by, a hint of mysticism which seems to make an appearance at crucial points in their arguments.

It seems clear to me that the adoption of this attitude has had the effect of alienating groups of people who might otherwise have supported conservatism. I am thinking here, of course, of academics, a disproportionately small number of whom are conservatives, and of the young, especially young intellectuals, who

[47]

are anxious to avoid linking themselves with anything smacking of unintelligence.

The best way of showing the disastrous nature of this effect is to ponder the contrasting attitude of the left, which could not be more different. It is hardly an exaggeration to say that all serious-minded socialists affect to be, and sometimes really are, familiar with some, at least, of the writings of socialist thinkers, especially, of course, Marx and Engels. I shall never forget one occasion when I was involved with a debate against a group of Labour Party Young Socialists. In the course of her speech, one of them confided to us that, despite her lack of a higher education, she nevertheless saw it as her duty to read the works of Marx, though she recommended others to start with some writings of Trotsky, since they were slightly easier reading. Whereas the eyes of conservatives glaze over if they are presented with facts and figures supporting their case, the left seem to seize upon such weapons and brandish them triumphantly against their ideological opponents. And with this conviction that theirs are the best arguments, and that reason is on their side, comes a confident and attractive self-assurance. No wonder so many generations of the young and intelligent — destined, of course, to occupy key positions of power and influence — have found the left so irresistible.

'Stupid' old right v. intellectual New Right

What I have said so far about conservatives and their attitudes is meant to apply only to the Old Right. The New Right is different. It is, I suggest, precisely in its view of the worth of ideas and arguments that the essence of the New Right is to be found; whichever pundit it was who coined the phrase 'New Right', in deliberate imitation of the label 'New Left', had hold of an important truth. For the New Right is distinguished by its willingness to develop a systematic point of view and to defend it by argument and the presentation of evidence, in a way strongly reminiscent of the New Left. Activists of the New Right are not afraid to dazzle their opponents with evidence and to quote from learned professors. In consequence, they enjoy some of that brash self-confidence which we used to associate with the New Left.

To anyone who has accepted my analysis thus far, an obvious question arises. Why does the New Right differ in this way from the Old? The answer to this query is best approached by considering a further question. Why was the Old Right so fearful of arguments and ideas?

The correct explanation, I suggest, is that the Old Right has never really been convinced that it had the best arguments. One suspects, indeed, that it is a fear of being clearly shown to be wrong which has underlied, and which continues to underlie, the Conservative

[48]

reluctance to argue. And there is one part of the Conservative position about which the Old Right is particularly bashful, perhaps even ashamed, and that is the support, muted though it is, which Conservatives have always given to the system of private property and free markets that we call 'capitalism'. They have in practice conceded nearly all of the radical criticisms levelled at capitalism, and especially the moral ones. They are reduced as a result to appealing to mere prejudice or mumbling highly questionable generalisations about selfishness and the incorrigibility of human nature. All this is made worse by the weakness that conservatism, by its very nature, has lacked a clear view of an ideal form of society. It is easy to understand why conservatives have so often been dismissed as unscrupulous and complacent apologists for the status quo and for groups with a vested interest in it.

Intellectual resources for the New Right

But the secret of the New Right is now clear. Its activists can stride into the arena of intellectual debate with complete confidence, because they believe that their case is strong. They are convinced that the power of reason is on their side, and so they need fear nothing from argument. In particular, of course, they are unembarrassed to proclaim their support for capitalism, which is not for them some sordid but necessary evil, but on the contrary a progressive and humane ideal.

But what are the intellectual resources on which the New Right has drawn and by which it has been so emboldened?

There are many strands one might consider. First the work of the so-called Chicago economists has altered our understanding of the problems of external effects, public goods and monopoly; and its extensive researches have served both to document the economic failures of government and to force a reassessment of alleged historical instances of certain kinds of market failure. Second, and still in the realm of economics, there is the Austrian school of economists, whose emphasis on time, uncertainty, ignorance and disequilibrium explains the value of certain features of real-world markets, such as advertising and price inflexibility, which used to be condemned as undesirable imperfections (Professor Israel Kirzner's *Competition and Entrepreneurship* is especially enlightening).

Third, if we cross to political theory, we will find poised between economics and politics the theory of public choice, which has illuminated the logic of voting procedures, bureaucratic behaviour and political activity in general and in consequence revealed the incorrigibility of political institutions (an introduction is Professor Gordon Tullock's *The Vote Motive*). Fourth, in the area of political

[49]

theory proper, the work of Hayek, with its extraordinary range, continues to inspire countless young people, inside and outside the academies, by its richness, elegance and erudition (a good guide to his writings is Eamonn Butler's *Hayek*). Nor should the novels and other writings of Ayn Rand be forgotten, since what they lack in intellectual depth and rigour they make up by their remarkable penetration and insight.

For this essay I direct attention to one specific development, namely, the publication in 1974 of Robert Nozick's *Anarchy, State and Utopia.*

Nozick's moral argument for capitalism

Nozick, who holds a chair in philosophy at Harvard, has described himself as a moral defender of capitalism. One of the reasons why his book came as such a surprise to mainstream political philosophers was that it contained a defence of capitalism based not on considerations of utility or practical necessity, but rather on the claims of that part of morality we call justice. Hitherto, where it had not been dismissed out of hand, capitalism was regarded as at best a moderately useful tool but whose use is attended with distasteful features and which requires careful control and limitation if it is to be used at all. Nozick's enduring achievement was to present capitalism as a *moral* ideal, consistent with the rights which justice assigns to persons, so that any economic efficiency it might bring in its train constitutes a purely additional, if very welcome, advantage.

Anarchy, State and Utopia dazzles with its brilliance and perplexes with its countless arguments, counter-arguments, examples and suggestions. It defies brief summary. Yet the core of Nozick's positive thesis can perhaps be put like this. Critics of capitalism who claim that it fails to satisfy the demands of distributive justice have typically assumed the correctness of what Nozick calls an end-state theory. End-state theories specify a profile of distribution to which each person's holdings must correspond if they are to be just. The most popular end-state theory is egalitarianism of outcome, which requires that everyone's holdings be equal. Nozick makes three fundamental criticisms of end-state theories (of which egalitarianism is only one example).

First, it runs wildly counter to intuition to suppose, as end-state theorists do, that what happened in the past is irrelevant to justice. For consider the distribution not of goods but of 'bads', that is, punishment. Whether a person is imprisoned or merely fined seems to depend, in justice, on the gravity of the crime: on what the person *did*. An end-state theory of punishment would be a palpable absurdity. And what is true of punishment is also true of the distribution of things that are good. It seems to matter whether a person's car was bought or stolen. In general, it looks as if justice requires us to see how holdings arose, and not simply to consider whether they form part of some distributional 'profile'.

Nozick's second criticism of end-state theories is that they necessitate interference with liberty. Suppose you walk into a room full of people with a box of apples and that you distribute them in accordance with your favourite end-state theory, whether equally or otherwise. The appropriate distribution is now realised, and justice prevails. Suppose, however, that someone has the temerity to eat his apple, or to give it away, or to trade it for a riper one. *Justice no longer prevails*, since the appropriate distribution is no longer realised. If an end-state theory is correct, justice can be maintained only by prohibiting such disruptive actions. Hence the supporters of end-state theories must pay a high price in sacrificed liberty.

The third criticism Nozick makes is best explained by asking a question about the example of the previous paragraph: where did you get the box of apples? End-state theories treat goods to be distributed as, to use Nozick's phrase, manna from heaven. But we do not simply *find* them: crops have to be planted and harvested, natural resources have to be got out of the ground, consumer goods have to be produced, services have to be provided. In giving people enforceable claims to things of this sort, end-state theories give people enforceable claims to the actions of other people: such virtual slavery cannot be demanded by justice.

It is from such powerful negative considerations as these that Nozick fashions the so-called entitlement theory of justice. It is, of course, not an end-state theory but on the contrary what Nozick calls a *historical* theory. The essence of it is that any distribution of holdings is just so long as it arises from a process which violates no one's rights; we avoid violating persons' rights if our dealings with them are purely contractual and *voluntary*; hence any distribution of holdings is just if it arose from voluntary transactions. Since transactions under capitalism are, in the required sense, contractual and voluntary, the distribution of holdings under capitalism is just. Nozick offers a playful slogan, a satirical dig at Marx, to encapsulate his view: to each as he chooses, from each as he is chosen. The entitlement theory has played a large part in the moral rehabilitation of capitalism.

The left's response 'pitifully inadequate'

Given the existence of these rich intellectual resources on which the New Right has, albeit indirectly, drawn, it is only natural to wonder how the left, with its strong tradition of valuing reason and evidence,

[51]

has responded. The short answer is that its response has been pitifully inadequate.

A typical reaction is simply to ignore the arguments presented and to assail the motives of those presenting them. Normally there is more than a hint of the suggestion that they are only in the pay of some sinister interest. This is all hopelessly confused.

To begin with, the question of what reasons (in the sense of grounds) someone has for holding a view is logically distinct from the question of what motivates the person to propound the view. Suppose I am promised that I will be paid £100 every time I proclaim and defend the thesis that two plus two makes four. Then, clearly, I will go around doing this as often as I can. My reason (in the sense of motive) for doing so will be my desire to be enriched. But that does not cast any doubt upon the cogency of my arguments for the thesis; and it most definitely does not tend to show that the claim that two plus two makes four is false.

Furthermore, it is simply wrong to suggest that capitalists prefer a free market economy. They do not. The reason is that in a free market there would be no monopolistic privileges — tariff barriers, subsidies, regulations and so on — serving to protect existing capitalists from new competition. Capitalists hate that kind of unstable environment where their profits are always at risk. What they want is not, to be sure, full-blown socialist planning, but rather some sort of corporatist mixture of socialism and capitalism where they not only find shelter from competitive pressures but also have a taste of the pleasures of political power. More fundamentally still, even if the maintenance of a free market economy were in the interests of capitalists, it would not be in the interests of any individual capitalist to expend the resources necessary for lobbying for it, because if he did so, the benefit would go to all the other capitalists regardless of whether they contributed anything to the expense. In short, capitalism would be a public good. That is another reason why the worst enemies of capitalism are capitalists.

Nove's flawed critique of market capitalism

The other main response on the part of the left, Old or New, to the Right does at least recognise that there is a case to be answered, but fails to appreciate its strength and complexity. A good illustration of this sort of reaction is provided by parts of Professor Alec Nove's *The Economics of Feasible Socialism*. The author is certainly no friend of Marx's ideas on socialism, which he considers 'very seriously defective and misleading'. Many of those who have come to similar conclusions about Marxian socialism have, of course, joined the New Right, but Nove is not among them. Accordingly, when in a prefatory section

[52]

entitled 'Socialism — Why?' he presents his reasons for persevering with some sort of socialism, he does virtually nothing except attack a New Right position.

My aim in referring to Nove's discussion is not to refute him, though that would be ridiculously easy, but rather to indicate his complete failure to come to grips with the radical defence of the free market. He knows that F. A. Hayek and Milton Friedman are associated with it, but although he mentions their names a handful of times, there is no reference to any book written by either of them. Neither is there any hint of an appreciation of the profound differences between their approaches — Austrian and Chicagoan, respectively — to the working of a market economy.

The trouble with Nove's critique is that he seems quite oblivious of the plausible replies to each of his specific criticisms. In the course, for instance, of associating himself with the currently fashionable concern over stocks of raw materials and energy, there is no mention of basic statistics, such as those presented by Professor Julian L. Simon in his brilliant book *The Ultimate Resource* which contradict the gloomy prophecies of the merchants of ecological doom. More fundamentally, Nove makes no reference to discussions by theorists of the economics of property rights who contend that it is *common* property institutions, and not those based on *private* property, which give rise to over-exploitation of natural resources. This omission emerges most clearly when Nove offers as an illustration of market failure the widespread phenomenon of over-fishing. For fish are typically common, not private, property. If over-fishing illustrates anything, it is the urgency of the requirement to establish private property rights in marine resources, including fish.

Another cluster of criticisms made by Nove centres around the allegation that on today's world 'enormous business corporations and conglomerates dominate a whole series of vital industries'. No evidence for this claim is cited, and the meaning of the emotive word 'dominates' is left unexplained. It is left almost wholly obscure precisely what is supposed to be bad about large corporations or highly concentrated industries. Nove mentions 'administered prices', which are not responsive to supply and demand as they should be. But the study by Professor (and Nobel Laureate) George Stigler and J. K. Kindahl found no evidence connecting inflexible prices with concentrated industries (*The Behaviour of Industrial Prices*, 1970).

Perhaps Nove's contention is that big companies gain excess profits at the expense of their customers. But recent work by another Chicago economist, Professor Yale Brozen, casts doubt on this claim, too. He failed to find any evidence showing a persistent relationship between concentration and high rates of return (*Journal of Law and*

Economics, 1970, and his new book, *Concentration, Mergers and Public Policy*, 1982).

What these examples show is that Nove's critique is completely emasculated by his failure to take into account the evidence and argument for markets and capitalism. It may be, of course, that Nove has assiduously studied this literature and privately devised brilliant replies to it. Nor do I rule out the possibility that the criticisms made by Nove are not adequately met by the economists I cited. The argument is simply that Nove fails to engage with them. All that I am maintaining is that he provides a splendid example of an intellectual response to the New Right which fails to do justice to the intellectual foundations on which it rests.

The New Right and morality

But we have come to a point where further clarification of the New Right's attitude towards capitalism is necessary. For while it is clear that it is prepared to give enthusiastic and unabashed support, there remains the question of how, and how far, this support is contaminated by a more genuinely conservative tradition emphasising the desirability of the enforcement of morality, the importance of authority and nationalism. Without detailed knowledge of the particular beliefs of members of the New Right, this question cannot be satisfactorily answered.

What is clear, however, at any rate to me, is that the phrase 'New Right' has all the wrong connotations. Although I suppose I have to admit to being a part of the New Right, it is simply not true that my views are 'right-wing'. Right-wingers favour immigration control; I hold that it violates peoples' rights and retards economic growth. Right-wingers harbour predjudices against, amongst others, women and homosexuals; I welcome the liberation of women and homosexuals, which capitalism has helped to bring about. Again, political right-wingers insinuate that welfare beneficiaries do not deserve any money; I too oppose welfare payments, but on the different ground that, no matter how deserving people may be, of praise, gratitude or other reward, they do not have a right to it enforceable against others. Right-wingers are always to be found giving wooden-headed support to the police, no matter how clear it is that they have done something wrong; I regard the police as no different from any other nationalised industry — inefficient and giving its customers bad service.

Radical libertarianism

If my earlier arguments are correct, the New Right has drawn its intellectual ammunition from the arsenal of libertarianism. Yet libertarianism is a radical doctrine, perhaps the most radical doctrine in modern politics. It embraces not just economic but also the deepest social and moral issues. My fear and suspicion is that those who style themselves members of the New Right are still more or less encumbered by the baggage of a traditionalist, authoritarian and nationalistic conservatism with which the radicalism of libertarianism is blatantly inconsistent. They should, therefore, clarify where they stand on the wider issues. If they reject the libertarian position, they must give a satisfactory account of how they think they can reconcile the apparently disparate elements of their political beliefs. But adherents of the New Right who embrace the full implications of libertarianism would surely be well-advised to jettison the label 'New Right' and call themselves instead libertarians, or classical liberals, or (best of all) simply liberals.

If, as I hope, that is what they do, their decision will perhaps mark a crucial turning-point. For traditionally the attitude of intellectuals towards capitalism has been one of ill-disguised contempt. If the rise of the New Right either is, or becomes, a harbinger of a new assessment by intellectuals of the worth of a system of free markets and private property, there will be no one who does not have grounds for rejoicing.

CHANDRAN KUKATHAS

Another essayist from Oxford emphasises the nature of the origins of the New Right and the interrelationships between its six intellectual tributaries.

Chandran Kukathas was born in 1957 in Kuala Lumpur, Malaysia. His father was a radio broadcaster turned Malaysian diplomat and finally journalist. His mother was a teacher.

He was educated at a primary school in Kuala Lumpur and a High School in Canberra, Australia. He graduated with a BA in History and Political Science from the Australian National University in Canberra, and an MA from the University of New South Wales with a thesis on the political philosophy of David Hume prepared while a Teaching Fellow in the Department of Government at the Royal Military College, Canberra. Since 1982 he has been writing a doctoral thesis, at Linacre College, Oxford, on the political thought of Hayek, and began a one-year lectureship in philosophy at Lincoln College, Oxford, in October 1985.

He explains the emergence of governments more sympathetic to the market as a reaction to the failure of Keynesian demand management rather than to the advent of a new political philosophy. The New Right is not a political *movement based on ideas but an* intellectual *departure unconnected with political allegiance: 'it lacks a natural constitutency'.*

The New Right is at odds with the old Right, which emphasised 'authority', as well as with the New left, which deified the state. The New Right shares with Old Right conservatives hostility to wealth redistribution based on notions of 'social justice' but shares with Social Democrats suspicion of the state's attempts to strengthen politically-defined moral values or to strengthen its authority. The New Right must not be confined to one political grouping.

5

POLITICAL IDEAS AND POLITICAL INTERESTS

CHANDRAN KUKATHAS

> If the idea is good, it will survive defeat, it may even survive the victory.
>
> (Stephen Vincent Benét, *John Brown's Body*)

I. The putative success of the New Right

The political success of the 'New Right' has been much exaggerated. This is not to say that its impact has been negligible but, rather, to emphasise that the term New Right identifies a set of ideas rather than a set of interests. The electoral successes of 'right-wing' governments in North America and Britain do not bear witness to a triumph, or even to an ascendancy, of the New Right. The changes in government policy in favour of slightly freer markets and less inflationary monetary policy have not come in response to the arguments of a New Right philosophy but as a reaction to the perceived failures of 'Keynesian demand management'.

Put most simply, the changes in government policy are the consequences, less of the success of a new political philosophy, than of the recognition that increases in government spending, designed to boost demand, would not operate to increase output and reduce unemployment to specifiable amounts. That the economic policy developments of the late 1970s and early 1980s betray a management 'reaction' rather than a 'counter-revolution' is confirmed by a number of observations. First, this reaction has not been characteristic only of governments commonly regarded as 'right-wing'. As Samuel Brittan has often observed, the most characteristic features of financial Thatcherism were initiated and pursued (albeit reluctantly) by the Callaghan-Healey Labour Government. More recently, the Australian Labor Government has initiated policies of monetary restraint and set about deregulating the financial system in accordance with the recommendations of the Campbell Report which their Liberal Party predecessors ignored. And the Labour Government in New Zealand, following its victory over Robert Muldoon's National Party, has begun to remove the battery of subsidies and central controls maintained by its 'right-wing' predecessor. Secondly, none of the 'right-wing' governments allegedly pursuing the policies of free-market economics has been eager to remove major obstacles to *international* free trade. The Conservative and Republican governments of the UK and USA have been as anxious to maintain European steel production quotas, or 'voluntary' agreements restricting the importing of Japanese cars, and to limit imports from the Third World, as any other European government. And thirdly, inasmuch as these parties have sought to develop free markets out of a conviction that 'free enterprise is a necessary condition of cultural and political liberty' (Sir Keith Joseph), or an inseparable part of 'an open, pluralistic and free society' (Sir Keith Joseph again), they cannot (yet) command the support of an electorate or an intellectual elite which still clings, more or less tenaciously, to ideas which uphold the welfare state.

For these reasons I would argue that the New Right is not a political movement underpinned by a set of shared theoretical claims but an intellectual movement independent of political allegiance. My purpose here is to consider the difficulties confronting this movement in the light of the truth that, as a body of ideas in the competitive arena of democratic politics, it lacks a natural constituency. The next two sections consider how the New Right might best be characterised and what strengths their fundamental ideas possess. From here we should be better able to assess the theoretical as well as the practical difficulties which must be overcome if these ideas are to achieve any success in the world about which they theorise.

II. Defining the New Right

The term 'New Right' is often used to label a variety of political theories from conservatism to individualist anarchism. But applied to such a wide range of viewpoints the adjective 'new' loses its explanatory value. If the term is to have any useful function it must distinguish a set of ideas from *two* other major political outlooks: the 'left' and the '*old* right'. Although the philosophy of the New Right is at odds with that of the 'left', it is no less in conflict with the politics of 'old right' conservatism. Yet while these labels which have entered the vocabulary of politics distinguish broad political outlooks, they remain vague and unsatisfactory. 'New Right' must be given clearer content. Which attitudes characterise the New Right? Which groups and individuals share them?

The philosophy of the New Right is distinguished from the conservatism of the 'old right', and from the social democratic outlook of the 'left', by its attitude to the state and, more particularly, the dominant institution within the state: government. For conservatives, such as Roger Scruton, the state, which comprises 'not just government, but also territory, language, administration, established institutions all growing from the interaction of unconscious custom and reflective choice', is 'the completion, and also the champion of society' (Scruton, *The Meaning of Conservatism*). Although they do not call for the expansion of the *scope* of state power, their primary concern is not the freedom of the individual but the maintenance of the strength of the state's legitimate power: the maintenance of *authority*. And while they repudiate the claim that the state should be concerned with the redistribution of wealth according to abstract principles of 'social justice', they equally see it as 'inescapable that there should be family law, planning laws, laws which regulate the days and times when men work, drink or seek recreation, even laws which control the nature of permitted intoxicants' (Scruton). Because they see the preservation of society as the most important (and difficult to attain) precondition of human flourishing, their pre-occupation is with *authority* as the vitally necessary precondition of order.

The social democrat is concerned primarily with the redistribution of wealth in accordance with principles which propose that social justice requires that individuals be entitled to receive resources to meet their 'basic needs' or to receive a more 'equal' share of those resources. The state, in this case, is the agency through which redistribution is effected. And while they are by no means always hostile to the constitutionalism so highly valued by conservatives, they emphasise the importance of the machinery of democracy in settling distributive questions. Since they are not as concerned as the conservatives with the preservation of order, they are generally less enthusiastic about the reinforcement of authority and the regulation of morality. Thus they are less likely to condone the invasion by the state of individual *privacy* than they are to endorse its invasion of individual *property*. This viewpoint is adopted by a range of modern thinkers from self-proclaimed liberals such as Ronald Dworkin (*Taking Rights Seriously*) to critics of liberalism such as Raymond Plant (*Equality, Markets and the State*); and their writings manifest a concern, primarily, for individual *welfare*. While many social democrats would deny that they are socialists, preferring the title of liberal, some among them see no substantive difference between the terms social democrat and democratic socialist (for example, Bruce Ackerman, *Social Justice and the Liberal State*).

The New Right attitude to the state differs from the attitudes of the conservative and the social democrat insofar as its primary concern is the scope of state power — whether that power be exercised through the law or through the democratic process. And, without exception, the advocates of the New Right view argue that the power of the modern state has exceeded its proper bounds. Thus while they share with conservatives a hostility to the idea of wealth redistribution according to principles of social justice, they also share with social democrats a suspicion of attempts by the state to reinforce particular moral values or to strengthen its own authority.

Yet they do not share the social democrat's tendency to distinguish between the infringement by the state of certain political liberties (such as freedom of speech or of association) and its infringement of economic liberty (through wage controls, redistributive taxation or business and labour regulation). Indeed, insofar as New Right thinkers see themselves as the standard-bearers of liberty, they argue that liberty is not to be disaggregated into separate liberties requiring separate justifications. Rather, individual liberty is the primary value, and it is any curtailment of that liberty that requires justification.

While it would be convenient to label the members of the New Right 'liberals' it would also be misleading. For not only is the right to use the word 'liberal' much disputed but also not all those falling under the purview of the New Right would admit to being liberals. Indeed, they defend a common outlook from a variety of moral and economic perspectives. Within the New Right six major schools or thinkers can be identified:

1) the Chicago school of economics, whose most famous exponent is Milton Friedman;

2) the Virginia school of Public Choice theory, most strongly associated with Gordon Tullock and James Buchanan;

3) the 'Objectivist' philosophy of Ayn Rand;

4) the minimal state libertarianism most commonly associated with Robert Nozick;

5) the anarchist libertarianism of Murray Rothbard;

6) the 'classical liberal' philosophy of limited government of F. A. Hayek.

The works of these schools or theorists do not all share the same immediate purpose. Some seek simply to demystify the workings of the state, and of government in particular, and to show that it is far from a neutral or impartial referee regulating individual relations. Thus the public choice school attempts mainly to demonstrate that government leaders and civil servants, no less than trade unionists and industrial lobbyists, are all economic agents bent upon securing their own interests or the interests of their groups. Others seek to show that, in most areas of society, the involvement of the state leads not only to less efficient production of goods and services but is also often counter-productive or harmful. Thus Hayek and Friedman argue for a reduction of state regulation of business and labour and of state provision of welfare services; and Thomas Sowell argues that racial minorities have suffered to the extent that governments have sought to ameliorate their conditions through regulation of working conditions and welfare services. Some New Right advocates criticise the workings of the state on moral grounds. Thus Rand and Nozick reject all state activities other than those essential for the defence of society against internal and external aggressors; and Hayek argues that the state may act only to provide defence services and certain public goods (which include a welfare safety net) if it is to stay within the bounds established by the rule of law; while Rothbard rejects the state completely as an institution which is incompatible with morality and human freedom.

While the New Right has gained little acknowledgement in the past, it is now achieving considerable attention. This is evident not only in the growing number of institutions, beginning with the Institute of Economic Affairs, investigating and defending the claims of the New Right, but also in the new attitude that many of those hostile to these ideas now take them seriously enough to want to refute them (a recent example is Nicholas Bosanquet, *After the New Right*). To see why it is taken seriously we should look now at the general strengths of the New Right's case — before we turn to the problems which confront it and the reasons why it still has considerable distance to travel.

III. The arguments

It is difficult to discern a core of argumentation that is common to all New Right theorists, not only because they approach questions from different perspectives, but also because they disagree considerably over many important issues. Disputes persist between the anti-empiricist economics of the Austrian School (which includes Hayek and Rothbard) and the neo-classical orthodoxy of the Chicago and Virginia (public choice) schools. Equally, Rothbard has been fiercely critical of the Nozickian minimal state and Rand has charged liberalism and the liberals with undermining the moral basis of capitalism and the free society. Nevertheless, there exists a family of arguments, shared by these writers to varying degrees, which form the heart of the New Right's attitude.

First, they share a favourable view of capitalism. But here a possible source of confusion must be removed. For when 'capitalism' is discussed by its critics, it is taken to refer to the set of historical circumstances that followed upon the decline of feudalism. While capitalist society is taken to be characterised by the existence of market or exchange relations among individuals, the persistence of laws and governments which intervene in these exchanges (usually to benefit the stronger) is taken to be equally a part of 'capitalism'. But the New right's defence of capitalism does not extend beyond the defence of the market free of state intervention. Thus when Rand or Friedman or Hayek extol the virtues of 19th-century European capitalism, they do not thereby endorse all the laws or government actions of Victorian Britain. Indeed, Hayek has argued the case for legislation to reform the law dealing with master/servant and landlord/tenant relations — law often made to suit the interests of the more powerful. Nor does this defence of capitalism extend to the defence of capitalists who are recognised not as upholders of the free market but as interested agents who frequently seek to alter laws and restrict market exchanges to favour themselves. Following Adam Smith, they observe that capitalists seldom associate if not to conspire against the public. And such conspiracies never succeed so well except with the sponsorship of the state.

The second major claim shared by the New Right is that central organisation is not an essential prerequisite of order: the absence of governmental regulation does not mean chaos. Thus Professor Buchanan argues that there is only one principle in economics that is worth stressing: the principle of the 'spontaneous order' of the market (*Freedom in Constitutional Contract*). And the strength of this position derives largely from the success of the New Right economists in particular in demonstrating that attempts to secure social improvements through the ordering mechanisms of the state invariably prove to be not merely futile but counter-productive. Two different, but compatible, explanations for this have been developed: one by Hayek and the other mainly by the public choice school.

Hayek's explanation stems from his account of 'competition as a discovery procedure'. What is most significant about human society, he argues, is not that individuals differ in their tastes or preferences but that they differ in their circumstances and in their knowledge. The problem that this condition poses is economic in the widest possible sense of the term. For the economic problem is not one of calculating how existing scarce resources or goods are to be allocated or distributed to those who require or prefer them. Scarcity is only one aspect of the problem. The more serious problem is *discovering what is scarce* or valuable. A crucial aid in the solution of this problem is the price mechanism, for prices direct attention to the *relative* scarcity of various goods. But, more fundamentally, value can be discovered, and prices can discover these relative values, only in conditions in which individuals are free not only to set prices for their wares but also to produce and market their goods.

A number of important benefits flow from this freedom. First, the knowledge of relative scarcity embodied in prices guides producers to create goods and services which are most likely to conserve scarce resources and not to create goods for which there is unlikely to be any demand. Second, in the free market the continual and systematic disappointment of the expectations of those who fail to produce the values sought by others quickly eliminates practices which waste resources (both human and material). And because loss-making enterprises disappear more quickly, the costs of disappointing expectations are less tragic as individuals are left better able to adjust to gradually changing circumstances. Had British coal mines been subject more directly to economic pressures rather than to political ones, there would never have been a need for a pit-closure *programme* putting entire communities out of work at a stroke, and turning out into the labour market thousands of people with the same skills to compete for the same jobs. The early collapse of loss-making enterprises also informs other potential producers of the investment potential of those industries.

Third, and most important, a condition of freedom in which individuals are free to produce and market their wares, or to purchase the creations of others, enables individuals to discover values which no one may have realised existed before. Individuals do *not* always know what they want or where their interests lie any more than producers always know what consumers want or what would satisfy their customers' interests. In a competitive market it is true not only that producers compete to satisfy public demand but also that they compete to *persuade* individuals of the *existence* of new or different kinds of values. And it is also true that individuals seek to discover what they value by purchasing, hiring, or testing the goods that become available to them. Thus Culture Club's first concert was an entrepreneurial risk not only for the band and its promoters, but also for those who paid to discover whether or not Boy George was worth listening to.

The threat posed by the regulatory state, given the nature of the human condition in which resources are scarce and knowledge is dispersed, comes from the discoordination of individual plans effected by the very attempt to coordinate them in accordance with pre-determined objectives. The harm is created not by human planning but by superseding individual plans by a single enforced plan drawn up by agents who do not have, and cannot possibly acquire, the *knowledge* necessary for such a task.

The most persuasive example of the harm created by state planning appears in attempts to maintain low-cost housing through rent control. At a time when groups of all political persuasions are decrying the appalling condition of rented homes in Britain, labouring under shortages exacerbated by the Rent Acts of 1965 and 1968, it is sobering to note the *absence* of a housing problem in San Francisco a month after the 1906 earthquake destroyed half the housing facilities.

[63]

In the absence of rent control virtually every one of the 225,000 people rendered homeless, less than half of whom left the city or sought shelter in temporary camps, secured housing so rapidly that the first re-issue of the *San Francisco Chronicle* made no mention of any housing shortage but advertised more than 65 dwellings for rent (Friedman and Stigler, *Roofs or Ceilings?*). While prices for rented homes rose (encouraging new construction), higher prices also prompted others to let accommodation at competitive prices to the extent that inexpensive flats and houses were always available. (Interestingly, in the rent-controlled San Francisco of 1946, the shortage of rental homes was, according to the Governor, 'the most critical problem facing California'. There was no *physical* shortage of housing: owners simply found it too costly to let their homes at low rents and chose instead to sell. In 1906 there were 3 houses for sale for every 10 listed for rent in the *San Francisco Chronicle*. In 1946 730 houses were listed for sale for every ten listed for rent.)

It is no part of Hayek's claim that, given free markets, all good things will be available. Individuals and groups continually encounter and attempt to solve problems which sometimes prove insurmountable. The argument for the free market is grounded, rather, in the contention that problems are less likely to be solved if options are closed by the imposition of unjustifiable contraints upon individual experimentation or by the imposition of a single solution for all individuals.

The dangers in the political process

While the public choice theorists would not quarrel with the Hayekian defence of the free market, they have developed a separate argument against the growth of state involvement in the regulation of enterprises in society. Unlike the Hayekian argument which emphasises the difficulties which confront any central authority given the nature of the *economic* problem, the public choice argument points to the *political* obstacles which lie in the way of good decision-making by the state. Even if the economic problems were surmountable by a central agency, what guarantees that the decisions taken by the state will correspond to collective desires? And if the state does make decisions in the public interest, what assurance have we that the *results* of government action will conform to its intentions? The public choice reply is that not only can there be no such assurance, but, more likely, state actions will reflect the interests of individual politicians, political groups or other powerful and organised interests rather than the collective interests of society.

What public choice theory demonstrates most clearly is that the actors in politics are as much interested agents as the actors in the market. Moreover, politics is an arena in which interests compete to persuade (or even force) those who wield political power to legislate or administer rules in their favour. These interests are manifested in a variety of types of organisation ranging from trade unions and industrial lobbies to civil service departments and arts councils. Almost invariably, such organisations or interests call for a particular policy, a subsidy, the banning of a particular activity or the increasing of a government-funded budget, in the interest not of themselves but of a wider community or of society at large. The chairman of the US Committee on Armed Services was invited by the president of the Footswear Industry of America to protect the footwear industry *on national security grounds*. In time of war, he argued, America 'won't be able to wait for ships to deliver shoes from Taiwan' and 'improper footwear can lead to needless casualties and turn sure victory into possible defeat'.

Yet on almost all occasions the government action called for coincides less with any national interest than with the interests of special groups. None of this is to suggest that organised interests are necessarily composed of selfish individuals, hostile to the interests of society or of their fellows. Yet the bargaining processes of *politics* encourages 'rent-seeking' (procuring favoured treatment) when its costs are lower than the costs of securing policies which benefit everyone. It is less costly and more profitable to obtain a subsidy or tariff protection in the political process than it is to promote free trade in the market. The results are less favourable for everyone inasmuch as rent-seeking through government is, at best, a zero-sum game. As a purely redistributive activity, it incurs costs without adding to total output. Indeed, it often turns into a negative-sum game because the assignment of special privileges by government, through subsidies or tariffs, encourages others to devote fewer resources to the production of goods and services and more to rent-seeking. In May 1979 Sir Keith Joseph, as Secretary of State for Industry, charged the British Steel Corporation with the task of breaking even in 1980-81. BSC's subsequent loss of £660 million led to the 'reconstruction' by the Government of BSC finances, writing off £3,550 million in BSC public debt, and granting a further subsidy of £730 million for 1981-82. The resulting lobbying by the British Independent Steel Producers Association caused the government to start giving financial assistance to independent steelmakers (John Burton, *Picking Losers . . .?*).

In drawing attention to the nature of politics as the bargaining arena of competing interests, public choice theorists points to a conclusion of particular importance for the New Right. For they argue that, while organised interests are able to articulate their demands for a larger share of the goods available through the agencies of the state, groups which are not able to organise receive correspondingly less attention from government. They are less able to articulate their concerns because they are not able to organise. Thus working trade unionists can form effective, organised lobbies, while the unemployed, because they lack resources and face enormous costs in organising people who are geographically and difficult to identify, are less able to form strong pressure groups. Unsurprisingly, British governments in the 1970s and 1980s have continued to bow to the pressures exerted by the well organised and employed rather than respond to the plight of the jobless.

This generalisation can be taken further. Since politics favours those who are organisationally powerful, the political process tends to shift the objects of political competition from the politically weak to the powerful. Thus, as we would expect, the majority of the beneficiaries of income redistribution undertaken by the state are not the poor but those with stronger political influence. Hence Professor Tullock observes that the bulk of income redistribution comprises a shifting of money among people in the middle-income bracket. And this activity produces three main externalities, all of which are 'public *bads*': a significant portion of tax is used simply to raise money for the transfer of income or to deliver the subsidy, and large quantities of resources are devoted to the political manoeuvring necessary to carry out the transfer (*Private Wants, Public Means: The Desirable Scope of Government*).

Public choice theory has indeed gone some way to demystify the operations of the state and provides a number of (empirically corroborated) replies to the often-asked question: 'Why doesn't the government do something about it?' Yet many recognise that explanations of behaviour are inadequate in debates which hinge, largely, on moral issues. So now we must turn to the final aspect of New Right philosophy and their claim that the extensive (and expanding) state is morally unjustifiable.

The immorality of the political process

While Nozick, Hayek and Friedman regard the extensive state as morally unjustifiable, for Murray Rothbard any state is an extensive state. Even among the defenders of a 'minimal' state there are disputes about how minimal the state should be. In the face of considerable disagreement over fundamentals among these theorists, it would appear impossible to specify any one view as common to the moral outlook of the New Right. There is, however, at least one central agreement.

They all recognise the inadequacy of 'democracy' as a basis for any

[66]

moral justification. That a majority of individuals endorse a proposal is neither necessary nor sufficient to make it morally acceptable. In one way this is a view most people would accept. Few would argue that I should be forced to live on soy beans and alfalfa sprouts because a democratic majority voted that I should, or even that everybody should. But what the New Right claims is that there are many issues on which decisions are taken and laws are passed on the basis of democratic consent, despite the absence, in their view, of adequate moral justification for making that issue the subject of democratic decision-making. Just as a democratic state may not tell me what to eat, neither may it tell me what safety precautions I should take *for myself* when driving my car or designing my house, or tell my union what voting procedures it must use, or tell my grocer when he may open his shop. The objection raised here is not against democracy as a decision procedure but against the extensive scope of democracy. In the moral philosophy of an intellectual anarchist like Rothbard, of course, the scope of democracy is contracted until it disappears.

But is there a moral theory that is shared by the New Right? In one sense the New Right articulates not one moral theory but several. Thus Rothbard draws his conclusions about morality from a theory of natural law. Ayn Rand seeks similar foundations for morality, emphasising that her philosophy follows from a correct understanding of man as a rational being. Hayek sees morality as the product of human evolution and thinks that the correct moral conclusions will be reached through the rule of law provided that judges respect the contraints imposed by the demands of consistency among rules of conduct — by the (Kantian) test of the ability to universalise moral prescriptions. James Buchanan sees the correct moral theory as that which is articulated by a social contract which respects the interests both of those favoured and those disadvantaged by the rules of the status quo. If there is a common core of agreement amongst these New Right theorists in moral philosophy, it is the shared view that there should not be enforceable, uncontracted obligations within a particular domain of human action. Where they differ is over the scope of that domain and over the way in which it is to be identified. Rothbard would argue that the domain within which this principle applies includes all human action. Buchanan, on the other hand, would maintain that it is not of unlimited scope but is defined by the contractarian procedures he defends.

While the arguments advanced by the New Right have by no means been embraced by a majority of people, even in the small world of academia, they are receiving serious attention. So much so that many adherents of this political philosophy seem to think that the major debates have been won and that political success awaits them. I

[67]

suggest that, in spite of the strength of the New Right case, important problems have yet to be solved.

IV. *Problems facing the New Right*

The major problems stem from the nature of politics and particularly from the deficiencies of the political process which they have gone so far to expose. For while the processes of democratic politics serve best the interests which are powerful enough and organised enough to take advantage of them, the obstacle remains that this is the arena within which the New Right has to compete. Here a number of difficulties arise. Most obviously, the New Right is not a powerful interest in any country and lacks the funds necessary to exert political influence or the numbers necessary to be regarded as electorally important.

One solution calls for the advocates of New Right thinking to enter politics in an attempt to implement the changes they favour. This strategy would be accomplished either by forming new political parties, or entering and seeking to change existing political parties — in the way that communists have sought to change the political direction of the Labour Party. To some small extent this has happened, both in the USA and in Britain. While this approach may bring some success in the short term, the actors in politics will remain subject to the pressures of politics. And for the reasons outlined by the public choice school, the parochial interests of influential sections of the electorate will generally assert themselves over the ideas of politicians. Thus Sir Keith Joseph's proposals to make wealthier parents pay for a part of their children's tertiary education costs crumbled in the face of resistance from the middle-class Tory voter and his representatives on the Conservative benches in Parliament. As long as organised interests dominate markets across the economy and government is led to intervene on their behalf, no government inspired by the New Right will be able to put things right. And as long as the ideas of the New Right are at odds with the perceived interests of the electorate in a democratic polity, its chances of bringing about significant changes will remain slight.

For these reasons what is more important than electoral victory is changing people's perceptions of where their interests truly lie. This is not to deny the success of the Thatcher Government which has, in its privatisation measures for example, brought about changes considered politically impossible in the late 1970s. Yet it must be recognised that, while some restrictions of individual freedom have been lifted, some new ones have also been put in place (compulsory car seat belts, for example) and many old ones remain (like zoning for comprehensive schools). If New Right ideas are to hold sway in the

[68]

long term, changes are necessary not only in a government's inclinations but also in the outlook of the public generally and, more particularly, of the people to whom governments turn for counsel.

The first and most important task of the New Right must then be to solve the theoretical problems evident in their writings, particularly since their intellectual opponents, while conceding certain arguments, are also marshalling their responses to the advocates of freedom and market. Here the claim that requires most careful re-examination is that the reduction of the scope of the activities of the state is a sufficient condition for progress toward freer and more prosperous societies.

For as Professor Mancur Olson has shown through his study of *The Rise and Decline of Nations*, organised interests or, as he calls them, distributional coalitions, may persist in societies in which government is not the source of coercion or social pressure. Indian castes, for example, exhibited all the features of cartels, controlling entry into lines of business, keeping craft mysteries or secrets, and setting monopoly prices. While individuals across the world may not differ in their basic motivation to improve the lot of their families and themselves, the nature of the prevailing systems of entitlement or of 'property rights' may have as important an effect on the outcomes produced by the market as any set of rules imposed by government. This condition requires the generation not only of ideas about how the market might be reinvented in areas in which it no longer exists, but also of arguments in moral philosophy to justify the development of particular forms of property rights.

The most stubborn obstacle to the success of New Right ideas lies in the fact that, in politics, interests rather than ideas predominate. But if there is a reason that this obstacle is not insurmountable it is that people's perceptions of their interests, and of the interests of others, are governed by ideas, including the ideas of economists and political philosophers. Recall Keynes' familiar remark that politicians are often the unwitting slaves of some defunct economist. If so, what the New Right requires more urgently than the continued electoral success of its favoured political parties is the intellectual and popular success of its ideas. The measure of this success should consider not merely the number of New Right proposals adopted by the Conservative Party but the distance travelled in the same direction by the Alliance or by Labour. What is least desirable is that the ideas of the New Right become tied to the political interests of any one party. For then the interests of party would prevail over the ideas which it claims to espouse. If this were to happen, the danger would lie not in electoral defeat but in securing false victory.

[69]

GRAHAM DAWSON

The fifth essay in this group on first principles expounds the philosophical and economic content of the New Right.

Graham Dawson was born in 1946 in Birkenhead. His father began life as a clerk, was unemployed in the 1930s, worked as a labourer on a building site, joined Bowater as a casual labourer and rose to be chief wages clerk.

Dr Dawson was at a state primary and a grammar school near Liverpool. He graduated from University College, Oxford, in 1968 with a degree in Politics, Philosophy and Economics, and from Liverpool University with a B.Phil. in 1970. He won a doctorate in education at Keele University in 1981 and is working in his spare time for a doctorate in economics at Liverpool University. Since 1984 he has been Head of Economics at Birkenhead School. From 1975 to 1984 he was a part-time Tutor in Philosophy to the Open University.

In the 1960s he was Secretary/Treasurer of the Oxford University Democratic Labour Club, a social democratic-type breakaway group from the Trotskyist Labour Club.

Dr Dawson is an occasional contributor to Economic Affairs *and has written for philosophical and educational journals.*

His epigrammatic prose outlines the reasons for the New Right reaction against basic tenets of the New Left. The New Right rejects both the Old Left and the 'Dead (Conservative) Centre' for accepting Keynesianism.

The New Right is not original, but it is now fashionable, perhaps even chic.

6

THE OLD AND THE NEW LEFT ARE OLD HAT

GRAHAM DAWSON

My essay is divided into four parts; the first two are broadly philosophical and the second two more directly on economic policy. Part I expounds what I take to be the principal ideas of the New Left. Part II criticises them and sets out how I see the general philosophical perspective of the New Right. Part III discusses the economic policies of the post-war consensus and describes the events which set me on the New Right road. Part IV indicates the economic policies that seem to be most urgent.

Economic collectivism and social disintegration

To be on the political Right is to be reactionary. The New Right is a superior and opposite reaction to the New Left, which had most of the action in the 1960s and '70s. Its first manifestation was in the protest movements of the '60s, which took 'the form of opposition to the Viet Nam War, struggles for Civil Rights, Women's Lib and Gay Liberation, and Environmentalism' (S. M. Lipset, 'Whatever happened to the proletariat?', *Encounter*, June 1981). New Left thought exhibited five main characteristics.

(i) *The discovery of the new proletariat*. The New Left could not conceal its disappointment with the working classes of the Western industrial nations for having let down the Marxist side by failing to stage the proletarian revolution. The diagnosis of the workers' condition was that they had contracted the dreaded *embourgeoisement*. They had fallen victim to the false needs of the consumer society, in which people buy the goods they have helped to produce not because they 'really need' them but because they have been brainwashed by advertising into falsely believing they do. In devoting their time and energy to the satisfaction of 'false' needs, workers are distracted from the frustration of their 'real' needs. They remain docile and repressed, instead of becoming active in the social revolution which alone can satisfy their 'real' needs. It was, therefore, up to a somewhat heterogeneous proletariat, comprising students,

[71]

women, blacks, gays and Third-World guerrillas, to initiate the revolution (Herbert Marcuse, in *One-Dimensional Man*).

(ii) Post-materialism. This is the assumption that the affluent West had solved the problem of wealth-creation once and for all. Wealth would go on reproducing itself without anyone having to lift a finger or fire a brain cell. All men of goodwill should therefore turn to redistributing it away from the grabbers to the deprived. Industry and commerce must make way for social work. The entrepreneur must do as the sociologist-king tells him.

(iii) Economic interference. Once economic activity is thought to be a form of grabbing, of acquiring for oneself what should rightfully be held in common ownership, there can be no objection to placing as many restraints upon it as possible. The more taxes, forms, licences, rules and regulations to be paid, filled in, taken out, complied with and observed, the better.

(iv) The permissive society. The Freudian concept of repression found a place in New left thought. Civilisation required some restraint on the sexual impulse, it was admitted. But Victorian morality, for instance, was held to be a device for preserving capitalist relations of production in particular rather than civilisation in general. Affluence had rendered the capitalist system, which included the severe repression of sexual drives, surplus to requirements. So there could be a non-stop ride all the way from Victorian straight lace to 'whatever turns you on' (Herbert Marcuse again, in *Eros and Civilisation*).

(v) The routinisation of violence. Marx had predicted a violent revolution. But he saw it as a revolution to end all revolutions by abolishing private property, the cause of all social conflict. Those who took part in the protest movements of the '60s saw violence differently — as the weapon of first resort in every local disturbance. Occupations, 'demos', flying pickets and intimidation became everyday occurrences, like muggings and vandalism. We are still waiting for the Proletarian Revolution.

The New Left combined two main strands of thought: economic interventionism and social *laissez faire*. A philosophical defence of this way of drawing the boundary between social control and individual freedom was offered in *A Theory of Justice* by John Rawls. The significance of the book for the New Right is that (in the words of *The Times Literary Supplement*) it makes the task of the reactionary so clear:

> ... the liberal ... wants to say that governements have no right to censor, no right to dictate private conduct; and he wants to fight off the conservative who claims that governments have no right to tax their citizenry for welfare purposes. ... *A Theory of Justice* neatly separates out a group

of political and civil liberties which are all but absolutely inviolable, placing them in a different category from the rules about such things as property rights which enable economic activity to proceed.

Market economy and ordered society

The task of the New Right is simply to turn the clock back by reversing Rawls. There must be more freedom in economic affairs but less in social matters. I shall defend this opinion by trying to rebut each of the five New Left propositions.

(i) *Populism.* The New Right has rediscovered the people. The contempt for the ambitions and preferences of ordinary working people was always the least attractive aspect of New left theorising. Marcuse defined false needs as 'those which are superimposed upon the individual by particular social interests in his repression.' But what are people's 'real' needs, if not for jobs, money and some of the many things that money can buy? There is nothing false about needing somewhere to live, a holiday, a healthy diet, the freedom of movement that only a car can give, the cultural enrichment provided by books and the arts, and so on. What 'real' or 'true' needs were being 'suppressed' by the consumer society? It was preposterous to suggest that the Universal Californian Campus could satisfy needs that were somehow truer or more real than those met by the economies of the Western world. Hence the appeal of the Marcusean vision to the leisured offspring of affluent parents and to virtually no one else. Working people knew very well that the problem was not what to give the man who has everything, but how to get a bit more of what you want.

(ii) *Wealth creation.* Post-materialists think that there are only two things to be done with wealth. We can acquire it, which is greedy and materialistic. Or we can redistribute it, which is caring and compassionate. There is a third thing we can, and must, do. We must create wealth. But that is too much like hard work. What post-materialists fail to realise is that the creation of wealth is the most fundamental social service of all. Charity begins at work.

It is essential to encourage people to create wealth, because that is the indispensable means to the execution of many humanitarian tasks. Being starry-eyed about the ends of human action and incompetent about the means to achieve them is almost a national characteristic. Ever since Shelley panicked at the Industrial Revolution and went off to drown in the Mediterranean through a failure to master the practical art of sailing a small boat, we have been intent on making a land fit for ineffectual angels to live in. A survey by Japan's Ministry of International Trade and Industry found that Great Britain had produced 55 per cent of the world's post-war inventions, to the USA's 22 per cent and Japan's 6 per cent. Yet we appear to be so embarrassed at having invented something that we can hardly wait to see the Americans or Japanese exploit its commercial potential. We are in danger of becoming the Icarus of the industrial world, falling into the sea while a boat sails calmly on its way carrying heatshields for wax made in South Korea.

(iii) The moral superiority of the market. Economic interference is based on the paternalistic assumption that the moral values of state bureaucrats are superior to those of ordinary people. The paternalist concedes that the market economy is unbeatable at creating wealth, but claims that it does so only by producing trivia and conning people into believing that trivia are just what they have always wanted. The responsible role is to set yourself up in a Town Hall and cream off the profits of private industry to spend on socially useful nuclear-free zones. After all, you know what is best for everyone. You must do. You are a socialist.

What this means in the real world is that serving customers who are always right has been given up in favour of treating clients who have 'social problems'. State-sector workers owe their livelihoods not to the general public who pay them but to the local government and union bosses who use them to build their own empires. The Left has given us a hundred years of indigestible Marxist theorising — and what has it produced? The feudal system all over again, with a Trotskyite as lord of the inner-city manor.

By contrast the market economy is free in the sense not that it is a jungle of greed and exploitation, a Hobbesian state of nature where every man is at war with every other man, but that it gives people the chance to enter into obligations without coercion. The mutual benefit of the contracting parties is the motive. Buyer and seller, employer and employee, agree to be bound by a contract requiring each party to give up something in return for benefits received. A contract is not merely a soulless legal document: it is a formal promise. And the obligation to honour promises is the cornerstone of morality. To be outside the market is to be in moral jeopardy, not knowing whether you are foisting on a captive public what it is convenient for you to provide or meeting a real 'need' which people would *willingly* pay for if given the choice.

(iv) The objectivity of morality. Some advocates of the free market argue that consistency requires them to support the permissive society. However, universal libertarianism is dangerous and not in any way implied by arguments for the market economy. A Thatcherite utopia of self-help and self-discipline, of hard work and deferred gratification, is a long way from the Universal Californian Campus sought by Marcuse's disciples, where laid-back promiscuity and the

[74]

conspicuous consumption of narcotic substances would prevail. It is an immature over-simplification to regard the permissive society as the more consistent variation on the individualist theme.

There is a world of difference between the market economy and anarchic individualism. The fundamental error of inordinate libertarianism is to suppose that society consists only of individuals and the state; this view overlooks the existence of institutions without which individual human beings could never become complete persons. The private sector of the economy comprises households and firms as well as individuals; human society includes churches and nations as well as people. What makes someone the person that he is is the web of customs and traditions which he inherits from, and duties and loyalties which he owes to, family, employer, church and nation.

Accordingly, it is deeply mistaken to maintain that the real test of commitment to freedom is whether it allows people to act in ways of which one disapproves. For this implies that morality is a matter of merely personal approbation and disapprobation. Thus, the libertarian is obliged to espouse subjectivism, which precludes a rational justification of his doctrine. If his belief in individual liberty is only a personal preference, it has no better a claim on the allegiance of the rational man than the totalitarian's belief in the supremacy of the state.

The truth is that there are objective standards of right and wrong, which are grounded in the duties we, as social beings, owe to others.

(v) 'Order, order!' The decay of a shared public morality has weakened inhibitions against the use of force. To the degree that morality is seen as a matter of personal approval and disapproval, rational debate is bound to be overwhelmed by trials of brute strength. The permissive society is part of the same pattern of social disintegration as the routinisation of violence. Libertarianism is a degenerate mutation of true right-wing principles, which seek a balance between economic freedom and social stability.

Nice ends, pity about the means

The argument so far has concentrated on the philosophical assumptions of the New Left. It is now time to turn to the economic policies of the Old Left. The New Right believes, not only in wealth creation rather than post-materialism, but also in New Classical Economics rather than Keynesianism. To avoid repeating familiar criticisms of Keynesian economics, I shall describe three turning-points in the development of my own views.

The failings of the Old Left and — for many Conservatives accepted Keynesianism — the Dead Centre were largely of ill-advised means rather than ill-chosen ends. Three policy issues illustrate this weakness.

(i) International competitiveness. A recognition of the importance of creating wealth was implicit in the anxiety voiced by several post-war governments over the United Kingdom's declining international competitiveness and relatively poor growth record. It was Harold Wilson who said: 'The world does not owe us a living'. But his mixture of devaluation and deflation failed to revive the entrepreneurial spirit in British industry. This failure is hardly surprising, for the third ingredient in the Wilsonian confection was a sharp rise in income tax, not the best incentive to hard work and risk-taking. Yet the sentiment is essentially Thatcherite.

The mistake was that the robust commonsense of the diagnosis gave way to the over-protectiveness typical of Keynesian policy. It is no use saying we have to pull our economic socks up and then devaluing the pound so that our international competitiveness is apparently restored wihout anyone having had to lift a restrictive practice. If the external world is indifferent to our fate, government should not shrink from tolerating conditions which demonstrate the truth.

It was not until 1980-81 that a British government *acted* as if it believed that 'the world does not owe us a living'. In refusing to intervene in the foreign-exchange markets to reduce the value of the pound, Sir Geoffrey Howe placed the responsibility for earning Britain a living where it belonged: with the British people. It was up to industry to move up-market and sell on quality rather than cheapness; to get out of low-skill low-tech manufacturing into industries where our comparative advantage in technological and financial sophistication can make itself felt; to improve productivity, even if it requires redundancies; and to cut costs by carrying fewer stocks. These are real changes undertaken by the people rather than sleight of hand with the exchange rate performed by the government.

(ii) Unemployment. Sometime in 1966 or '7 I attended a meeting in Oxford addressed by Michael Stewart, then Secretary of State for Economic Affairs. What I remember chiefly is his defence of earnings-related unemployment benefit. As far as I recall, he argued that technological advance and competition from Third-World industries were about to render much of the manufacturing capacity of the UK obsolete. Resources, including labour, would have to be transferred to high-tech and service industries, a process which would increase unemployment, albeit temporarily. To persuade the unions to accept that a period or two of unemployment would become a normal part of a typical worker's life, the government had a duty to ensure that living standards for those out of work would not fall below those to which their earnings had accustomed them. Unemployment would

[76]

cease to be a stigma and a cause of fear, and the unions would co-operate in the modernisation of industry.

The argument seemed reasonable enough at the time, and the goal of a union movement which accepts the inevitability of industrial change remains desirable. But there is now evidence that un-employment benefits are, as Hermione Parker has put it, high enough 'to price the unskilled worker out of work especially if he or she has children to support' (*Action on Welfare*). Yet many trades unions continue to resist necessary change, as the miners' strike of 1984-85 amply demonstrated.

(iii) 'You can fool some of the people some of the time . . .'. The final episode is more theoretical. As a philosopher, I was aware that human actions are not the same as physical events. An action has a meaning for the person performing it; it makes sense to him in terms of his aims and assumptions, beliefs and values, hopes and expectations. Yet when I turned to economics I found the human dimension apparently absent. Keynesian economics regarded people as not really people at all but as a transparent medium quite incapable of deflecting government intentions. The government pressed whatever button its economic advisers told it to and exchange (un)employment for inflation as electoral convenience dictated.

Nowadays, rational expectations theory recognises that people use as much information as they can acquire. Workers are no longer seen as the hapless victims of money illusion, mindlessly assuming that every 10 per cent wage increase means a 10 per cent improvement in the standard of living, regardless of what is happening to prices. Instead, they will realise that a higher standard of living during a period of 10 per cent inflation requires a wage rise in excess of that figure. Consequently, government efforts to reduce unemployment at a cost of no more than 10 per cent inflation will be thwarted. A stable inflation rate is rendered impossible by the way in which people react to reflationary policy. Economic agents are seen to be precisely that: independent sources of action, interacting with the government rather than endlessly duped by it.

What are the implications for policy of my critique of Old and New Left?

Implications for economic policy

Three main principles have emerged from this discussion. First, the market economy possesses a dual significance, as the engine of wealth-creation and as the only morally defensible arena for economic transactions. Secondly, freedom and innovation in the econ-omic sphere should be combined with caution and continuity in the social realm. Thirdly, domestic institutions, especially the labour market, should reflect the truth that the world does not owe us a living. It is here that policy seems to be most seriously deficient. I propose three reforms.

1. *Abolish trade union immunities.* Unions have a constructive role to play, and many union officials do valuable work in improving conditions, dealing with specific grievances and so on, all through routine negotiation which would be unaffected by the loss of immunities. Unions cannot create wealth but they can obtruct necessary change and so undermine the wealth-creating process. It is inequitable to grant immunity from actions for damages to bodies which can make some workers better off only at the expense of others. If the jurisdiction of the common law were restored to all union actions, as Professor Patrick Minford has argued, unemployment could be reduced by 1 million over ten years. Trade unionists who say this measure would make unions completely powerless are effectively admitting that their power has been exercised *outside the law* that applies to everyone else.

2. *Set a maximum replacement ratio.* The message that the world does not owe us a living is bound to be muffled if the state acts as if it owes the individual a better living than he can earn for himself. Yet some people are better off on the dole. To ensure that every unemployed person has an incentive to take a job, a maximum replacement ratio of 70 per cent of net income in work should be set. This would reduce unemployment, according to calculations by Professor Minford, by 0·75 million over five years. No doubt someone will denounce this proposal as the product of 'Victorian values'. But it is good old eighteenth-century commonsense as put by Dr Johnson's Boswell:

> You cannot spend money in luxury without doing good to the poor. Nay, you do more good to them by spending it in luxury than by giving it: for by spending it in luxury you make them exert industry, whereas by giving it you keep them idle.

3. *Privatise state education.* There are no good reasons for having a state-run education system. There are good reasons for *not* having it: teachers are becoming as addicted to 'industrial action' as other public-sector workers; they have given up serving the customer who is always right in favour of treating clients with social disadvantages; and they are frequently out to promote an anti-business culture. The occupational hazard of teachers — that they believe themselves in sole possession of the right answers — exercabates these distortions. To the charge that state schools neglect the requirements of industry, many teachers would reply that industry is only good for exploiting its workers and manipulating its consumers. The only way to eradicate

[78]

that sort of bias is to expose schools now in the state sector to the discipline of market forces. It is foolish to leave the education of young people who, it is to be hoped, will consolidate Britain's recent economic recovery, in the hands of people many of whom are antipathetic to the very idea of commercial success.

So what is new about the New Right? The combination of economic change and social continuity is not original. What *is* new is the intellectual respectability of free market arguments and the electoral appeal of economic individualism and old-fashioned patriotism. To be on the political Right is fashionable, perhaps even *chic*. Labour's Clause IV on nationalising industry was always silly; now it is also boring. Union-bashing has been sensible since 1906 at least, now it is also self-evident. Reactionary *chic* is the flavour of the month. But fashion's swings and roundabouts are as unpredictable as fortune's slings and arrows. No wonder fortune is capricious: she is a woman, as Machiavelli, an unjustly maligned political thinker, recognised long ago:

> I hold strongly to this: that it is better to be impetuous than circumspect; because fortune is a woman and if she is to be submissive it is necessary to beat and coerce her.

It has taken a woman, who shows no signs of running out of radicalism, to beat the rest of us.

ROBERT MILLER

The final essay in this group examines the economic essence of the New Right — the scope it envisages for the individual entrepreneur.

Robert Miller was born in 1947 and educated at Worksop College, Trinity College, Dublin, and the University of Edinburgh.

After working in a firm of stockbrokers in the City of London, he was at the Centre for Policy Studies. He is now a consultant to the IEA and to several City firms — a discount house, a futures broker, and the London International Financial Futures Exchange. He has been an adviser to TV Channel 4 current affairs programmes.

He has written Hobart Papers for the Institute of Economic Affairs and contributes to financial journals.

His essay argues that much of the criticism on the Left or on the Old Right, including the Keynesians and other critics of the market, has been undermined by the evidence in recent years that the market is spontaneously capable of producing institutions and devices to deal with economic instability and its other alleged imperfections.

The New Right will be strengthened if it applies the economics of creativity and entrepreneurship to human action where it was thought inappropriate — not least, unemployment.

7

ENTREPRENEURSHIP — THE ESSENCE

ROBERT MILLER

On leaving Edinburgh University in the early 1970's, where I had studied amongst other subjects, the philosophy of the social sciences under Professor H. B. Acton, I had a short and unsatisfactory career as a stockbroker. I joined the firm when the *Financial Times* 30-share index was at 520 in late 1972 and left in early 1975 when it was around 180. If unsatisfactory, the job was not without excitement. On one day in early 1975 as the market bounced from its nadir we bought Thorn shares at 100p in the morning and could have sold them for 118p at the close of business. I then took a job with the Centre for Policy Studies in 1975 soon after it was founded.

From philosophy and economics to entrepreneurship — and poetry

This irregular path to economics was stimulated by the discovery that there was one school of economics which was fully in accord with my understanding of the philosophy of the social sciences. This was the Austrian school, which, unlike other groups of economists, did not pretend that it was searching for laws of human economic behaviour which would enable the economist, given initial conditions, to predict the future pattern of the economy in much the same way as meteorologists predict the weather. They might not do it very well, but at least it could be done in principle. But this approach to the social sciences was totally discredited by philosophers who argued that human behaviour could not be assimilated to that of the natural sciences, because it was essentially 'purposive'. In other words it made no sense to talk about human behaviour if it did not include a description of personal *intentions*.

   This *purposive* character of human economic agents was completely ignored by most of the standard schools of economics which attempted to 'model' the economy on the basis of historic patterns of behaviour. But this approach ignores the *creative* activity which characterises much of human behaviour of all types. That this creative feature of human activity should be ignored by economists was all the more surprising as it seemed to be the most interesting aspect of economic life in the western world — its continuous capacity for innovation. It was only in the writings of the then derided obscure economists like the 'Austrians' Hayek and Mises that there were intimations of this economics of creativity. They included the British G. L. S. Shackle who had declared that the businessman should be compared to the poet as both were essentially innovative — creating a new pattern of goods or words which was not logically contained in what went before.

This insight of the Austrian economists has still not been assimilated into economics, perhaps because it has devastating consequences for politicians and governments. Because of the creative capacity of human beings, it is impossible to predict the pattern of economic activity. Any attempt by government to formulate economic policy of any kind must therefore be doomed to failure, or at least to risk massive damage because of its errors and misjudgments, accentuated by the element of short-term political interest.

Entrepreneurship and the 'New Right'

Thus, even the whole apparatus of monetarism, which seems to epitomise the New Right, is based on a fundamental mistake. A monetary policy is as bound to be fundamentally inefficient as any other attempt to supply goods by a state monopoly. According to Milton Friedman, monetarism rests on the assumption of regularity in the behaviour of people towards money, and supposes that this regularity can be used to predict the future pattern of the economy in general and inflation in particular.

But this view fails to take into account what has become known as Goodhart's Law, named after the monetary economist at the Bank of England. Goodhart argued that as soon as the Bank of England attempted to control one measure of the money supply, such as M1 or M3, the money markets would adjust their behaviour accordingly, so that the measure of money being used became useless for its purpose. Here was a perfect example of a 'socialist' policy being rendered useless by the creativity of businessmen in the market. The infinite flexibility of financial markets means that it is exceptionally difficult or impossible for the Bank of England and the Treasury to develop a policy of monetary control. The solution is for them to abandon the concept of 'monetary policy' which, as Professor Hayek has recently pointed out, is only some 60 years old. Liquidity should be supplied by private enterprise for exactly the same reasons that consumers prefer the supply of motor cars by private enterprise rather than nationalised industry.

The significance of entrepreneurship for the New Right is not

[82]

limited to monetary policy — important though it is. The idea that the individual is a creative and innovative being whose views of business prospects may differ has other devastating effects on the ordinary understanding of the economy. The very idea that it is either valid or useful to describe the economic activities of a group of people as 'an economy' is fundamentally flawed.

The superstition of macro-economics and macro-forecasting

It is entirely misconceived for example to aggregate figures for capital to give a total value of the capital stock. Since the individual valuations on which the aggregation must be based reflect differing and possibly *conflicting* views of business prospects, the total will almost certainly be inaccurate. What is more, there can be no means of knowing in advance by how much the aggregate figure is inaccurate. But if the economy contains a multiplicity of differing and contradictory views, it makes no sense to manufacture artificial aggregate statistics which will conceal more than they reveal. In any event although the aggregate may remain the same, its constituents may have altered considerably, and the changes in the individual components may be ultimately of more significance for the economy than the simple total which is of immediate interest to the macro-economist.

The creative capacity of human beings destroys the sense and utility of the economic forecasting agencies which sell their wares to undiscerning companies and newspapers. What is particularly surprising is that, given the 'scientific' character of the forecasts, all the forecasts are different. We would be immensely surprised if the weather forecasters produced different predictions of the weather and retain what confidence we have in their skills, but this is what the economic forecasters expect of us.

The assumptions of those who even attempt to predict human conduct in general and economic behaviour in particular are unrealistic in the extreme. They do not describe real human beings, but cardboard men who never choose or think for themselves, but only react in the same stylised way to the phenomena which confront them. But people on the whole act for reasons that affect their view of the future, not as the result of causes that influenced the past.

There are also considerable practical difficulties in the way of the forecaster. It is undeniable that governments by their acts of commission and omission have an important effect on the economy and that they are run by politicians and civil servants with interest of their own that may conflict with the public interest. But of all the unpredictable things in the universe, the British party politician is about the most unpredictable.

There are also grave difficulties in assembling and co-ordinating all

[83]

the necessary information for a comprehensive 'model' of the economy that would be necessary for forecasts which were any better than informed guesses. Lord McFadzean, former chairman of Shell and Rolls Royce, once commented on the 10 million Soviet citizens who, in the absence of spontaneous market mechanisms, were estimated in the 1960's to engaged in the manual collection and processing of data. 'Academician Glushkov', he added, 'warned that if Russia attempted to simulate the detailed operations of the Russian economy, it would require "several quintillion relationships to be examined and appraised" and that would take several years even with "a million computers processing 30,000 operations a second."' Apart from any theoretical objections, forecasting is impracticable because of the impossibility of accumulating the requisite amounts of information.

What harm in macro forecasting?

At this stage we may ask: why is it that businesses and governments spend so much money on macro-economic forecasts when the whole enterprise has so many obvious flaws. In business this is particularly strange, because its supposed need for forecasts is based on a confusion; what concerns a business are the movements in the supply and demand for the particular goods and services in which it trades. For a company dealing in leather goods, the future movements of the GNP will be irrelevant if trends in the leather trade differ significantly from the course of the GNP. Indeed to rely on forecasts of the economy as a whole as guide to future progress of a business will be to divert attention from the dangers and opportunities which confront the businessman everyday. No econometric forecasts inspired Stephen Jobs of Apple Computers; nor could forecasts have prevented the near collapse of Acorn Computers.

For the private business, forecasts of changes in the macro-economic aggregates are useful only if they are good proxies for micro-economic particulars; but this is even more doubtful than the accuracy of the forecast, for as we have seen it is in the nature of the micro-components of macro-aggregates to change. Businessmen form expectations about the future and make plans of which many may be incompatible: they and the forecaster have no means of knowing in advance which plans will succeed and to what degree. Both will be able to guess, but this guessing reduces the forecaster to the modest position of one businessman amongst many in a competitive market.

Governments also claim that they require macro-economic forecasts so that they can manipulate the economy to carry out their programmes of full employment and prosperity. This claim is common to monetarists and to their Keynesian opponents. But it is not necessarily true, for governments can get out of the business of having 'policies' and can instead leave the field to spontaneous forces.

It is perfectly practicable for governments to leave 'policies' to individuals, for all governments do so to a greater or lesser extent. In the case of monetary policy the difficulties (described above) can be removed by admitting that there may be many different and conflicting views about the 'correct' supply of liquidity and allowing competition between the adherents of the opposing views. Thus, as Hayek has suggested, the supply of money and liquidity could be left entirely to competing banks and houses of issue. Competition would soon select which sort of money was most popular — that which was stable in value or indeed which appreciated.

It may be argued that, despite its obvious flaws, macro-economic forecasting is a harmless activity which keeps many people innocently occupied. But the practice of macro-economic forecasting encourages the belief that the 'economy' is a system to be manipulated and moulded in line with 'policy objectives', resources must be apportioned, and the 'national cake' cut in accord with the politician's view of other people's 'needs'. This view of the economy is ultimately incompatible with a free society because it involves the wholesale imposition of the planners' value judgements. The use of macro-economic forecasting is a small but significant step on the road to serfdom. For once economists and officials have a description of the economy as a whole, it is all too easy for them to attempt to mould it to either their own advantage or that of their section of the bureaucracy. A 'model' of the economy has exactly the same relationship to reality as a model railway to a real railway system. It is identical, except that the model leaves out the most important element of the real railway — the human beings.

Entrepreneurship and economic stability

The significance of entrepreneurship for the New Right is that it shows how collectivist techniques of economic management are fundamentally flawed in ways that have yet to be fully appreciated. It is also important as, in recent years, entrepreneurial action has begun to tackle some of the problems of economic instability which had led many economists to think that there was a role for 'policy'. This is not surprising, because businessmen are continually required to deal with all the ordinary uncertainties of industry, and government-induced instability is only one difficulty amongst many which they face.

An interesting example has been the explosive growth of trading in commodity and financial futures markets over the last ten years. Innovative commodity exchanges have adapted old methods of

[85]

trading in commodity futures to allow businesses which are subject to interest rate and other commercial risks to 'hedge'. Futures allow businessmen to fix in advance what they will have to pay or receive and thus to insulate themselves from adverse price changes.

Futures trading in US Treasury Bonds for example has been developed with outstanding success by the Chicago Board of Trade. It is now the most actively traded commodity futures contract in the history of the world. The new market allows traders collectively to form a pessimistic view of the future course of bond prices without setting off the cumulative deflation that Keynes claimed was a major cause of recession. Instead of pessimism leading to a destabilising flight into cash and liquid assets, the new markets absorb extremes of pessimism and optimism about interest rates without provoking the surges in the demand for cash that Keynes thought was one of the chief causes of the cycle of boom and slump. Pessimists about bond prices do not have scramble for cash, because they now can sell interest rate futures contracts with much more convenience and without the dire effects on the economy predicted by the Keynesian theory. Whether or not we accept the Keynesian analysis, the new markets show how entrepreneurs can adjust themselves to economic instability. They counter the view common to most critics of capitalism that the system is inherently unstable. Economic creativity is the great stabiliser of the economy.

Entrepreneurship and the New Right

This is a direct response by spontaneous market forces to reduce the difficulties for business of economic instability. Not only do these new markets provide insulation for those who are averse to risk and want to play safe, but they also serve the advantage for society by reducing the instability that gave rise to them. Futures trading in interest rates was the market's response to government-induced volatility in interest rates and inflation. A development which may be of exceptional interest is the introduction of futures trading based on the American Consumer Price Index (CPI) which will make it possible to 'hedge' against unanticipated increases in the rate of inflation. By buying CPI futures it would be possible to insulate a company from the effects of accelerating inflation faster than expected. Inflation would lead to profits from the rising price of the inflation futures contracts. Such trading has started on the New York Coffee, Sugar and Cocoa Exchange, and it may represent another attempt by the market economy to deal *spontaneously* with government intervention and with the problems presented by economic instability.

This capacity of entrepreneurship to cope with the problems presented to it by government is of exceptional importance for the future of the New Right, because it finally removes one of the last excuses for intervention available — that free markets are incapable of dealing with economic instability.

Entrepreneurship is creativity in everyday business. It is only recently that economists have begun to realise its true significance. The older economics which dealt in the relationships between economic aggregates and averages has proved ineffective, because it could not accommodate the truth that human beings are not automata, doing the same old things in the same old way. The strength of the New Right in developing its arguments will depend in large measure on how much it can apply the theory of entrepreneurship or economic creativity to parts of economics and politics where it was previously thought irrelevant.

Entrepreneurship is of fundamental importance in monetary economics, the development of financial institutions and the study of the problem of unemployment. All the unemployed are entrepreneurs — potential creators of economic value to a greater or lesser extent. Economists should ask what is frustrating this inherent creativity. The answer does not lie in macro-economics but in the market.

III

CRITIQUES

JOHN BURTON

Three critiques of intellectual error comprise group III. The first essay demolishes the notion that a compromise between supposed 'extremes' yields the best of both: it could produce the worst.

John Burton was born in 1945, within the sound of Bow Bells, the oldest of the essayists, aged 39 when the essay was commissioned in March 1985. He was educated at a local private school and at a grammar school in Worthing. He graduated with a First in economics at the University of Wales and obtained a Master's degree at the London School of Economics in 1969.

His career was in University and Polytechnic teaching from 1969 to 1985, when he joined the Institute of Economic Affairs as Research Fellow and later Research Director.

He has written books, contributed to learned and popular journals, lectured in Western Europe and North America, and advised government organisations and private enterprises.

He describes how his doubts about economic policy under Harold Wilson were reinforced by research into national economic planning and incomes policy, trade union power (used for 'plunder'), the tripartite corporatist planning by government, TUC and CBI, and industrial policy engineered by quangos endowed with power and public money but no responsibility.

He believes that a major reason for the conversion of younger scholars from socialism to liberalism has been the experience of the failure of the Middle Way urged by politicians of all Parties.

8

THE MUDDLE OF THE MIDDLE WAY

JOHN BURTON

Throughout the 20th century there has been a quest, conducted both in the minds of academics and intellectuals and in the experiments of Western governments, to find a Golden Mean between a free and a collectivist society/economy.

The idea of a 'middle way' is usually attributed to Bismarck. In Britain the idea received explicit attention in 1938 in a book, *The Middle Way*, written and published by a Conservative politician, Harold Macmillan, later to become Prime Minister in the post-war years, and who is now sitting in the House of Lords as Earl Stockton.

But the idea pre-dates that publication and its circulation in the political arena. Economists and other social scientists/philosophers in the UK had been discussing it long before. In economics specifically there had been the development of 'welfare economics' from the first decade of the 20th century. Moreover, the publication of Keynes' *General Theory*, with its notion that the economy can be boosted by appropriate dollops of extra government spending, pre-dated Macmillan by two years. But Pigou's notion of a gap between the private and 'social' costs and benefits of economic activity, requiring state action to fill it, came as early as 1920.

Both of these developments pointed in the same direction. The market system of a free society was not perfect. Therefore, it was argued, government should step in where the market failed, in order to rectify the situation. Thus arose notions of regional policy, environmental policy, income re-distribution policy, 'trade' policy (i.e., various forms of protectionism), macro-economic policy, industrial policy, health-care policy, nationalisation, and so on. The list is endless.

In the post-war period, under the influence of a political consensus about the middle way, these policies were put into effect, and Britain became a 'mixed economy'.

As a young man at university, I was strongly attracted to these ideas. It seemed eminently sensible to me that, if there was unemployment, any sane government should 'shift the LM curve to the right' (indulge in monetary expansionism) or 'shift the IS curve upwards' (spend a lot more). If pollution existed then, obviously, government should step in with appropriate regulations, taxes and subsidies in order to 'equate marginal social cost with marginal social benefit'. If people were poor, then, again obviously, they should be helped — through the state.

My enthusiasm for the mixed economy during my undergraduate years was enhanced by the promises of Harold Wilson. It was becoming apparent by the mid-to-late 1960s that my country was going into relative economic decline, compared to the French, German, Japanese, American and other economies. Something, clearly, had to be done — and fast.

Harold Wilson promised us a 'white-hot' technological revolution' and industrial regeneration: a new economic dynamism. It was all very heady stuff, and I voted for it. Britain would be great again (with a capital G), the economy would be stabilised at full employment, moving ahead fast, catching up with our rivals, and getting the benefits of an 'economic miracle' as seemed to have occurred via *planification* in France. Sir Alec Douglas Home playing with his matchsticks (as he himself represented his understanding of economics and economic policy) did not sound a very impressive alternative.

The emergence of doubt: the failure of national economic planning

My gradual conversion to the 'New Right' — a term that I disclaim and indeed reject — was not a matter of any grandoise intellectual transmogrification from one orthodoxy to another. It was the result of experience — experience at first hand — with economic problems, and patient study of them.

My education in economic realities started, while I was still at university as an undergraduate, with the (in retrospect) grotesque failure of the National Plan of 1965.

There had been an earlier attempt at *planification* in Britain, under the aegis of the National Economic Development Council (NEDC) in 1962, under a Conservative Government. The NEDC was supposed to harness government and 'both sides of industry' *via* indicative planning. It set 'targets' for this, that, and the other, but the record shows that, in the words of Professor Alan Budd (*The Politics of Economic Planning*):

> Between 1961 and 1966 total output rose by 2·9 per cent a year compared to the NEDC target of 4 per cent. Productivity appeared to grow no faster than in the previous five years ... manufacturing investment grew by 0·2 per cent a year, compared with the target of 3·3 per cent.

Nothing was learned at the time from this failure. The incoming Labour Government of 1964 set about an even more ambitious exercise in indicative planning under a newly-created Department of Economic Affairs, which 11 months later produced a National Plan. The NEDC target of 4 per cent a year growth was replaced by one of 25 per cent growth over 1964-1970 (about 3·8 per cent a year). Here again the theory was that by talking about higher growth, and publishing a large tract upon it (The Plan), the growth rate could be miraculously jacked up by government.

It did not happen. In July 1966, the National Plan was abandoned in the wake of a sterling crisis. Moreover, it is simple, in retrospect, to see that the 'plan' *could not have worked* in any event. Companies had been asked to fill in forms about what they 'thought would happen' to their sales and output assuming 25 per cent growth from 1964 to 1970. Few believed in the latter assumptions, and some must have filled in their forms with the appropriate degree of cynicism, not to say hilarity.

Professor Dennis Lees — a member of the Advisory Council of the IEA — was then at the University College of Swansea and my tutor. In 1968 he delivered a virtuoso inaugural lecture on 'The Uses and Abuses of National Planning' which pointed to the main theoretical flaws in the case for this form of governmental intervention. The problem is that the future is *inherently* uncertain. Thus, what is needed is an economy which has the capability for 'flexible response' to swiftly-changing (and unpredictable) circumstances, peopled by economic actors — entrepreneurs and consumers — with the incentive to do so. And only a market economy can provide that system. Any straightjacket laid down by government reduces the necessary flexibility. Moreover, 'indicative' planning — which does not involve directives from government — neither reduces the uncertainty about the future nor provides any incentive for firms to follow the 'guidelines' of the plan. It is simply an expensive exercise in grandiose delusion.

I had begun to see the force of such market-economy arguments towards the latter end of my undergraduate years. Later experience and research was to confirm and reinforce these doubts about the 'middle way', and its constituent delusions, especially three on which I worked: wage and price controls; trade union power; and industrial policy.

Incomes policy and King Canute

In the late 1960s I undertook postgraduate training in economics at the London School of Economics. To supplement my student grant I also did some work during vacations for the National Board for

Prices and Incomes (NBPI), created under the Wilson government to contain the problem of inflation.

The UK was then experiencing its first major dose of 'stagflation' — a combination of rising unemployment and high (if not rising) inflation. According to the 'Phillips curve' — which produced the proposition that a reduction in unemployment could be 'bought' by an increase in inflation induced by monetary/fiscal expansion by government — stagflation simply could not happen: yet it *was* happening.

Clearly the world had gone wrong. The answer given by many macro-economists was that wage and price inflation might be held down by an incomes policy. (More technically, the policy aim was to 'shift the Phillips' curve downwards', so that a lower rate of inflation would obtain for any given rate of unemployment.) In terms of the equation structures of *simpliste* Keynesian models — which assume there is such a thing as 'the' wage level and 'the' price level — this solution sounded convincing.

As part of my travails for the NBPI I was sent off to investigate the market in office and 'temp' labour in and around London. Visiting a large number of companies I was disturbed to discover that there was no such thing as 'the' wage rate, as my macro-economic textbooks and the lectures I listened to took as a basic assumption. I was to discover that company wage, fringe, and personnel policies — the packages of benefits they offer employees — vary widely and are of infinite complexity. This is one example of Professor Hayek's more general proposition that social and economic systems are essentially complex phenomena, quite different in character from the relatively simple systems studied by physicists, chemists, and other students of the natural sciences. Attempting to control 'the' wage level and 'the' price level in a complex modern economy with an intricate division of labour and vast (and changing) product lines was, I began to realise, yet another delusion of 'middle way' thinking. The argument has superbly set out by Samuel Brittan and Peter Lilley in *The Delusion of Incomes Policy* in 1977.

This flaw of the left-right consensus on the 'middle way' has been overwhelmingly confirmed by econometric research into the impacts of incomes policies in the post-war period in numerous countries and by historical research into the effects of wage and price controls over four millenia. Governments, it appears, may perhaps and very temporarily — say, for a year or two — reduce inflation by wage and price controls, but the eventual result is always that they fail and are abandoned.

Either repressed inflation emerges, with shortages in white markets and inflation in black markets, or the controls system breaks down entirely and is discredited and discarded.

King Canute once sought to demonstrate to his subjects that he could not hold back the mighty forces of the sea. Government cannot hold back the forces of the market by incomes policy, especially in a highly complex, modern economy.

Trade union power and the general problem of organised interests

An essential feature of the post-war middle way consensus was its devotion to the corporatist notion of 'tripartism'. Specifically, the trade union movement was to be included, alongside big industry (in practice the CBI), in the deliberations of government. In this happy scenario, Big Government was to bring together 'both sides of industry' in the forum of quasi-state corporatist institutions (such as the NEDC), agreements would be reached, and consensus would reign.

In the 1960s I had regarded this as a 'balanced' approach to industrial organisation and to the formation of public policy. The 1971-2 and 1973-4 miners' strikes — which involved the deployment of massed secondary picketing (intimidation by large mobs), and which inflicted severe damage on the British economy — suggested to me (then a young lecturer at Kingston Polytechnic) that something was wrong in all this reasoning. Concentrations of power, I began to realise, were clearly dangerous to economic and political stability; and organised sectional interests, armed with immunities from the law, and in effect above the rule of law, were potentially a severe threat to the survival of both liberty and democracy.

The corporatist ethos of British politics reached its zenith (hopefully never to return) in the Social Contract episode of 1974-79, in which the trade unions were given a direct voice in the formation of government policy, across the board, in return for co-operation in the working of an incomes policy. Theoretically, if the economic policy of corporatism/fiscal is correct, this should have been merry for all.

To the contrary the outcome was distinctly unamusing, if not damaging. What (predictably) the unions wanted from government were new powers, new pro-union legislation, and an entire absence of restraint. This the Wilson/Callaghan Governments granted in ample measure. Between 1974 and 1979 a virtual revolution occurred in British labour law, with the passage of numerous pro-union Acts of Parliament. In one case, the Employment Protection Act of 1975, the legislation was drafted by the trade union lawyers, passed to the Secretary of State for Employment, Michael Foot, and enscribed in a statute, virtually unchanged.

This, to me, was a clear example of the inherent danger of corporatism — that it leads not to consensus but to the abuse of government power in the favour of organised sectional interests. The result is therefore not consensus but plunder through the deployment of government power and legislation, and thus the enlargement, not the containment, of the potential for resentment, and social and political conflict.

In late 1978 the Social contract broke down, to be replaced by an extremely vague 'Concordat' between government and the unions. Wage inflation had started to rip again, and incomes policy had in effect been discarded. Thus extensive new powers had been granted to the unions — and remained on the statute book — while the wage restraint these measures had supposedly bought proved to be illusory and short-lived. Some contract!

In early 1979 I wrote an analysis of the growth of trade union power, drawing attention to these and related matters, *The Trojan Horse: Union Power in British Politics*. At the time, it was not 'the done thing' in academic circles to discuss and analyse these matters. I was duly and regularly rounded upon both in staff common rooms and book reviews by my peers. The general reaction was that I was being 'unfair' not to analyse the power of organised business interests to gain sectional advantage — which I had indeed done in an essay published almost simultaneously, *A Critique of the Subsidy Morass* — whilst other academics thought it virtually indecent to analyse trade union power at all.

My central argument — that to give *any* sectional interest unique legal privileges and immunities, and to treat them as above the role of law, must inevitably be dangerous to the general interests of the community as a whole — received little or no attention in academic quarters. In the light of the incidents that developed in the year-long partial miners' strike of 1984-85 — including some 5,000 acts of violence (most against working miners), the virtual operation of a private army some 4-5,000 strong, arson, mob rampage, and murder (not to mention a cost of something like £3bn to the British taxpayer) — I think my worries on this score may be seen to have been vindicated by events.

Adam Smith had made the same point on the special legal privileges of the clergy and the monasteries, during the Middle Ages, in his *Wealth of Nations* of 1776. He argued that the total exemption of the clergy from secular jurisdiction, as during 10th to 13th centuries, throughout the larger part of Europe, represented an immense danger to the 'liberty, reason, and happiness of mankind' and to the authority and security of civil government. And power was duly and grossly abused during that period.

The danger is universal: it applies to the Church as much as to trade unions or businesses. In the words of Henry C. Simons, 'power has no use save its abuse'. If governments grant special privileges to selected groups — whether in the form of legal immunities, exclusive monopoly rights, special bounties, or any other — they are to the general detriment of society as a whole. Only equality before the law — the rule of law — can protect liberty, and prevent the abuse of power by privileged groups.

These are old classical liberal truths that the so-called New Right have rediscovered.

The chimera of industrial policy

Harold Wilson had proclaimed of a 'white hot technological revolution' sponsored and promoted by government *via* industrial policy. What we got from his 1964-70 government was very different: the Industrial Reorganisation Corporation (IRC) appointed with the task of promoting mergers in British industry in order to promote efficiency. Amongst other failures, it created the financial disaster later to be known as British Leyland. Out of the 70 cases that the IRC handled in the 4 years of its life perhaps only one may be claimed to have been a commercial success — the GEC/ACI merger. In most cases the IRC simply provided funds to private companies at far below the price on the capital market for comparable projects. It is very doubtful if the borrowers from the IRC would have been able to borrow on the open market for such projects. In short, the IRC proved to be yet another experiment attesting to the existence of 'government failure' (as public choice economists use the term) in directing the economy.

What we also got from the 'white-hot technological revolution' were a number of sectoral policies for (supposedly) high-tech industries which proved to be a veritable herd of white elephants — such as aluminium smelters located in outlandish places and Concorde.

I recounted the subsequent development, and lurches in, British industrial policy, in some detail in an essay *Picking Losers . . ?* in 1984. The story is, throughout, much the same: dismal. The history of what is grandoisely called 'industrial policy' — which simply means the allocation of taxpayers' money to favoured or fashionable technologies, enterprises and industries by bureaucrats and politicians — demonstrates repetitively that it is markets, entrepreneurs and venture capitalists who 'pick winners' in the economy, not government. If politicians or bureaucrats were good at picking winners, we would have expected Silicon Valley to be located somewhere to the east of the socialist Iron Curtain, instead of in capitalist Santa Clara County, USA.

On the contrary, what governments, under the aegis of industrial policy, seem to be exceedingly good at as my doing is, in 'backing losers'. In case after case, in what has been proclaimed by government to be a testament to their economic wisdom, subsequent events have demonstrated the miserable reality, at often vast cost to the taxpayer.

[97]

This is not to deny the occasional winner picked by government. But it seems only to demonstrate the truth of the old adage that if a chimpanzee were given enough time and a typewriter (now, of course, it would be a word-processor!), it might eventually come up with *Hamlet*.

Experience in the '60s and '70s has taught us in this arena of the mixed economy that — as with the lessons recounted above — government should let well alone. The idea of regenerating the economy through industrial policy is a chimera. What government needs to do is to get its fingers out of the market economy — and especially out of the business till and the consumer's pocket — so that the economy is allowed to regenerate itself.

The Muddle of the Middle Way

This essay was not intended to be an exercise in self-indulgence (although, as Samuel Brittan — another convert to economic liberalism — once remarked, there is probably nothing more pleasurable for a writer than to write about himself). I have given a personal account of some main factors — many others could be added, but for the well-known severity of our Editor's pen — that led me away from the delusion of the 'middle way', and towards a general position that has been termed 'the New Right' but which, for intellectual reasons, I would prefer to term as 'the new liberalism', or as the resurgence of (classical) liberalism (blended with some new economics). But I think that my personal story is a more general significance, and indeed has been a common experience.

A major factor in the conversion of younger scholars, and many others (such as businessmen, taxpayers, and consumers) to the general idea of a free society and economy under the rule of law has been the lessons of experience.

The Middle Way was offered to us as a Golden Mean by economic theorists and sociological intellectuals who were playing at being Buddha in describing (what they thought would be) the attainment of Nirvana. In the post-war period this catchy idea of the middle way proved to be highly saleable in the political market; and politicians — being a curious species of entrepreneur — sold it by the bucketload. Thus the post-war 'consensus'.

But by 1975 we had had three decades of experience with the Golden Mean of the Middle Way, a type of economic system that Ludwig von Mises has more aptly and accurately labelled as 'interventionism'.

In short, after 30 years — and now 40 years — the chickens have come home to roost. People often shirk the lessons of experience for a considerable time, not least because change is often costly, and is virulently opposed by vested interests. But eventually, in a society in which freedom of expression persists, the evidence will out, and flourish.

The evidence of government failure to install Nirvana *via* the Middle Way has mounted cumulatively over these 40 years in virtually every arena of government interventionism. The catalogue of government failure and overload is now so large that it would take a new British Museum to house it.

When ideas fail, and especially when repeatedly so (we have, for example, had some 17 attempts at implementing an incomes policy in post-war Britain), (some) people will eventually start searching around for an alternative, an answer, a new 'paradigm'. They browse through bookshops and perhaps pick up an IEA monograph reasserting simple and basic economic principles. They may then go on to read learned works by the master expositors of classical liberalism. This is what happened to me, and in my certain knowledge, to many others who share my general views.

Old lessons, both of economic history and the economic 'principles' that were developed to explain them, eventually get relearned — at least by a few intially. Then, through a complex process of human interaction, they get disseminated to a wider audience.

From the Middle Way to the New Enlightenment

Thus is the case-history, as I see it, of the so-called 'birth' of the so called 'New Right', especially amongst the young (who can learn lessons quickly). It is a gradual social process of escaping from delusion, and the restoration of reality. This is what the new liberalism amounts to.

After four decades of experience we have to face up to reality that the mixed economy proved simply to be a grossly *mixed-up* economy (as the late Harry G. Johnson was to describe it). Instead of the Golden Mean we are supposed to get, the middle way proved to be a recipe for economic sclerosis through seemingly never-ending intervention in order to cure the ills caused by earlier government failure. Our economy has become a shambles of government regulations and tax laws, subsidies and controls, the total complexity of which no human being could ever comprehend. It has also become a sparring ground on which organised interests curry favours from politicians and government, or indeed threaten them with vote losses, and even violent overthrow, if their incessant demands for specific acts of government intervention in their sectional interest are not met.

The middle way of the mixed economy is an *inherently* unstable political and economic system, a form of Hobbesian war of all against all, conducted through the political marketplace. I now believe it possible to demonstrate, through the application of the most basic, and uncontestable, of economic principles, why this is *inevitable*, and I tried to explain why in an essay in *Hayek's 'Serfdom' Revisited*.

The Thatcher Experiment — the 'New Right' in practice?

It is widely believed that the Thatcher Governments of 1979 and 1983 to date have put the ideas of the new liberalism into thoroughgoing practice. Monetarism reigns; the unions have been tamed by the 1980 and 1982 Employment Acts; the welfare state dismantled; and privatisation proceeds by leaps and bounds.

Yet the experience has been found wanting. We now have over three million recorded as unemployed; and that figure, on most macroeconometric forecasts, is likely to grow rather than wilt. Thus there is a growing theme amongst opinion-formers that the policy prescriptions of the 'new liberals' do not work in practice.

Siren songs (and singers) from the past

Consequently, a yearning has developed amongst some intellectuals for a 'return' to the Middle Way. We should have a 'mild' Keynesian reflation, yet another incomes policy (in its new format of an 'anti-inflation tax'), employment subsidies, and so on. This is the message of the new Employment Institute and the Charter for Jobs, which emerged in May 1985. Significantly, these developments were backed by leading political practitioners of the 'middle way', in all parties — Earl Stockton (the original Harold Macmillan), Lord Wilson, Mr Edward Heath. All of these former Prime Ministers were eminent advocates and exponents of government intervention and (indicative) planning, industrial policy, 'reflation' (read: inflation), incomes policy, and corporatism.

The old adage has it that 'old dogs do not learn new tricks'. This should now be amended to include: old dogs often return to their old trickery.

Newspeak vs Reality

It is a hallmark of British economic and political decline that much of our contemporary 'national' debate on economic problems is conducted in a form of Newspeak. The differences between rhetoric and reality, and the yearnings for a 'return' to a supposed Golden Age of the middle way — as conducted under 'Supermac' and 'SuperHarold' in the 1950s and '60s — are alarming to younger people who have studied the real genesis of our troubles in detail.

Mrs Thatcher had adopted the rhetoric of the new liberalism, but in most major respects has significantly failed to put it into practice. Thatcherism has turned out to be mostly a variant of the middle way — although now it is called 'consolidation'. There is some trimming here and there; some privatisation of state ownership (sometimes in tendentious form, as with British Telecom); some half-hearted ruminations on deregulation (as in the official paper *Burdens on Business* in March 1985).

There has been some minor — and mostly unused — qualification of trade union immunities in the 1980 and 1982 Employment Acts. The welfare state — the Fowler Commission notwithstanding — rambles on much as before, with gathering numbers of tax-eaters, a (despairing) state-defined caste of taxpayers, and now an increasing number of tax avoiders/evaders.

'Reflation' cannot possibly solve our fundamental difficulties, which are of a long-run nature, a sclerosis induced by decades of intervention, and the habits of mind, and of group action, that inevitably accompany such a politico-economic system. The siren-songsters of yesteryear, like old soldiers, must fade away if there is to be a serious chance of younger British people developing their skills and enterprise in what is a highly competitive world economy. 'Reflaters' should consider what happens when they inflate a balloon. Air is transferred from one space (the lungs) to another (balloon), at some cost of energy and puff. All of this is fine for a Christmas party, but it is not a serious way of making an economy grow. Transferring increased sums of money from taxpayers (lungs) to the balloon (tax-eaters) has the same general effect, with the additional vice that it adds to the numbers voting for tax-consumption instead of contributing to production. The balloon can only, eventually, explode.

As I write, in mid-1985, the camp of the economic 'balloonists' is growing more numerous, and more strident in its demands for 'puff economics'. Over the next few years, fateful decisions will be made, in this country, on the general direction of economic policy. Either the serious deliberations of the 'new' liberals will be taken to heart, and enacted in policy; or the balloon will go up and, eventually, pop. We who have our lives mainly ahead of us must escape the muddle of the 'middle way'. The New Right, the New Enlightenment, offers hope.

PETER CLARKE

The second critique is of Conservatives who enabled most of the objectives of the 1848 Communist Manifesto to be put into practice in Britain.

Peter Clarke was born in Venice in 1948. His father worked in printing, his mother was a civil servant.

He was educated at Scottish state primary schools, a comprehensive school in Barrow and a grammar school in Loughborough. He graduated from Bradford University and studied economics under Lord Balogh at Balliol College, Oxford.

After teaching economics at the Conservative staff college at Swindon and a spell as an economist in industry, he worked as a broadcaster for LBC and economics correspondent for the BBC. Since 1984 he has been with Channel 4's Diverse Reports: 'the only TV journalist in Britain licensed to argue for liberal causes'.

He has been chairman of the Selsdon Group and is now Director of the newly-formed David Hume Institute in Edinburgh.

He says the New Right 'merely wants to stop some people, mostly governments, from coercing other people'.

Just as the Democrats and Republicans in the USA have implemented the appealing ideas of the US Socialist Party, so, he argues, British Conservatives have implemented the ideas of Marx's and Engels' Communist Manifesto.

He maintains that Keynesianism and Marxism are discredited. 'The New Right has captured the future'; 'the intellectual initiative has been regained by liberalism'.

9

THE SOCIALISM OF THE OLD RIGHT

PETER CLARKE

It is a familiar idea that wise Tories do not think there is anything new in human nature or the folly of government. The predisposition to get everything wrong is common to the politicians in every nation, and only a reflection of the Fall and Original Sin. By imposing patterns of coercion on others, parliament and civil service magnify their errors. Tories seem to be able to laugh at the accretions of daftness called 'policies', or grow weary at the conceit of the people who can cause so much harm.

The very idea of anyone on the Right believing in 'Newness' is more illusion than paradox; but it does seem to me that the Austrian economists have an idea that is new and potentially very subversive to any school of progressives or rationalists.

The Austrian idea of price as a living, moving thing that connects people who know nothing of one another's needs and circumstances challenges the pretended scientific notions of much economics, and with it the vanities of policy-making.

The insight envelops far more than the value of commodities and services: it contradicts all utilitarian efforts to explain conduct and even ethics.

Like so many strands in the radical right the trail leads back to Frederick Hayek. His essay, 'The Use of Knowledge In Society' is the most important contribution to the New Right. I was pleased to find that Professor Thomas Sowell concurred. Hayek's 15 pages provide an open-ended manifesto for the New Right.

His argument gives a proper sense of awe at the miraculous nature of markets. Spontaneous orders, more the result of individual's actions, with no designers, will be more sensitive, creative, sophisticated, detailed and humane than any arrangements that could be described by any state agency.

Hayek's argument is that, just as language and music and to some extent law has emerged and evolved in a manner that cannot be explained by reference to designs or plans, so political relations could and should grow in an unspecified way with no useful resort to rationality or plan.

Tories can reasonably claim that Adam Smith, David Hume, Adam Fergusson and Edmund Burke were arguing nothing very different from this in the 18th century, but I believe Hayek has furnished the Right with a new coherence and momentum. It leaves us with a severely limited range of ambitions. We merely want to stop some people, mostly governments, from coercing other people. The New Right has little more than Acton or de Tocqueville to contribute to law. But we can muster a different language mostly derived from Hayek, and utterly different from the main body of long-fashionable academic economics and law.

Communism in a comprehensive

After a secondary school experience in one of the then novel and very chic 'comprehensive schools' in Leicestershire, where we learned race relations and woodwork, and were visited by journalists from London with progressive views, I entered the sixth form as a mild communist. It seemed plain to all of us that anyone with any intelligence or sensitivity must be a socialist.

My schoolboy dismissal of the Conservatives as mentally and morally inert was dented by Rodney Elton, the present Minister of State at the Department of the Environment, but then as a school-teacher quietly subverting us from our teenage socialism. Lord Elton taught me the macabre history of the French Revolution and converted me to an Anti-Jacobin. The story of the assignat inflation of the 1790s turned me into a pidgin monetarist. To side with Edmund Burke was thought perverse and dim, but he seemed wise and genial. By the time the UCCA computer had sent me off to university I had spent my year's pocket money on an early edition of Adam Smith's *The Wealth of Nations*.

College was a uniformly socialist environment. Again the brightest and the best always seemed to congregate on the left, leaving the Conservatives as the socially clumsy and slow-witted. Even the college Tory Association was committed to socialist prescriptions for everything. Under Mr Edward Heath the Government shared the view that state control was the answer to every difficulty. The only source of lively liberalism I stumbled upon was the thin seam of papers from the obscure Institute of Economic Affairs. They supplied me with a repertoire of ideas with which to tease the solidly socialist academics. Liberalism as provocateur was an attraction. Many IEA papers touched on a man called Hayek, and I found his magisterial *Constitution of Liberty* a satisfying manifesto. He even had the grace to conclude with a vivid account of 'Why I am not a Conservative'.

Free-market ideas seemed to have more attractions than the claims of competition and efficiency. Although the link was elusive they seemed to create liberty as a happy by-product. For all the economics I endured I didn't think there was anything valuable to be learned from the text books other than comparative advantage and marginal utility.

The Conservative Party seemed a spiritual desert empty of any integrity or purpose, although I found that Enoch Powell was making lucid and compelling speeches. I went to hear him; I was converted. Perhaps Toryism wasn't so hostile to ideas. Mr Powell treated his audience as adults with critical intelligence, not mouthing the weak truisms and stronger falsehoods that Conservative politicians appeared to prefer.

Chance took me to work for the Party, but under Mr Heath's charge the political latitude offered was minimal. The suggestion from a party employee that inflation could be a monetary disorder rather than the fault of greedy trade unions or Arabs was thought to be seditious. The party under Mrs Thatcher's leadership is a far more relaxed and eclectic body of people, but I still wonder why so much of the political energies of the Tories around the country are mostly spent in servicing a Party secretariat that remains socialist in its instincts.

Conservatism a mask for socialism

Working for Enoch Powell served as a postgraduate degree, with new seams of books and an insight into how unprepossessing the Parliamentary Party and Central Office can be. Mr Powell has the handicap of speaking plainly and truthfully, but the demand for those qualities in the political market are limited.

The political mission isn't to fight the socialism of the Labour Party or even the stunted syndicalism of the Liberals. The enemy for a libertarian is the forces of wetness in the Tory Party. They are the true bulwarks protecting our socialists inheritance.

Milton Friedman argues that the ideas of the Socialist Party in the United States were so powerful that, without ever winning any elections, it has seen almost all of its original 1928 manifesto implemented by the Democrats and the Republicans. Perhaps a small number of British liberals could re-win Britain for the Whig cause by infiltrating the minds of the politically active.

At school I had discovered, to my surprise, that Mr Harold Macmillan's Young Conservatives complacently supported the main planks of the Communist Manifesto of Marx and Engels. If the political culture of even the Conservative Party could have absorbed

[105]

the ideas of socialism, the mysterious process of osmosis or capillary action could possibly be made to operate in reverse.

1848 Communist Manifesto and 20th century government

When Friedrich Engels and Karl Marx identified the characteristics that defined a socialist society, they refined them down to ten points. It is marvellous to find that so many respectable complacent pin-stripped public figures, who would laugh at being described as socialists, doggedly endeavour to preserve (the fashionable verb is 'consolidate') the plans of the 1848 Manifesto. That may sound cranky, but recall what it was that Marx had on his list of objectives:

1. 'Ending private ownership in land.'

Engels and Marx did not envisage the outright expropriation of free-holders. They thought central planning would be far more effective. Property rights could be diluted to nothing without annexing all holdings. The Town and Country Planning Act is a model of socialist propriety, as are the Rent Acts, commended by Engels and endorsed now, we gather, by Peter Walker. Every communist country has a higher proportion of private housing than Scotland. Nominal private property should shrink, said the Communists. Two-thirds of the acreage of the UK are owned by the Crown Estate Commissioners, with government departments and quangos enveloping ever larger proportions of the remaining private land.

2. 'A progressive income tax.'

Marx would have been amazed at the enthusiasm of 'bourgeois' parties to build our ramshackle and oppressive income taxes. He agreed with the Victorian free-trade radical John Bright that any income tax beyond 25 per cent would cease to be effective. He thought people would lose their motivation to work, or evade such a tax. Under Tory Government nominal income taxes have been very slightly reduced, but the marginal rate paid by the average worker is nearly 50 per cent, and the lowest rate remains above Marx's threshold. Our tax rates are draconian, even in comparison with communist states.

3. 'The abolition of inheritance.'

Through death duties, capital transfer tax and capital gains taxes we have honoured the Communist Manifesto's ideal that a person's wealth should pass to the state. It is true that Sir Geoffrey Howe ameliorated some of these taxes, but even reformer Nigel Lawson has been unable or unwilling to scrap them, even though they harvest little revenue.

4. *'A National Bank with an exclusive monopoly of money.'*
Although Mrs Thatcher moved boldly and abolished exchange controls so that we are free to buy dollars or francs unimpeded by the state, the Government has not had the courage or will to tackle the entrenched and lawless powers of the state Bank of England. Before the nationalisation of the currency, with the centralisation of credit in the authorities, bankers could issue their own notes. They were free to offer what receipts for value they wanted, but they found that the public preferred gold-backed money. The Scottish banks, free of the nascent power of Threadneedle Street, evolved the most satisfactory system. Inflation was impossible as banks had to keep the value of their money steady, which was achieved by not inflating its supply.

5. *'The public ownership of railroads and transport.'*
Our railways are still run on sound communist lines. The Department of Transport is opposed to the liberalisation of British Rail. If the track is to be the state's, even private rolling stock has to be deterred. Nicholas Ridley is opening up the bus market, but the reform of the roads will be incomplete until taxis have been delicensed and deregulated. Aviation, unimagined by Marx, is tightly controlled on strict socialist lines with the spirit of monopoly preserved. For the moment British Rail and its sandwiches are secure parts of our socialist heritage.

6. *'The extension of public ownership, the cultivation of idle lands and a state forest organisation.'*
The theme of the Labour Party's Clause Four and the Communist Party's Clause Six is intellectually dead. No one with any common-sense believes in nationalisation. But we still have a surfeit of state corporations and quangos. The Government's privatisation pro-gramme is gaining in speed and confidence. Where Mr Heath's courage failed him after privatising Thomas Cook's and four pubs in Carlisle, Mrs Thatcher has been willing to take on the formidable vested interests of Morrisonian socialism.

Yet British Steel, the National Coal Board, the BBC, and other socialist limbs endure untouched.

In agriculture our success in Marx's terms is confusing. We have achieved the 'cultivation of idle land' by the lavish use of subsidies. Instead of buying our food where it is cheapest we force everyone to buy from expensive sources. The Small Farmers Association argues that half of the hundreds of millions spent has been directed to no more than ten thousand men — the prairie farmers of East Anglia. State Forests? The Forestry Commission, busy supplying us with pit props and railway sleepers to defeat the Kaiser, merrily runs up its losses. Neither Engels or Marx could have imagined the weird

[107]

economics of our agriculture, but the inspiration of 1980s policy-makers is certainly far from liberal.

7. 'Education of all children in state schools'.'

About 4 per cent of children manage to escape the state sector schools at enormous cost in taxed income. Poor Sir Keith Joseph, like his predecessor as Education Secretary Mrs Thatcher, gets no thanks for spending ever more and more money on state schools. Truency rises, standards fall. Illiteracy and innumeracy characterise local authority schooling. At their best they can only emulate private schools. Marx's ideal is preserved by Tories too cautious to offer choice to parents.

8, 9, and 10.

The three other clauses of the inspirational Communist Manifesto that otherwise still mesmerises so many Conservatives now sound sinister and sightly odd. They were: 'The confiscation of the property of all immigrants and rebels', 'the establishment of industrial armies' and 'the combination of agriculture with industry'. The Youth Training Scheme and the Development Commission are echoes of this style of thinking, but the sheer magnetic power of their evangelising for an all-powerful state is disconcerting.

Mrs Thatcher is serious about wanting to nurture a counter-revolution. But the socialist establishment, in all parties, is still too dominant for her to win. Luckily, a 'New Right Manifesto' can be compressed into one simple freedom — the freedom of contract. If individuals can form contracts through time and space, all other freedoms such as freedom of speech, or of trade, flow from the elementary ability to make voluntary agreements. Socialists hate anything that is spontaneous. That is why our ideas terrify them.

Professor Hayek, the nearest we can claim as an equivalent figure to Marx on the Right, argues that the most urgent reform is to break the state monopoly of money. Concurrent private currencies, he says, will resolve many other apparently unrelated problems.

What has Government Done to Our Money, an essay in 1971 by Murray Rothbard, first suggested the privatisation of money. Then it seemed an idea of only theoretical interest, but now Hayek raises it to the top of the agenda. It is a token of the seriousness of libertarian thinking that activities long reserved to the state can be challenged. Hayek's 1976 IEA book *The Denationalisation of Money* is one of the key documents of the New Right, (even though its author was an officer of the Austro-Hungarian Empire and a contemporary of Wieser and Bohm-Bawaerk).

The most debilitating sapping of the self-respect and coherence of the capitalist cause was the humiliating and apparently baffling experience of the 1930s Great Depression. We still live in the mental shadow of the inter-war years. They leave a question mark about the self-regenerating qualities that markets are meant to have — didn't such obvious failure demonstrate that the state must at least intercede to help its people? The whole dreary record of unemployment and recession and the depression of the trade cycle discourages support for the market. Milton Friedman, brilliant exponent of the market case, seems to under-rate the libertarian arguments that the Depression was caused by state price-fixing and credit-rigging. If Hayek is correct, the latter-day experience of monetarism has been an intellectual cul-de-sac. For 50 years liberal energies have been devoted to attributing importance to measuring the volume of new credit, not the value of newly-issued money. Hayek says wittily that we shouldn't think of money as a noun but as an adjective. Chicago frets about quantity; Vienna quality. Monetarists concern themselves with measuring magnitudes of types of new money created. But Hayek discusses all monetarist efforts as a panmetric folly. The 'moneyness' of new credit is a subjective attribute, not an easy barometer to read — indeed, the art of trying to read it actually affects it.

The abolition of the government monopoly of money would render inflation and deflation impossible — as the pressure of borrowers matched that of lenders. Market-generated monies would depend on *not* emulating the unhappy history of state currencies. By short-circuiting trade cycles, private money would also force governments to limit their expenditures to their revenues. It has been the failure of the New Right that so far this reform ranks as little more than a technical or theoretical aspect of finance. Hayek hasn't yet stimulated the moral fervour that Cobden and Bright generated for the Free Trade cause. But it is competing private currencies that will insure the survival of the extended order we call democracy.

Keynesianism is dead

Economics will be much more fun when the differences between Friedman and Hayek are taken as the main play in the theatre of professional rivalries. In the long run Keynesianism has proved to be dead. Economists used to teach their students that their discipline was about the effective or efficient allocation of resources by the use of data. The Austrian alternative is more elusive, humane, and true — that economics is about how knowledge can be relayed to others. The spontaneous knowledge-transmitting device of the market is a marvel.

The Austrian contribution has freed us from the vain hunt for mathematical or macro-economics uniform laws of behaviour that cadres of elected or chosen political people could apply to the rest of us. Knowledge is highly specific and individual. It is subjective, and therefore more usefully diffused through a market than through any designed order. Each of us has our own different time horizons and appreciation of opportunities — to be alive is to be subjective. Keynesians, and other schools of coercers, cannot accept this simple liberal quality; they have to assume there is a body of special knowledge accessible only to some, and that with these mysterious insights they can know how to compel and administer others. In a sense the Austrian idea of markets as spontaneous orders is very wounding to the pride of all intellectuals. It gives no room to the vanity of all planners or people who would like to improve others.

The rationalist presumption in favour of intelligent observation of patterns of behaviour allowing us to select the best institutions is confounded by the pure New Right position. There is evolution, but it is of group selection, not individuals, and it can only be understood in glimpses and retrospectively. The evolution of rules of conduct, or laws, or other institutions such as property, is different in this respect from biological evolution. Rules of property and of family behaviour are not thought out and then followed; they emerged haphazardly, and those groups that keep to unarticulated rules prosper. Utilitarian explanations of ethics are absent from the New Right.

It may be that we only return to rediscover Adam Fergusson's theme that social arrangements emerge 'as the result of human action but not design'. 18th century Edinburgh had developed all the arguments required to demolish the socialism of the 20th century. Most intellectual schools are concerned about technology, usually to argue that its very complexity demands state control. But the New Right seems to be utterly relaxed about the adaptations to the capital structure. If it is complex, it is markets that will comprehend and digest this complexity — not bureaucracies. Resources can be poured into equipment, and techniques of production refined, but unless individuals can integrate capital closely and intimately with their wants the grandest assets melt into liabilities. Markets adjust resources to the moving kaleidoscope of constant small changes in circumstances and understanding — always subjectively.

The sad pre-occupation of so many good economists in juggling statistical aggregates and searching for patterns is futile. When they think they have found one, and then seek to coerce everyone else to conform, they become dangerously presumptuous. In its pure form the sort of things the economists who use the methodology of the Austrians call 'knowledge' cannot be translated into statistics, and only very loosely into terms of price.

A change in price communicates knowledge in a unique way. It is

[110]

specific to those responding to the price change, but general as it ripples through the economy to others who have no knowledge of why and how the relative prices of a commodity or service have changed. Hayek describes the price mechanism as a co-ordinating device as a 'miracle'.

The miracle of the market

If someone had invented the market it would be claimed as more magical than language or music, but it was never designed and our understanding of its amounts to little more than glimpses. Painstaking and scholarly though Hayek is, his wisdom boils down to a huge doubt about how useful it is to ratiocinate about behaviour. Civilisation is based on a division of labour and purpose beyond the understanding of the social sciences. Convention, tradition, custom, and intuition, even myth, is far more important than anything contrived by a plan or a state agency. Hayek says he is best understood as a Whig, and that he repudiates Conservatism, but it seems to me that his appreciation of the mystery of culture makes him a Tory. Lacking only theological endorsement he offers more reconciliation with religion that ever David Hume or Adam Smith could. Hayek sees symbolic truth in religion. Edmund Burke described prejudice as 'latent wisdom'. By seeing merit in the superstition of religions Hayek says they can carry information and guidance.

Hayek's tolerance of, and even interest in, the function of religions as transmitters of 'symbolic truth' offers the New Right a link to the Old Right. We want to ensure there is a free market in gods, where the Old Right only wanted faith in one. The Fall and Original Sin amount to symbolic versions of the Invisible Hand. Self-interest is turned to the general good.

The New Right has captured the future. No one with intellectual self-respect believes in Marxism or socialism. The Keynesian system is losing its confidence and coherence. The intellectual initiative has been recaptured by liberalism, a power lost to the Left for almost one hundred years.

The radical idea of scrapping the grand superstructures of coercion built upon Bretton Woods, legal tender laws, exchange controls and the rest illustrates the newly-rekindled courage of right-wing thinking. 'Practical men' and politicians will struggle to preserve the socialist money system, but its decay makes the eventual success of a liberal monetary order ever more likely. The right traditionally cornered the market in gloom and pessimism, but now the left is losing its vitality and is on the defensive.

The New Right's horizon is bright. All we have to do is win over the universities. Then the political parties will yield to our ideas.

[111]

I referred to the denationalisation of money as the outstanding reform of the libertarian agenda, but the prospects of returning the schools to parents and away from the civil servants and local authorities is the reform I would rate as the most potent vote-winner for liberals in the Conservative Party.

Education reform the vote-winner

Either education vouchers or tax relief for school fees would reverse the flow of power in the haughty empires of the Department of Education. By returning purchasing power and the discretion of choice to parents, schools would be transformed — some so much that no doubt they would disappear while others would flourish. Yet since Mr Edward Heath taught the Conservatives to sneer at 'coupons' the theme of vouchers has been kept on the margin of Tory policy. The broad wish not to worry, still less offend, the civil service is at its worst in the Conservatives' humility in the face of the DES.

It may be that the SDP will be the first party to put education vouchers on their agenda. It will be a clever piece of democratic entrepreneurship if Dr Owen can steal the Tories' clothes on this issue. I still feel that it will be the Conservatives who introduce real choice into the school system.

With Sir Keith Joseph as Secretary of State, Dr Rhodes Boyson as Minister, Stuart Sexton and Oliver Letwin as political advisors, and Mr Ferdinand Mount in the Prime Minister's outer office musing over his 'Windsor Bypass' scheme (a device to give discretion back to parents) to free the schools, the opportunities for the birth of a voucher scheme could hardly have been better. Still the weight of the civil service, far more than any political opposition, inhibited Sir Keith from adopting a policy that appealed to all his honourable instincts.

The defeat of school vouchers is a cameo of the difficulty facing liberalism. It would be attractive, and certainly tidier, if we could enjoy the luxury of a new parliamentary Opposition that constantly harried the Conservatives to realise the potential of reforms that would give the dignity of choice back to people. The nearest we have in Parliament is the non-Party 'Repeal Group' organised, if that is the word, by Lord Harris of High Cross. By harassing the Government over modest items such as the opticians' monopoly or Sunday trading they have changed the flavour of some areas of political debate.

The prevailing assumption remains that 'social' spending is 'a good thing' and that politicians who fail to gift more resources to the welfare state will be characterised as mean-spirited and misanthropic. Tactically shrewd liberals have to find ways of out-bidding the vested interests of the socialists of every party. This is the elementary

[112]

beauty of the school voucher. It buys out the local authority school bureaucracies, and the teachers' unions, and authoritarian progressives of every sort.

If we could persuade politicians of no conviction but conventional ambitions that there are votes in vouchers the reform can be won.

Such thoughts lack the august and abstract charm of Hayek's vision, but while the ideals of an open society, or as he would say, 'extended order' are understood by so few, liberalism needs a few political guerrillas to subvert our socialist establishment. Socialism is a reactionary conceit, but by a paradox of history we can use only the Party of the Right to demolish it. The New Right will win if it remains obscure and lets the Tories think they believed in freedom all along.

MARTIN J. ANDERSON

The third critique is aimed at the unreasoned notion that the multifarious activities of mankind can be governed by politicians despite legal, financial and police power to coerce.

Martin Anderson was born in 1955 in Perthshire. His father is a graduate in aeronautical engineering; his mother was trained as a teacher. He was educated at a direct-grant academy in Crieff, and graduated with a Master's degree in mediaeval French and German from St Andrews University in 1977.

From his student Conservatism he has moved to a libertarian scepticism of all government.

He has written on public affairs and music for specialist journals, runs a one-man spare-time music book publishing house and, since 1980, has been Assistant Editor of Economic Affairs.

Martin Anderson uncompromisingly argues that the natural diversity of human beings ('chaos') cannot be reduced to a pattern for regulation by politicians. He draws on the Austrian economist Ludwig von Mises to explain his rejection of political order, and he denies that 'chaos' is disorderly since individuals are all purposefully working towards ends they have conceived and chosen for themselves: 'Human society is chaotic — but it is also coherent'.

This approach leads him to question the macro-quantification of the diverse human activities and their products and incomes upon which governments base policies. He questions attitudes found even among leading exponents of Austrian economics.

Like other essayists, he turns to the school of public choice to debunk the pretences of politicians to govern benevolently. Individuals who believe themselves to be over-governed, over-taxed, over-controlled, have no political mechanism by which they can escape.

The New Right must identify the groups that will benefit from liberalisation. But it has not yet learned to sell its ideas.

10

IN DEFENCE OF CHAOS

MARTIN J. ANDERSON

Haydn, like his God before him, began *The Creation* by banishing chaos. Most of the intellectuals prominent in the history of Western thought have similarly tried to banish chaos, to see in the diversity of human society some sort of grand pattern that could be identified. The motives have varied: once a pattern of behaviour has been recognised, it can be studied; equally, it can be exploited by someone in a position of power. Human history offers a sorry mixture of the two. But the 'chaos' to which most intellectuals have refused to give room is nothing less than the diversity of human behaviour and of the natural world which gave rise to it. It is the acceptance of chaos — of uncertainty, infinite variety and complexity — in the world-view of most of its advocates that makes the position of the 'New Right' not only stimulating but also attractively modest.

Enough of the other contributors to this collection of essays are taking issue with the title for me to dispense with the dissociative prelude I had initially intended. Unlike many of those (inside these covers and outside) who have adopted libertarian or classical liberal attitudes, my own intellectual development began in the backwaters of traditional Conservatism; to write an essay for a book called *The New Right* is potentially an embarrassing reminder of earlier naivities. My disagreement with the title is quite simple: it is a complete misnomer. 'The New Right' is new insofar as it has shed the intellectual falsehoods of previous centuries and offers a coherent body of thought with which to rebut criticism. It is 'right' only in the sense that it is not 'left'; but it is not made of chocolate either, and a form of classification which attempts to define objects, attitudes and so on, solely in terms of what they are not is unlikely to be a particularly useful tool of study.

Ludwig von Mises, whose work underpins many of the attitudes held by the 'New Right' (for which I shall prefer the term 'libertarianism' — again, it is adequately defined by others in this book), begins his major treatise *Human Action* with a potential self-contradiction: 'Economics', he writes, 'is the youngest of all sciences'. He goes on to define human action as purposeful behaviour and the field of the economist as the study of human action. But the assessment and analysis of purposeful behaviour is almost as old as the species, and the science of economics, in its broadest sense as the study of all human behaviour (its effect but not its cause; that is the psychologist's domain), thus cannot be much younger than the practice of human procreation. What has encouraged the development of libertarianism as an internally consistent body of thought is the expansion of the scope of economics to analyse *all* human activity, and it is this expansion which exposes the fallacies of *a priori* assumptions of the nature of human society. The 'New Right' draws much of its inspiration from the writings not only of economists but also of historians, psychologists, and thinkers in other disciplines, as Chris Tame shows.

Apriorism — the visitation upon the object of study of assumptions already held by the observer — has been a constant feature of Western intellectual history. (My use of 'apriorism' here should not be confused with the term 'aprioristic' with which the Austrians describe their methodology. The Austrians conceive of economic science as aprioristic in that it is essentially deductive, that is, from certain self-evident axioms and hence, in this sense, aprioristic. Most Austrians would naturally contend that these axioms are based squarely in empirical reality. Von Mises is lucid on this point in 'The Epistemological Problems of the Sciences of Human Action', *Human Action,* Part I, Chapter 2, and in *The Ultimate Foundation of Economic Science,* Van Nostrand, Princeton, 1962, pp. 17-21.) Apriorism colours political and religious thought as far back as history can trace. Indeed, religion would be impossible without it, since religious belief, in its assumption of the existence of a god or gods, is nothing more than institutionalised apriorism. My early rebellion against religion (I was baptised, I am told, under protest) had expanded during four years at the University of St Andrews into a general opposition to the state. I can remember the astonishment of a feminist friend that a member of the Conservative Association, as I then was, should be handing round a petition to object to proposed restrictions in the availability of abortion.

Under the tutelage of eight years' working at the Institute of Economic Affairs that early dislike of religion has hardened into a complete rejection (as far as humans can achieve it) of apriorism. The insights of the Austrian School, acquired at the IEA by osmosis, into the nature of human society both allow the student of human behaviour increased scope for his investigations and insist that he go about them with a far more modest notion of what he can achieve — in short, that he admit chaos to his notion of what constitutes society.

'Chaos' is defined in *The Shorter Oxford English Dictionary* as 'a state of utter confusion and disorder'; it may thus seem odd that I am so eager to see human society characterised as chaotic. What is convincing about the idea is that it is utterly individualist, that it regards society as a fruitful object of study only because it is a collection of *individuals*, each 'behaving purposefully', as von Mises would have it, to his or her own ends. It is chaotic in the sense that an external observer may well perceive nothing more than 'a state of utter confusion and disorder'; the participants in that process are acting towards their personal *chosen* goals that may not be apparent to the observer. There are, of course, institutions that reveal broader patterns in human behaviour, institutions which Hayek describes in his *Studies in Philosophy, Politics and Economics* as 'the result of human action but not of human design'. Money and language, for example, are unlikely to have developed in isolation but arose in response to a demand from individuals for means to speed up the transmission of information between them. Thus there are collective or 'social' phenomena, but these have their sources in individuals wants and urges.

Nothing disorderly about chaos

In *The Confusion of Language in Political Thought* Hayek suggests the term 'cosmos' to describe the spontaneous *order* that is human society. My adherence to 'chaos', rather than adopt the term of a mind much wiser than mine, is in the hope that, by choosing the more graphic term, I may draw attention to the argument there is nothing disorderly about chaos — at least, for the student of human behaviour. My point is that human society is chaotic — but it is also coherent.

The immense variety of human activities is bound to require some form of simplification if it is to be studied with any degree of success. But accuracy is thus instantly precluded: the very act of simplification *falsifies* the object of study. Simplification is not itself objectionable, as it is necessary for the rational study of anything; the difficulty arises when social scientists begin to perceive their explanatory devices as themselves reality, and to propose courses of coercive action based on their misconception. Since chaos — or society — cannot be studied systematically without simplifying it to the point at which it is no longer chaotic (or it would change as we tried to analyse it), we are left with the assumption that economics (and especially macro-economics), like any other 'social science', can offer only an approximation to the truth, and an approximation which, by its nature, is false. The danger of the approach which is thus prepared to allow distortion of reality in order to encourage understanding of society is that *these are the premises on which government is founded.* Laws, fiscal policies, social security schemes, state regulations all have to be

[117]

formulated broadly: if each government diktat were devised so as to accommodate the requirements of individual people or institutions, none would ever be made; even if it were technically possible (which it isn't — *cf.* Hayek's 'Two Pages of Fiction on Socialist Calculation', *The Journal of Economic Affairs*, Vol. 2, No. 3, April 1983, and Andrew Melnyk's response in the following issue) to construct such minutious decrees, no legislature could deal with the complexity of, say, a tax code that went into so much detail — indeed, the very idea is absurd. Thus governmental policies have to be concerned with macro-economic effects. But if the world is chaotic, and if economic analysis can offer only falsifying approximations of the micro-economic realities it purports to observe, it follows that *no* government can ever be fully aware of the incidence of the laws it promulgates or taxes it imposes. Taxation and welfare policies, laws prescribing or proscribing activities the state smiles or frowns on (wearing seatbelts, smoking cannabis; paying taxes or dodging them; taking out a mortgage on a house; driving at 45 m.p.h. in a built-up area) — all will have effects on human behaviour which those who construct or enforce them cannot possibly foresee, effects perhaps even opposite to those intended.

The British Government, for example, regularly produces statistics which suggest that the total size of the British economy can be assessed as so many million pounds' worth of economic activity per annum. It attempts to measure relative incomes of participants in that economy. It depends for the accuracy of its figures on the honesty of citizens who may have found that, in the absence of an adequate political mechanism, the only means of registering their dissatisfaction with over-government is to conceal the extent of their economic activity. Their participation in the 'black' or 'underground' economy, to a degree which is *ipso facto* undiscoverable, may thus mean that the entire taxation policy of this (or any other) Government is wildly arbitrary, that a law-abiding minority is taxed to provide welfare benefits for a majority of the population which is busy earning a handsome living in that part of the economy which escapes state surveillance. One eminent economist privately suggested to me that the black economy might encompass as much as a quarter of all economic activity in the UK. Naturally, he said, he was reluctant to record his hunch anywhere in print because the inevitable absence of corroborative statistics would invite the derision of his peers. The implication of his and similar estimations of the volume of unrecorded economic activity is that they point to the ultimate redundancy of *all* macro-economics, that Austrian economists can parcel together Neo-classicals, Keynesians, monetarists, Marxists and other birds of an apparently dissimilar feather as having put all their eggs in a basket — of which one of the sides is missing.

The issue of tax evasion starts up a red herring which I should like to shoot down before it flies any further. That is the question of morality and the allegation that markets are not concerned with it. It is an issue as irrelevant to economics as the colour of Beethoven's hair is to his music. The late Lionel Robbins wrote (in *The Journal of Economic Affairs*, Vol. 1, No. 4, July 1981) that 'only acts which are free ... are susceptible of moral judgement. Acts done under compulsion ... are neither wrong nor right: without free-will they fall into the same category as bad weather or other manifestations of natural forces'. 'Morality' need thus detain us no further.

No morality without markets

The desire to understand what happens in society — whether one's income is derived from explaining human affairs (as a 'social scientist') or exploiting them (as a politician) — is a deeply rooted part of the human psyche. Just as early philosophers found it impossible to conceive of a world that was created without purpose and they thus invented gods, it seems equally difficult for almost all contemporary analysts of human affairs to admit that economic activity is chaotic. The notion of the unfathomable complexity of economic activity (what I have here called chaos) is derived principally from the work of the Austrian School, and especially from refinements in the work of Professor Ludwig Lachmann, now based in South Africa. That the insight of chaos will be resisted by most thinkers was recently illustrated with a joyous irony.

Since I have no degree in economics and yet spend my day editing its practitioners, it was decided at the IEA that I should attend a course in Austrian economics run in Milwaukee by the Institute of Humane Studies. I duly spent a week there in June 1984. One of the four distinguished academics teaching there, to an audience consisting largely of well-disposed post-graduates (most of whom would have considered themselves members of the 'New Right', if without accepting the label), was Professor Israel Kirzner, perhaps the best-known coadjutor of Ludwig von Mises, with whom he studied in New York for many years. Professor Kirzner delivered several of the introductory lectures at the course, during which he emphasised the importance of what American Austrians call 'process' — the idea that economic activity consists of a *sequence* of acts, each of which takes account of information revealed by earlier acts; it must therefore occur *over time*. One of the chief complaints of the Austrians about the Neo-classical school of economic analysis (of Milton Friedman and other economists at the University of Chicago and elsewhere) is that it ignores the importance of process, that it conducts its investigations as if the world were static, as if chaos could somehow be made orderly for the duration of study.

This objection was eagerly received by the young Austrian Turks at the Milwaukee seminar; but the enthusiasm soon turned to dismay when these four outstanding Austrians began to chalk on the board the standard, *static* supply-and-demand diagrams of Neo-classical methodology which show the interaction of economic forces in isolation. They have to, since the construction of a 'model' (whether chalked on a blackboard or keyed into a computer) requires assumptions ('parameters', if you must) against which those forces can be assessed. It may be that the most fundamental lesson of Austrian economics is thus that the finer forms of analysis cannot be taught without the inevitable betrayal of its most basic assumption (rather like Groucho Marx's refusal to join any club which would have him as a member). If 'pure' Austrian economics defies teaching, we might reasonably have expected Professor Kirzner and his colleagues to offer more than a disclaimer for the impasse before carrying on to more advanced economic theory.

But it got worse. Halfway through that week in Milwaukee, Professor Kirzner was asked by one of the students (not a committed Austrian this time) whether it wasn't a weakness in the Austrians' position that they could not devise an index of co-ordination, that is, for example, that they could not rank national economies (or constituent parts of them) according to their relative efficiency. He agreed that it was indeed a weakness and that they would have to do much work on that aspect of their 'paradigm'. I interjected, aghast, that it was surely one of the most basic tenets of Austrianism that such an index was technically impossible to construct, that it wasn't a weakness in the paradigm but one of its glories.

I relate this unsettling tale not to controvert Professor Kirzner, whose work I hugely admire and from whom I have learned no little, but to illustrate the all-pervading tendency in the social sciences (in which I include politics and its practice) to *a priori* thinking. Two further examples will help comfort Professor Kirzner with some distinguished company. The first is the parallel offered by Ludwig Lachmann to help understand movements within an economy: he compared each economic event (each purchase of a pair of socks, each rise in the oil price) to the movement of a particle in a kaleidoscope which would be reflected by corresponding movements elsewhere in the kaleidoscope/economy. The 19th–century Cambridge economist Alfred Marshall offered a similar analogy when he compared movements in prices to the movements of 'balls resting against one another in a basin' once one of them has been disturbed; they would resettle more or less swiftly according to the amount of friction in the basin — or the economy. Neither of these economists would suggest that

[120]

economic activity takes place in discrete, disjunct stages, nor that it is anything other than constant, and furiously so. My objection to their analogies — and to any other models of the economy, for all that even the most advanced computer simulation can deliver is a form of analogy or abstraction — is that they are finite, that they exclude chaos.

Government is unavoidably ignorant

A pragmatist will already have objected to my argument: of course, you must simplify, even falsify to a degree, if you are to explain the world; you simply have to accept that deficiency as part of the price of comprehension. It is an objection I would be happy to concede, if it were not that the governments which control the lives of all of us do so with little awareness, it would seem, of the micro-effects of their activities. And that it is technically impossible for them to gauge those effects leads us to a harsher conclusion: that government must then be an elaborate sham. Most citizens of most countries appear to be aware of this falsehood: we drink after hours, we break trading laws, we disguise taxable income, commit adultery (more readily in Bradford than Tehran), ignore speed restrictions, shoot pheasants out of season. (There are obviously 'crimes' most of us would not commit, with or without government; in which case the state is only buttressing constraints on behaviour that society has thrown up spontaneously.) So how has government survived? Even in the 'liberal democracies' of the West the state has grown to a size which the wide-scale disrespect it incurs cannot seem to shrink.

To answer the question we have to backtrack a little. Even if we assume that most individuals in any society will accept some sort of minimum state (that, say, they care about poverty or armed aggression and cannot imagine that an unprompted — chaotic — market economy will yield institutions to prevent these unwanted commodities; in which case, one might add, the fault lies with their imaginations), we must turn to a different branch of economic analysis, public choice or 'the economics of politics', to shed light on the growth and survival of governments.

Whereas Austrian economics is intensely individualistic in its approach, 'public choice' (a misnomer for a discipline which examines how the public is *denied* choice) assesses the behaviour of groups of individuals and the interaction of different groups with different incentives. Not surprisingly, public choice economists have concentrated their attentions on government, since the apparatus of government uses coercion (through laws supported by the threat of physical violence), and coercion is patently an attractive device for acquiring economic advantage. The history of the human race is

[121]

characterised by the institutionalised coercion of one group by another (group rather than individual, because it would be impossible anywhere other than in the tiniest society for a single member to dominate without the collusion of his peers): clan chieftains, royal families, military dictatorships. It doesn't take much reflection to realise, for example, that the much-vaunted democracy of classical Athens was based on a slave economy. And so if a mediaeval observer had been told that a form of government would develop in Western Europe which would allow the relative liberties of, say, near-universal suffrage (other than in Liechtenstein, prisons, royal palaces and lunatic asylums) and freedom of speech and of association, he would have shaken his head and advised against such unrealistic flights of fancy — rather as one might tell a modern anarcho-capitalist that his vision of a government-free world is attractive but 'politically unfeasible'.

Public-choice analysis can offer an appealingly straightforward explanation of the relative delimitation of the scope of government in the Western democracies, and one which avoids recourse to the sanctification of British parliamentarianism which often seems the One True Holy of Conservative historians and philosophers. Under the fierce glare of public choice, government can be seen as nothing more than an institution formed by collusion between interest groups. (The American journalist and political commentator Arthur Bentley stumbled on this truth in his book *The Governmental Process* (1908), but concluded naively that the result was a system in which opposing interest groups kept one another in balance.) This insight can be applied to *all* systems of government to rob them of their moral legitimacy. Whether forms of control development through agreements reached between church and tribe, mediaeval British barons and monarchy, East European *Nomenklatura* and army, they all derive their 'authority' from a superstructure of interests supported unwillingly or unwittingly by the taxpayer/citizen. The relative liberty accorded, say, the British citizen by the government which controls his activities may well be an object of approval in the eyes of most commentators, but any governmental institution remains an instrument of *coercion* no matter how 'enlightened' it may first appear.

History reinforces the public-choice insight that restricted government is possible only when interests form behind that restriction. The British parliamentary system, for example, developed solely because enough groups perceived it to be in their direct interest and therefore fostered its institution. It can thus be seen that the prescriptions for policy that follow from public-choice analysis rest on a huge irony: that a political mechanism to restrain the activities of interest groups can be achieved only if sanctioned by other interest groups. The

[122]

constitutional solution proposed by some public-choice economists to restrain the growth of government will thus prove ineffective unless extra-governmental interest groups can be persuaded to support its establishment. The citizen/taxpayer/consumer is unlikely to perceive much direct benefit in political agitation, and will prefer to register his discontent through existing political mechanisms and by concealing what he can of his income from the state. Unlike pressure groups within government or with access to governmental privilege, who will happily pursue their goals with much raucous lobbying, the interests of the individual are best served by keeping his head down (especially if he is the courageous recipient of undeclared income).

The 'New Right' is anti-state, anti-politics

It is this discrepancy that reveals what I feel to be the major task of the 'New Right'. It must propagandise mercilessly against the state. It must stress unremittingly the enduring moral bankruptcy of government. It must constantly compare the burden borne by the taxpayer, to fill the governmental trough from which the interest groups are feeding, with the benefits received by the swine at the trough. Karl Marx may seem an odd bedfellow for James Buchanan and Gordon Tullock (the chief American exponents of public choice analysis), but his prescriptions for instituting social change reveal that he understood very clearly how interests must be manipulated if 'society' is to be changed. If the impertinence of government interference in our private affairs (and they are all private in essence), is to be eliminated, we must underscore relentlessly to our unorganised fellow-taxpayers their direct interest in the unremitting attentuation of the state.

There is no overt way of doing this other than straightforward propagandising; any other will bring the full panoply of the law crashing down on the head of the dissenter. Since the interest groups have so roundly captured the coercive institutions of the state (and government itself is no more than a grandiose interest group, an elaborate network of brokerage, selling power and privilege), those who feel themselves over-governed over-taxed, over-controlled (a resentment not confined to the 'New Right') have no political mechanism they can use to alter the world around them. This assertion may be more obviously true of the Soviet Union than of the United Kingdom, but any distinction is otherwise tenuous: where, for example, does the voter who 'chose' Mrs Thatcher's Government to remove the hand of the state from his pocket turn, now he finds that she has thrust it yet further in? Speaking at a recent lunch at the IEA, Professor David Myddelton of the Cranfield School of Management argued that to free itself of the shackles of interest groups the British economy required a government that wouldn't worry about re-election but would instead set itself the Herculean task of mucking out Whitehall's Augean Stables of political and pecuniary interests. To which I said: 'Fine. Where do we buy one?' The ugly truth is that no form of government has yet been devised that will allow it to cure itself of the diseases that the body politic will inevitably attract.

So what can government — this Government, or any other — do? The first two terms of Mrs Thatcher's regime allow little hope that the British political system will produce in reality the 'friends of liberty' that the Conservatives proclaimed themselves before the 1979 Election. Perhaps the best we can hope is that a few embattled Ministers in this or the next (Social Democratic?) Government might liberalise the activities in their own portfolios, against opposition from their civil servants and, very probably, from fellow members of their cabinet, in the expectation that once the state has been removed other interest groups will fill the vacuum. If Sir Keith Joseph, for example, had succeeded in forcing through the education voucher despite the organised opposition of officials and teachers, he would have found that before long a very different interest group had formed — parents and pupils, who would resist as fiercely any attempt to remove the power that they had acquired. Libertarians, in politics or pubs, must learn from Marx, who saw that the key to the instigation of the social changes he advocated lay in the astute manipulation of vested interests. (A market will readily develop between libertarians who supply arguments from theory and empirical analysis and those eager to purchase such ammunition for political debate!) Until the 'New Right' has identified the groups, organised or otherwise, that will benefit from economic and political liberty and has informed them of those benefits, we are wasting our time, for no one will be listening. There is a market for these ideas, if hardly yet a free one. We must learn to sell the product.

IV

PARTY APPROACHES

MARC-HENRI GLENDENING

Five essays are grouped by personal political approach: Conservative (philosophic and economic), Social Democrat, Labour and non-party libertarian.

The first Conservative essay is by Marc-Henri Glendening, born in 1959, the son of an artist. His step-father is an antiquarian bookseller.

He was educated at a primary school and the Purcell School of Music, and graduated in Political Science from Warwick University in 1982.

He was an active Liberal from 1976, serving as an Agent at the 1979 General Election. He changed to the Conservatives in 1981, and in 1984 was elected chairman of the Federation of Conservative Students and to the General Purposes Committee of the Party.

Marc Glendening writes as an independent-minded, philosophically-inclined Conservative. He reached his position by two routes: a belief in the supreme value of individual choice and the conviction that the post-war 'social democratic' settlement was redundant. It became urgent to reverse the drift to mixed economy corporatism and economic decline. The state would have to be insulated from electoral and interest group pressure by constitutional safeguards.

The conventional Left/Right labels are meaningless. A more important division is between those who favour and those who oppose change. The economic-liberal, Conservative New Right in favour of change would then be on the left, and the 'social democrats' of all Parties opposed to change in the mixed economy on the right.

11

THATCHERISM AND LIBERTARIANISM

MARC-HENRI GLENDENING

In the first part of my essay I describe the ideas that led to my becoming a libertarian conservative. The second half examines the concept of the 'New Right' with particular attention to what critics call 'Thatcherism'. And I discuss points of tension on economic and social policy between the different modes of thought among Conservatives.

Two main principles

My moral commitment to the ideal of a polity that maximises the scope for individual human beings to give material expression to personal values and perceptions of self interest is grounded in two ideas. The first is ontological: the contention that the natural condition of human beings is freedom (defined as an absence of physical coercion). The second is epistemological: the denial that moral propositions can be shown to be objectively correct.

The first idea I possessed in the form of an intuition before I was aware of the existence of libertarianism as a political philosophy. It was articulated and systemised at a later time by reading Jean Paul Sartre's *Being and Nothingness*. Sartre maintains that absolute personal freedom is an inescapable consequence of the structure of consciousness. Through the act of directing consciousness inwards (introspection), the individual can make himself aware that he is more than a determined object. The very act of attempting to perceive oneself in terms of being an object is in itself proof that one is qualitatively different from an object, since inanimate objects cannot be conscious of themselves by definition of what they are.

For the football hooligan or heroin addict to seek to explain his past behaviour in terms of such environmental influences as peer-group pressure, lack of employment prospects, psychological depression, or anything else except themselves is, Sartre would have argued, 'bad faith'. They are attempting to define themselves in terms of mere objects who could not have done other than they did. Human beings, by virtue of their ability to engage in 'reflexive' consciousness, are agents who are at all times completely conscious of what they do. People are quite literally condemned to be free, regardless of whether they accept responsibility for their actions or nor not.

Existentialists are not necessarily drawn to libertarian conclusions. Sartre, a Marxist, quite clearly was not. They can say in all consistency, 'Man is born free but is everywhere in chains — bloody good thing, too'. Observations of what *is* do not tell us of themselves what *ought to be*. But humans do evaluate ethically what they perceive to be reality, and aspects of reality in turn contribute towards the formulation of moral and political values. An acceptance that the reality of the human condition is one of free choice is, arguably, a necessary but insufficient condition upon which a commitment to liberty as an idea is based. (There is not much point in defending freedom if you don't believe individuals are capable of exercising it.)

By adopting the existentialist thesis one is in a position to pose a question: 'Given that other human beings are free and have the equal capacity to make decisions for themselves (though not necessarily the ability to achieve their desired objectives since liberty and power are quite separate concepts), what circumstances, if any, would justify my utilising coercive means to try and dissuade others from exercising their free choice in certain ways?' I came to the conclusion that no such justification could be found because the subordination of the choices of others to my personal priorities presupposes a superior moral status commensurate with my own values. This is a claim that is not tenable owing to reasons relating to the second, epistemological argument.

The argument, in a nutshell, is that statements containing moral propositions cannot be shown to be true either 'synthetically' or 'analytically', that is by recourse to testing, matching observations of the real world to the hypothesis put forward, or by analysing the logical structures of the hypothesis. Contentions to the effect that: 'It is right that the rich ought to be forced to give some of their money to the poor', or 'All men should bow to Mecca ten times a day', cannot be tested in accordance with a scientific methodology because their validity cannot be refuted. Moral correctness and superiority does not reside in natural, physical, and empirically observable phenomena and properties. It is sometimes said that the purpose of moral propositions is to provide people with principles which can instruct them how to behave. Perhaps it is more pertinent to believe that is is not what ethical statements tell us, but what they *fail* to demonstrate that is a better indication of how we should behave, or, and more importantly, how we should *not* behave towards other equally sentient, choice-making human beings.

[128]

Given that there are no such entities as 'objectively correct moral truths' only competing *subjectively* derived ethical codes, the proper role of government and the law is not to enforce moral righteousness but to prevent individuals and groups of people from imposing their own self interests and/or ethical values upon other citizens through coercion. The coercer in any given situation cannot justify his act of violence to the victim by any methodology; this is the real reason why there must be strictly enforced laws against murder, rape, theft, and so on. Of course some will retort, and quite rightly, that the moral axiom I have presented itself cannot be verified or refuted. This is true. But personal values must come from somewhere, and the foundations of the non-aggression principle I have proposed as rooted in subjectivist relativism is arguably as valid as any other. It can also be maintained that there is a qualitative difference between moral principles that seek to impose ways of life upon human beings which are not of their own choosing (which is what all collectivists seek to do) and those which attempt no such thing.

The internal contradictions of social democracy

The second major influence on my political outlook was a realisation that the social democratic settlement that had been the legacy of Labour's 1945 victory was, by the late 1970s, redundant. The symptoms were quite obvious. Unemployment was rising and had been since the late 1960s despite the efforts of successive governments to control it through 'pump-priming' Keynesian demand-management exercises which had failed. The Phillips curve, the belief that there was a magical trade-off between inflation and unemployment, was dead. Despite the existence of tri-partite, corporatist industrial relations structures for the 'grandees' of big government, big business and the big unions, shop-floor militancy was on the increase. The third pillar of social democracy, the welfare state, was also in crisis as its cost to the Exchequer soared and its capacity to fulfill its basic functions deteriorated.

For some the remedies to the difficulties that Britain was facing were to be found in a bit of waste-cutting here, more negotiations there, a bit more public expenditure and the creation of new Royal Commissions to look into this or that. To others the causes were the inevitable consequence of the very structure of the mixed economy, a contradictory system which contained the seeds of its own eventual destruction. This view comprised three components: thesis, antithesis and synthesis. The thesis refers to the social democratic settlement, brought into being through the nationalisation of the 'commanding heights' of the economy, the undertaking by the post-war state of a comprehensive range of open-ended welfare commitments and responsibility for full employment. The dramatically enlarged public sector was to be dependent for its survival upon the expropriation of large sums of money created by the wealth-producing private sector. An essentially parasitic relationship was set in motion.

Two antitheses were triggered off as a consequence. The first was an expansionist dynamic within the public sector that could be attributed to the formation of a host of well-organised groups with a very well-formulated sense of self-interest and plan of political action designed to capitalise on the new state of affairs. These interest groups included those engaged directly in the provision of public services — miners, civil servants, teachers, hospital ancillary staff and so on, and those who, nominally in the private sector, stood to benefit directly from national and local government services, hand-outs and protection from competition. The myriad of public-sector producer-groups and their clients in the private sector all had a direct vested interest in lobbying politicians for additional funding to be devoted to themselves, and against being exposed to market competition.

Because the benefits of increased state expenditure are concentrated in the hands of the politically organised few who gain directly from it and because the costs of appeasing groups of producers/beneficiaries are spread thinly over the many politically-unorganised private sector workers, it has paid vote-maximising political entrepreneurs to pander to the demands of the few with monies of the many. As a consequence of lobby-group pressure, combined with the electoral exigencies of vote-buying, public expenditure continues to rise inexorably, and there is a continual movement away from the mixed economy towards the predominantly collectivist, corporatist state. Government now consumes close to 50 per cent of the national product, and around 30 per cent of the workforce is employed in the public sector. Conservative Chancellors elected on manifestos promising to cut state spending congratulate themselves on reducing its percentage increase.

The second antithesis is contractive rather than expansive. The private half of the mixed economy equation, under the growing weight of the public sector edifice, shrinks in size. Ever-higher taxation, inflation and local rates, combined with a thicket of bureaucratic regulations, eventually take their toll. These increasing state burdens are counter-productive. They serve only to exacerbate the financial pressures that already exist on the 'over-loaded' state because jobs lost only add to the cost of public expenditure and un-competitive sections of industry join the queue for subsidies. Thus the vicious cycle continues unabated and propels the political economy downwards towards economic decline and rising unemployment.

Ultimately, unless drastic measures are taken, a situation is

[130]

reached whereby government can no longer pay off all the groups it has made promises to because the private sector cannot, or refuses to, be squeezed any further. A cash-flow crisis is reached which threatens the continued existence of large elements of the public sector itself. Serious political instability is a distinct probability on a scale which make slick Channel-Four doomsday plays about post-industrial Britain look almost true to life.

The third stage of the dialectical triad now comes into play. At the point at which the public sector negates the private sector, and so itself in the process, a clear and distinctive choice presents itself. It could take the form of a totalitarian state which restores law and order and full employment through a series of Draconian measures. All productive factors, including labour, are placed under centralised control in a far more systematic and brutal manner than with the faltering corporatist model. Or it could take the form of a new and liberal society in which the means of production, distribution and exchange are liberated and returned to private ownership. The state ceases to be the tool of parasitic interests which produce only 'deficit value', but which use it to exploit the politically vulnerable. Government instead becomes the safeguarder of a self-regulating series of private-property relationships involving millions of individual economic agents — ordinary people — whose ability to accumulate wealth is dependent solely upon the ability to satisfy the demands of others in non-coercive economic activity.

Reversing the drift

Having adopted this analysis of Britain's crisis, and its likely conclusion, I then had to confront two questions: 'What immediate steps can be taken to begin the process of reversing the drift towards corporatism and catastrophe?' And 'Given that the problem has arisen because of the intimate inter-relationship between politics and economics, can the inner contradictions of the mixed economy be corrected within the confines of the current Parliamentary system which gave rise to them in the first place?'

These questions must be answered by those who are concerned about creating the foundations of a free and prosperous political order.

My personal response to the crisis was to leave the Liberal Party while in my second year at Warwick University and to join the Conservative Party via its student wing, the Federation of Conservative Students (F.C.S.). I harboured no illusions about my new Party because a considerable proportion of its Parliamentary membership were (and are) mixed economy corporatists. But it was apparent to me that the relatively new Thatcherite leadership had begun to develop at least something approaching a public choice analysis of the crisis of social democracy, even if it lacked a viable strategy to carry out the essential drastic surgery. I was also of the opinion that the Conservative Party could provide a potent vehicle for the mass education of the electorate about the horrors that awaited them unless the mixed economy were dismantled. It was imperative that the people be made to understand what had been the real agent of the coming collapse. This would make easier than it would otherwise be the task of mobilising popular support for the free market, rather than the totalitarian, alternative that would eventually present itself as a panacea for Britain's troubles.

While winning the battle of ideas is important and every means must be utilised through the Tory Party, the media, and single issue and local community organisations, free-marketeers should also turn their attention to a radical restructuring of the state in order to insulate it from electoral and interest-group pressure. Concrete proposals such as a politically-appointed civil service, a written constitution including a Bill of Rights, a balanced budget and flat-rate tax amendments, and an elected upper house, (elected in thirds with as much power as the lower chamber) will have to be considered.

What is the New Right?

The kind of ideas that have been referred to in the first part of this essay would no doubt be described as of the 'New Right' in the pages of *Marxism Today* and those other fashionable journals that decorate the coffee tables of the radical chic. But the terms 'right' and 'left' have no political significance in themselves. They are given meaning by merely virtue of the well-known and often-repeated cliché that those who desired change in a liberal direction in immediate pre-revolutionary France sat on the left of the Estates General and those who sought to preserve the existing feudal non-capitalist status quo sat on the right of the chamber. The political usage of the words 'left' and 'right' became, for reasons that are not clear, divorced in meaning from their precise, original 18th century context.

It has been assumed for some time that a person who has a predisposition against a predominantly free market economy and in favour of the most important economic decisions being made in a collectivist manner is on the 'left'. (Fascists, for some unknown reason, are exempt from this classification). The division disregards the existing state of affairs. Thus status-quo socialists in the Soviet Union are still referred to as on the left whereas anti-establishment political dissidents are sometimes labelled 'right-wing'. In an equally confusing manner free-marketeers, fascists and feudalist reactionaries are all bracketed together as 'right wing', again in defiance of political reality.

If the more original definitions of left and right were to be applied to Britain today is there a case for saying that those who, according to popular parlance, are described as of the 'New Right', should be thought of as left-wing? Yes — because an important characteristic of the New Right's prospectus is a large helping of economic liberalism. Even if the more common pro-change, anti-change dichotomy is adopted, both the Conservative (so-called) New Right and radical socialists are very much on the left, since both seek to dismantle the mixed economy and replace it with something very different. The real right-wingers could be said to be, therefore, the social democrats of all parties who wish to freeze the present and keep the status quo.

Both types of application of the words 'left' and 'right' — for v. against change, and for v. against the mixed economy — are equally inadequate because they imply that politics can be interpreted in terms of uni-dimensional continua in the form of liberalism — non-liberalism, or anti — pro status quo. Anti-liberalism covers a multitude of sins; it is possible to desire reform for a wide variety of objectives. It is for this reason also that an individualist — collectivist range of measurement is inadequate. Not only are there varieties of collectivist modes of thought; for all except the purest and internally consistent ideological models (that is, either completely individualist or totalitarian) a one-dimensional spectrum would fail to illustrate the type of issue upon which intermediate categories of thought are either for or against state intervention.

With reference to the non-socialist philosophical orientations that fall within the conservative family (and outside it) it is very important to be able to make qualitative as well as quantitative distinctions. What is of interest, for example, is not only that Thatcherite Tories will differ from Social Democrats in the amount of governmental interference they are prepared to sanction, but also how they respond to differing clusters of issues. Thatcherite Tories might be expected to be more individualist on economic policy than Social Democrats but more statist and interventionist on civil liberties.

It might be rather more satisfactory to attempt to measure competing ideologies according to a two-dimensional scale measuring individualist – collectivist inclinations on separate axes: economic and welfare on the one hand, and social/civil liberties on the other. Even this approach, while arguably an improvement on the right — left measure is itself an over-simplification. It excludes other dimensions and other criteria that could be considered. An axis which deals with foreign policy is ruled out because it does not lend itself to a criterion that seeks to measure state interventionism.

[133]

The two-dimensional approach is however of some use when examining the most influential mode of anti-socialist thought in British politics in recent times — 'Thatcherism'. This is particularly convenient since by common consent there are two distinct Thatcher agendas, the economic and the social, with a quite different treatment for each in terms of state interference.

The economic agenda

The first agenda is essentially liberal in nature. Political ideas periodically come in and out of vogue. Changes in the configuration of objective social and economic circumstances as they arise dictate concomitant changes in the appropriate response. So it is that liberal ideas have undergone something of a dramatic resurgence within the Conservative Party since the advent of Mrs Thatcher's leadership. The growing influence of free-market ideas was not the result of pressure from the grass roots and upwards but of the intellectual initiatives of leading figures within the Party (such as Sir Keith Joseph) who were dissatisfied with the collectivist 'middle way' policies that had characterised the Heath administration.

What marks these ideas as 'new' if not 'right-wing' is that they are distinguished by the challenge they pose to the very constraints and foundations of democratic political economy within which all governments from World War II up until 1979 worked.

Perhaps the best precis of the Thatcher project are contained in Sir Keith Joseph's two pamphlets *Why Britain Needs a Social Market Economy* and *Stranded on the Middle Ground*, published by the Centre for Policy Studies (the think-tank for the free market Tories in the late 1970s). In them Joseph argued for a break with Keynesian techniques of demand-management, for a monetarist regime of sound money, a dramatic altering of the balance between the private and public sectors in favour of the former, and a significant shift of the electorate's perceptions of what government could achieve.

Another key component of this new radical strategy has been to neutralise the damaging influence of the trade unions. As Hayek (among others) has argued, what is important in determining the degree of unemployment is not the aggregate amount of wages but relative wage increases between firms. The institution of the closed shop, by establishing a 'property relationship' between the worker and his job, bars non-unionised labour from taking up employment in unionised firms at competitive wage rates. By preventing the laws of supply and demand from taking their course in the labour market and by keeping some workers in employment at artificially high rates, unions therefore cause unemployment in uncompetitive sectors of the economy. It has been the closed shop which has inflated the 'natural rate' of unemployment, and traditional Keynesian techniques have been powerless to affect the process. Unions no longer suffer from 'money illusion' and as a consequence marginal wage rates remain unaltered, with the result that unemployment is unaffected. The irony is that Keynesian reflationism itself contributed to the demise of 'money illusion' as workers got wise to the reduction of the real value of their pay packets through monetary inflation.

The new Conservatism is characterised by a new-found emphasis on micro-economics. Deregulation and significant tax cuts (at least in theory) are seen as a means to unleash the wealth and job-creating potential in the economy that had lain dormant because of decades of excessive state interference. By putting their faith in market forces the new Conservatives are not afraid of the changes that free-market capitalism, being an essentially progressive mode of production, as Marx recognised, will bring about if left to its own devices. Free enterprise results in the decline of communities as workers have to be prepared to uproot themselves in order to find new centres of employment. Decaying dinosaur industries are replaced by the 'sunrise' businesses of the future. Entire landscapes become transformed, the corner shop giving way to the supermarket with its economies of scale.

Thatcherism has brought sharply into focus the competing streams of thought within the Conservative Party. Its interpretation of the Conservative mission has come under sustained attack from elements within the Party that had previously enjoyed hegemony.

The dissidents are grouped around the Tory Reform Group and, within Parliament, Francis Pym's Conservative Centre Forward. The 'wets', as they are commonly called, have very skilfully sought to perpetuate the myth that they are the true inheritors of the mantle of traditional Conservatism. Interpretations of history (true or false) can be powerful political tools because they can succeed in bestowing a veneer of legitimacy upon certain philosphical currents while simultaneously calling into question the authenticity of competing currents.

It is difficult to summarise the foundations of the 'wet' position because its protagonists dress up the essence of their approach with flowery and (deliberately) obscure language. They talk of 'One Nation', 'Community' and the 'Politics of Consent' (the title of Pym's personal manifesto). These concepts defy precise definition and so avoid a commitment to particular policies — which can be logically deduced from first principles. The Tory 'wet' can adopt or jettison virtually any set of policies according to how he or she perceives changes in mass opinion, without fear of being charged with betrayal and contradiction. In practice 'pragmatism', another nebulous term much used by the Sir Ian Gilmours and Peter Walkers, is nothing more than a euphemism for electoral opportunism. The slavish devotion of the Tory corporatists to the essential ingredients of consensus politics can be traced back to the new statist climate of opinion heralded by the 1930s and the restructuring of the political economy that followed Labour's 1945 victory. The exigencies of winning sufficient votes to enable the Conservative Party to reclaim its position as the natural party of power demanded then, as now (the 'wets' believe), that the Tory leadership concede vast amounts of moral, economic and analytical territory to socialism. Tories should stay close, in terms of policy, to whatever happened to be the 'centre' of the political spectrum.

Crude psephological calculations are one thing, philosophical integrity another. It can be argued that classical Conservatism was characterised by ideas which have implications for practical policies rather different from those advocated by the Conservative Centre Forward. The principle idea is a profound pessimism about the capacity of state-imposed reform to produce beneficial consequences.

It was Edmund Burke, the intellectual grand-daddy of modern Conservatism, who savaged the belief inspired by the late Enlightenment that the methods of the natural sciences could be applied to economics and politics. He interpreted society in terms of a self-regulating organism whose rhythms and traditions, if disturbed, could have harmful secondary effects.

Burke believed that humility and caution were important virtues. He therefore had nothing but disdain for the arrogance of intellectuals who wished to 'start the world all over again', according to their own abstract principles and who in their social engineering '. . . consider men in their experiments no more than they do mice in an air pump . . .' (quoted in Freeman, *Edmund Burke and the Critique of Political Radicalism.*) For this reason he approved of the free market because he saw it as part of the natural, organic development of the nation. For Burke the proper role of the state was to uphold private property and to facilitate the functioning of commerce. He was opposed to any attempt to redistribute economic rewards because material inequality '. . . grows out of the nature of things by time, custom, succession, accumulation, permutation and the improvement of property'.

The classical Conservative's instinctive scepticism about the efficacy of state interference provides a crucial point of convergence with more modern types of anti-collectivist thought such as those of the libertarian Austrian and Chicago schools. Libertarians reject economic planning as a non starter. It presupposes that central planning can have access to the necessary knowledge to run an efficient economy — information that is dispersed amongst millions of

[136]

individual human beings all capable of varying their behaviour and altering their desires at any one time.

For Hayek the free market is the result of human action but not conscious design. Its conventions contain within themselves more wisdom in the form of inherited experience than an individual would be capable of amassing on his own. Hence Hayek's objection to 'constructivist rationalism', the imposition of political blueprints upon society by arrogant reforming politicians, is that it serves only to create economic chaos and social disharmony. It is the concept of a society and economy that evolves according to the spontaneous and peaceful interaction of the individual people who go to make it up that ties Hayek to Burke.

It is the Tory 'wets' who are fundamentally out of step with the classical premises of Conservatism. It has been reflationist gimmickery and the establishment of the mixed economy which have been in large measure responsible for disrupting the delicate equilibrium of British society. They have created socially divisive by-products: inflation and an interest-group rat-race for other people's economic resources — the inevitable result of the collectivisation of economic decision-making.

Conversely, it has been the Thatcherites who have attempted to apply ideas and intuitions that owe their orgin to traditionalist Conservative thinking. In having debunked the discredited themes associated with post-war consensus politics, Thatcherism can be said to be both a new and an authentic form of Conservatism.

I thus think entirely appropriate to reject the notion that there is such a phenomenon as the 'New Right', and I propose the concept of a neo-Conservatism in its stead. This category can be divided into two main sub headings — Thatcherism and libertarianism. Although there is broad consensus between them on issues that are commonly thought of as economic, it begins to disintegrate on some issue of non-economic policy.

The social agenda

Thatcherism is usually presented as two conflicting and contradictory themes, economic liberalism and social authoritarianism. This interpretation is flawed because it fails to understand the foundations of Thatcherism — which are instinctive and pragmatic rather than morally derived. It fortifies its intuitions with impressive theory which serve to create the impression that it is an *a priori* system of politics, which it is not.

Because Thatcherites have no pretensions about constructing a philosophically inter-related whole they do not seek to erect permanent and unabridgeable boundaries between the public and private spheres of politics. Mrs Thatcher's followers have adopted many of the key characteristics of the free-market critique of collectivist economics, but they have done so on essentially utilitarian grounds — that monetarism, deregulation and privatisation will facilitate economic recovery. Such policies will increase the scope for individual choice, which is welcomed by the neo-Tories because they have a bias towards liberty.

Yet a bias for personal choice is not the same as a belief that human beings have a natural sacrosanct right not to be interfered with. The Neo-Conservatives have no inhibitions about sanctioning extensive intervention in peoples' lives when they feel it necessary to satisfy some broader social good. In the Thatcherites' own terms there is no theoretical or practical contradiction in doing this, some would go on to contend that placing severe restrictions on personal activities acts as a support mechanism to the first (economic) agenda. For the market to operate successfully, it is argued, certain social underpinnings are necessary which are quite different from the ideas most associated with the market, namely, free choice and the cash nexus. Such notions as obligations, patriotism, virtue, authority and paternalism, they continue, must predominate in other contexts if the social stability capitalism demands is to be maintained.

The most articulate, and controversial, exponent of socially-interventionist Conservatism is Roger Scruton. He argues in *The Meaning of Conservatism* (1980) that individual liberty must be subordinate to the 'higher value' of the authority of government. The state must be prepared to utilise its full legislative and coercive muscle in '... any area of social life which is vital ... to the strength of the social bond'.

The law, Scruton claims, is the expression of social consciousness. The law must go beyond seeking simply to protect the individual from physical attack and the theft of property. State intervention is justified wherever the existing order is felt to be in need of protection.

There can be no right, for example, to redecorate one's house if that conflicts with the prevailing character of the immediate environment; the marketing of sexual material and the performance of certain sexual acts which are out of step with society's prevailing sexual mores should also be regulated. Subversive ideas are also proper targets for censorship. There must be a common moral order, and since (Scruton is relieved to note) the majority of people are not moral libertarians, it will not be one based on permissiveness. The law must enshrine the traditional values of the society from which it emanates. The state also has a place, many Conservatives argue, to set the moral tone through legislation, to lead rather than just follow public opinion.

The idea which serves as a key element in fusing Thatcherites and libertarians — the concept of spontaneous social evolutionism — fails to produce such unity when applied to morality. Ideas and actions concerned with technical matters and economic problem-solving are imitated by individuals, and if they are found to be successful according to specific criteria, they are adopted; if not, they are discarded. No such test in reality can be applied to moral beliefs since, by definition, they do not relate to physical properties in the world and are concerned with how men *ought* to lead their lives rather than how they now behave. Libertarians believe that there should be a free market for ethics and that individuals should be free to adopt whatever beliefs and life style they choose so long as they do not violate the equal right of others to pick contrary ideas. The essence of libertarianism is that human beings are left free to determine their own priorities and decisions relating to their own lives in the sphere of economics, religion, politics, sex, culture and so on. Many libertarians, being legal contractarians, see it as improper for the state to impose arbitrarily derived moral values upon individuals; this is not a function that falls within its jurisdiction. In doing so it is exhibiting raw power, not authority. The state is negating the very purpose for which it should exist — the defence of individual freedom.

There are less fundamentalist arguments, which non-libertarian Conservatives can employ against the notion that government is the proper agency to bring about a moral reconstruction of society. First, politicians are not the most appropriate group of people to be the moral guardians of society since they, like their citizens, possess original sin and are therefore morally flawed. Why should it be presupposed that MPs are any better equipped to legislate for morality than, say, the Kray twins?

Second, as many Christians would argue, it is impossible to save souls by coercing bodies. There is no such thing as a forced conversion. Men can behave morally only when they have the option of behaving immorally.

Third, what is to be the method employed by which the fallen men and women of Westminster will ascertain what are the proper virtues to be inflicted upon everyone else? Some might say that the wishes of the majority should be translated into law, that this should be the yardstick of what is and is not morally acceptable. If the prerequisite half-plus-one of the electorate were of the opinion that all Quakers should be put in death or that all people of non-British stock should be forcefully repatriated, could this be said to be an objectively correct moral position to hold simply because a majority were of this view?

[139]

Majority viewpoints contain no intrinsic moral properties in themselves.

Fourth, governments have increasingly tended to collectivise morality (like economic decisions), and the result is a decline in respect for moral values once widely held. The welfare society has led to a withering away of the belief that individuals have a personal obligation to look after people less fortunate. Theft of private property has become more acceptable, with the public exaltation of concepts such as redistribution and 'need before profit'. The dangerous notion that crime is a socially induced phenomenon has only encouraged persons from relatively 'deprived' homes and backgrounds to commit crimes on the grounds that 'society is to blame'. The logic of this belief is that everybody but the criminal is responsible for his action. It is welfarism, not vice, that should be the paramount target for Conservatives, libertarian or otherwise.

Lastly, the invention of ever more 'victimless' crimes, such as offences relating to prostitution, selling certain types of merchandise on a Sunday, the private viewing of video 'nasties' (however that genre of film is defined) and pornography, has meant that the agents of law enforcement are having to devote an increasing amount of time and resources to arresting and prosecuting individuals who have not in any way violated the property rights of other citizens. Meanwhile, those criminals who have engaged in 'other-regarding' activities of a serious nature are given more opportunity to get away unpunished.

Conclusion

There is little doubt that many issues divide people who are opposed to socialism. Even amongst those who agree that the paramount project of politics must be the pursuit of liberty in all spheres of human existence, there will be differences on whether the implementation of particular policies will on balance maximise or minimise freedom. Abortion, drug-taking, the public display of pornographic materials, conscription during war, and even the provision of a nuclear defence deterrent are all classic examples of issues that can divide pro-freedom thinkers and activists.

The traditional response in the past within Conservative circles to intellectual divergence has been to bottle up genuine debate and urge 'unity' (on terms dictated by the Party hierarchy) at all costs.

In an age when political activists are considerably more aware of, and interested in, the relationship between philosophy and action, stifling dialogue and debate will result only in unnecessary and counter-productive factional sectarianism. A better appreciation of the precise nature of the similarities and differences between

Thatcherites and libertarians will make it apparent that there are considerable areas of agreement to serve as focal points for powerful united action to deliver Britain from collectivism.

TIM JANMAN

The second Conservative essay is by Tim Janman, born near Bournemouth in 1957.

He was educated at Sir William Borlase Grammar School in Marlow, Buckinghamshire and graduated in chemistry from Nottingham University.

From 1979 to 1982 he worked in industrial relations for Ford Motor Company and is now in marketing at IBM (UK) Ltd.

He has written widely for political publications and been active in Conservative politics. In 1980-81 he was Senior Vice-Chairman of the Federation of Conservative Students and since 1983 has been Chairman of the Selsdon Group, established in 1973 to emphasise the case for the free market in the Conservative Party. In 1985 he was adopted Conservative Prospective Parliamentary Candidate for Thurrock, Essex.

He argues that his Party had lost its way. He is critical of the old Right, 'downright protectionist and patrician'. He feels frustrated with 'the Tory Party for impotence [and] lack of political will to reverse' socialist measures — especially the Heath Government, 'often more left wing than the Wilson Government'. He is an uncompromising free market liberal on economic policy, populist on social issues. He found inspiration in Hayek, Popper, Powell and Friedman. He argues that the New Right should move the economic system back to private property, individual freedom and responsibility, and competition.

Tim Janman outlines seven main policies that bind the New Right together: on inflation; public expenditure; free trade, competition and denationalisation; trade unions; health services; education; defence.

12

A CONSERVATIVE'S APPROACH

TIM JANMAN

My first real involvement in politics was in the two election campaigns of 1974, when the Conservative Party leadership, with hardly a Conservative thought left in their collective heads, almost managed to cling on to power, due to the amazing loyalty of Tory voters and party workers (myself included).

Many people may have predicted that a new commitment to right-of-centre policies would have come about after the socialist years of 1964 to 1970. This did happen to some degree, but a much stronger catalyst for a new analysis of what the right policies should be came in 1975, when many instinctively right-wing conservatives, from young university students like me to senior constituency activists and Opposition spokesmen (Sir Keith Joseph predominantly) realised that a major crusade had to be launched not only against Marxist collectivism but also the sheer limpness of paternalistic social democracy.

Until 1975 I had always identified myself with the existing right of the Tory Party, but unlike the New Right, which I believe was born in 1975-76, the old right was either disinterested in economic policy or downright protectionist and patrician in its economic stance.

I do not view an instinctively right-of-centre Conservative as the same political animal as a libertarian. My definition of a Conservative is a nationalistic liberal (as was Churchill), who combines support for liberal economic policies with a dislike of the welfare state, a feeling for the identity of his nation, and the need for social cohesion within it, as opposed to the virtual anarchy as espoused by many libertarians.

On many issues, such as drugs, capital punishment, abortion, and international movement of labour, libertarians will cling to theoretical arguments and so-called moral principles about individual liberty in the same way as a left-wing socialist; a Conservative is more likely to consider the consequences for society as a whole and take each policy issue as it comes.

[143]

Constituents of the New Right

Thus, in my view, the two fundamental groupings in the New Right, as born in the middle 1970s, were firstly existing conservatives like me, who wanted a much stronger free-market approach, plus more purist libertarians, who obviously had that goal as a common objective, and who were then attracted to the Conservative Party, as the best vehicle for the New Right economic crusade.

Further support (albeit of debatable value) has during the 1980s been gained from Conservatives who dislike the right of the party but who will support right-wing economic policies to curry favour with the leadership, until there is a change of leader resulting in a more social democratic style. This third grouping will then show their true instincts for consensus, compromise, bowing to minority group interests, and spending large amounts of the electorate's money to buy votes.

So in the middle 1970s, whilst maintaining my traditionalist conservative views on social issues such as law and order, immigration and drugs, I became part of the New Right crusade, working for the election of a Conservative Government committed to deregulation, denationalisation, privatisation, lower government expenditure and taxation, more choice in education and health, and a general reduction in the degree to which individuals looked to government to provide them with support or goods and services.

In order to support these ideas I did not find myself going through any great ideological change. My political view from an early age had been to see a repugnant self-defeating economic suicide in government coercing money from some groups in order to subsidise the domestic or industrial inefficiency of others.

Subsidising people to have children, in a world of finite resources, or to grow un-needed food, or manufacture over-priced, unwanted goods, had always in my mind seemed an anathema to commonsense and honest government. It so happened that many young conservatives, in my view quite independently, were thinking the same thing in 1975, after the inability of the Heath administration to stop the rot. And together we all looked for inspiration and guidance from the likes of Hayek, Popper, Powell and Friedman in order to form one loud united voice. The New Right was born; and in 1979 with the election of Mrs Thatcher, and in 1980 of President Reagan, those who had battled hard during the 1970s saw new hope for a society based on merit, the 'protestant work ethic' and responsible individual freedom to be forged from the ashes of a failed social-democratic-based mixed economy.

Although the new 'New Right' was new, perhaps in the uncompromising attitude of many of its supporters, I think that terms such as 'radical right' are rather misleading, and were coined because some

[144]

people felt this made the movement sound more fashionable, and therefore more likely to gain support amongst young people.

The exact opposite is true. The New Right is 'reactionary'. It is a reaction against decades of increasing state intervention and rising taxation, resulting in a stifling of individual enterprise and risk-taking. Although sometimes in a more humane and sophisticated form, the New Right seeks ultimately to move the economic system and society as a whole back towards what it was, with its economic structure based on private property, individual freedom *and responsibility, and competition*, and not towards something totally new and unknown.

This is precisely why I support the New Right. Within the context of their time and place, vigorously free market economies such as Victorian Britain have been far more successful in generating wealth, maintaining individual freedom, and keeping real poverty down to its minimum, than any socialist system has ever achieved, or will ever achieve.

Where the 'New Right' has been 'new' is in the ferocity with which this new generation of conservatives and allies have been prepared to stand up and verbally and intellectually confront socialism and the social-democratic mixed-economy consensus.

Once again, this determination is based not solely upon a hatred of socialism but upon the huge frustration felt by many at the impotence of the Tory Party when in power — its lack of political will to reverse measures taken by socialist administrations. This failure was particularly acute under the 1970-74 Conservative Government which, on many policy areas, on any objective political scale, was more left-wing than the preceding Wilson Government.

Fortunately to some degree, this impotence has changed under Mrs Thatcher, who quite clearly has done much for the New Right in Britain today, — in my view as a traditional Conservative, and not a libertarian.

Much of what the present Government stands for unfortunately never becomes more than rhetoric (like cutting government expenditure). And there are many policy areas where the Government has taken nearly six years to do nothing.

Yet Mrs Thatcher and some of her Ministers have achieved a considerable amount in changing people's attitudes, particularly to the economic facts of life. And they have given ordinary people with commonsense much more confidence in what they believe.

Ronald Reagan in a speech this year at a banquet of the Conservative Political Action Conference in Washington said:

> The greatest triumph of modern conservatism has been to stop allowing the left to put the average American on the moral defensive. Average Americans held true to certain

[145]

beliefs and principles that for 20 years the intelligentsia were telling us were hopelessly out of date, utterly trite and reactionary. You want prayer in the schools? How primitive, they said. You oppose abortion? How oppressive, how anti-modern. The normal was portrayed as eccentric, and only the abnormal was worthy of emulation.

To a lesser degree, Mrs Thatcher has achieved a similar shift of political climate in Britain. But just as the 'old right' had its weaknesses, so in my view does the New Right. Before going on to discuss policies as such, I should expand briefly on this contrast between the old right and the New Right.

Old and New Right

The right in Britain until the mid-1970s had never been particularly vocal on economic policy, nor imaginative. It had concentrated mainly on foreign policy and on domestic social issues such as law and order and coloured immigration. Nor had it been prepared to re-examine many monopolies which benefited certain middle-class professions, or to question agricultural subsidy on a vast scale. In other words, the old right was rather selective in its support of free markets, in addition to being very gentlemanly in style, and not prepared to debate sacred cows such as the National Health Service.

The strength of the New Right is that it is genuinely meritocratic: it no more believes in a conveyancing monopoly held by solicitors than in the state monopoly of the NCB in coal. And it is prepared to argue intelligently the case against a large bureaucratic welfare state.

But the New Right has one glaring weakness, which in my view holds true for the Thatcher Government as well. I have one or two doubts about the New Right's strategy (particularly on education), but by and large I support 'New Right' policies, which if put into effect will create a major transformation in British society. It has to be accepted that implementation of such policies (deregulation, de-nationalisation, welfare state reform, rationalisation of social benefits, tax reduction, and much more) will, in the short term, bring some people up with a bit of a jolt, and that campaigning purely on these policies will be difficult.

The weakness of the New Right is that (unlike Mrs Thatcher) it does not seem to include in its political repertoire any skill or even premeditated desire to take on the progressive left in social policy. There are many policy areas such as Northern Ireland, the EEC, capital punishment, and law and order, the race relations industry and others where the New Right seems either scared or incapable of attuning itself to the wishes of the British people. Supporting and enacting policies in these areas, which have widespread popular rather than political consensus support, would provide the sugar to help the bitter pill of more competition and removal of subsidy and state ownership, with all its inherent overmanning, go down with the electorate.

The hard-headedness and economic policy of the New Right, combined with the populism of the old right on social issues, would provide an alliance invincible in British politics for a very long time to come.

Policies for the New Right

The second half of this essay examines the major policies of the New Right, and assesses progress to date. Many of these policies happen, not by coincidence, to be those that by 1975 the Tory Party had virtually surrendered to the consensus left — which advocates more state control and public expenditure, to plan and pay for a moribund egalitarian society.

Seven main areas of policy bind the New Right together as I see it:

(a) control of inflation through disciplined money supply policy;
(b) reducing public expenditure and therefore the role of the state and taxation;
(c) belief in free trade, subsidy-free competition, de-nationalisation and privatisation;
(d) major reform of British trade union and industrial relations law, plus mass deregulation;
(e) replacing as far as possible the state health service with a private health service, and reducing social benefits;
(f) working with our American allies to combat the Soviet war machine;
(g) a voucher system for education, leading ultimately to a totally private education system.

There are of course others; and there are issues on which individuals within the New Right feel very strongly, like Ulster; but I believe that anyone who examines the viewpoint of the New Right on these seven policy issues will receive a clear picture of what it stands for, its guiding philosophy, and what it wants to see for Great Britain.

I fully support the view of the New Right on all these policies with the exception of education (below), although even then it is a qualified exception.

Why does the New Right, made up of individuals like me, support

[147]

these policies? And what are the consequences of implementing them?

It is quite clear, from both historical and current evidence, that free-market-orientated economies are far more efficient and success-ful in creating wealth and delivering a higher standard of living to the societies they serve. The next issue is the degree to which wealth should be re-distributed in such a society (if at all), and if so through what mechanism. In addition, to what degree should the state intervene in the market place, to control monopolies of capital and labour, the balance of power between employer and employee, and the rules of commerce to protect businessmen and consumer alike?

The object of the New Right is, I believe, to support policies which on the one hand catalyse wealth-creating activity and severely reduce the role of the state in providing goods and services but, on the other, use the power of government to provide a safety net for the genuinely needy, and rules and regulations to protect businessmen from each other, and of course consumers from fraudulent practices. This, to me, seems a perfectly honourable political object and for the good of society as a whole. So let me briefly outline the motivation behind each of the seven main new-right policies.

(a) *Control of inflation via monetarism*
Money is no different from any other commodity. If there is too much supply chasing too little demand, its value (purchasing power) will fall. It is quite clear that governments which print or borrow excess money not financed by taxation create inflation, although with a time lag, and that there is a strong and permanent link between money supply and inflation.

Allowing for 9 to 18 month time lags, this Government's money-supply policy, and the rate of inflation, taking into account the rate of economic growth bear out this relationship and prediction. Inflation is the worst enemy of a democratic capitalist society. Not only does it seriously erode the return on investment, which it thus deters, but it also causes severe strains on the democratic system of government. As the long-term economic consequences of inflation proceed — unemployment coupled with high inflation — the conse-quences can be politically disastrous for a civilised democracy.

The New Right has been strongly identified with monetarism, and rightly so. It is the only school of economic thought that has consistently put forward theories on the value of money which have been vindicated by the fullness of time and empirical evidence.

Friedman (unlike Hayek), quite correctly in my view, states that no-one except government — not even trade unions — can create inflation. It is therefore important for the stability of our society that New Right monetarist macro-economic policy continues.

[148]

(b) *Government expenditure/taxation/role of the state*
Some of the seven policies overlap, particularly those concerned with
the economy and industry. The New Right has not only an economic
commitment to controlling government expenditure and therefore
inflation and taxes, but also a philosophic commitment to ensuring
that the consumer has choice between many private suppliers of
goods and services. Each time an expenditure decision is made by an
individual, he is voting on how the country's resources should be
spent. This system is far more democratic in giving individuals what
they desire than are tax-funded bureaucratic monopolies which tell
people what their 'choice' is — in travel or energy or health or local
utilities, with money being coerced from individuals by the state to
pay for these flatulent and largely inefficient state industries and
local government services.

The economic consequences of high government expenditure are
in the long term suicidal. The public-sector industries become more
and more inefficient, and therefore, often owing to increased number
of employees, politically stronger. This growth results in an even
stronger wealth-spending public sector that bleeds the wealth-
creating private sector — and leads to a politically élitest system
rather than an economic one. The outcome is typical of planned
socialist and communist economies: not contentment, the
containment of poverty, and political stability, but the exact reverse.
The New Right, as I see it, believes in an economic meritocratic élite,
and therefore minimum government, low public expenditure and low
taxation, allowing people to spend their money as they see fit, not as
the state dictates.

(c) *Competition, denationalisation and free trade*
One of the weaknesses of the old right was that it could not grasp the
necessity for free trade. No British manufacturer has a God-given
right to sell his goods to the British public. Such a head-in-the-sand
attitude only helps the Luddite leadership of the British trade union
movement, who seem mainly to divide into two categories — the
subversive militant and the uncomprehending, who do not want to, or
cannot, understand the economic facts of life.

If British goods are competitively priced and of good quality, of
course consumers will support native suppliers. But if these
conditions are not met, why should they? More seriously, why should
they be compelled to, as some on the old right and the new left
believe?

I would put forward two caveats to this strong free-trade position.
The first is that it is difficult for British companies to compete when
they are faced with high tax demands, undemocratic, legally
protected monopolies of labour, and masses of government regulation

[149]

and bureaucracy. The second is the unwillingness of countries like Japan to practise what they preach. I favour very strong retaliatory action against the Japanese and other nations that through unnecessary regulations effectively operate strong import controls against the USA and Western Europe.

It is also quite clear that the extra on-cost of slothful, bureaucratic, inefficient public-sector monopoly provision is far higher than the margin required by efficient private companies, operating within a competitive environment of meeting customers' demands and having to keep their costs down, to make a profit and therefore survive. This defect of public monopoly applies just as much to local government services and the NHS as to the major nationalised industries. The New Right has catalysed a new confidence in the natural belief of the British people that free enterprise does a better job than a nationalised monopoly.

(d) Trade unions and government legislation

In any modern civilised market economy the government will lay down a framework of laws within which the game is played: air safety regulations, motor insurance, bankruptcy laws, and so on. These laws are there to protect the basic foundations of the modern social market economy: i.e., trust, individual responsibility and a sense of natural justice — of good and evil. But during the last 50 years there has been an increasing tendency for government to intervene in a destructive rather than a constructive fashion. The New Right has been at the forefront of the campaign to achieve two objectives:

(i)   de-regulation of the labour market and the housing market,

(ii) repeal of socialist legislation designed to protect trade unions from the law and reform of the rules within which they operate.

Over the last 20 years various Acts of Parliament have been passed supposedly to improve the lot of employees. Quite predictably, the overall effect of legislation such as the Employment Protection Act, the Health and Safety at Work Act, the Equal Pay Act and laws on Wages Councils has been to raise production costs by causing rigidity in the labour market. The net result has been increased unemployment.

Another major cause of unemployment has been the antics of British trade unions over many decades. Although undemocratic both in their method of finance and of the election of national leaders, they have continually abused their power of labour monopoly, strongly aided by socialist legislation which put the employer in a hopeless situation in the labour market.

Although British trade unions do not create inflation, the New Right does believe they have been major perpetrators of un-employment in the UK. Their contribution to British society has been almost entirely harmful. The New Right has been adamant in the view that, no matter what confrontation came as a consequence, British trade unions had to be reformed and their unique legal privileges stripped.

(e) *Health and social services*
Providing a safety net for the genuinely needy is not the same as the state also providing 95 per cent of health care and making people better off out of work than in it.

The safety net should be provided through a tax credit system to ensure that people can pay for health care. 80 per cent of the NHS could then be put into the private sector, hence abolishing the requirement for national insurance contributions for all health services.

A state pension fund is also an absurdity, and will inevitably go bankrupt.

The husband of a family with two children has a net income, while unemployed, equal to that of an employed man earning gross £7,800 a year. For people at the bottom end of earnings in the labour market, it pays them to live off the state. The New Right has been fearless in stating the case for reviewing benefits in order to eradicate such major anomalies, which heavily distort the labour market and are in effect a subsidy for unemployment.

(f) *Education*
Another characteristic of the New Right has been the commitment to vouchers, and ultimately a completely private education system run in conjunction with tax credits. This, in my view, would be a major improvement on the state-run comprehensive system.

I have always been a passionate supporter of the state-run selective structure, which educationally was a very fine system. Both options have major attractions, but selection, if the willpower were there, would be much easier to accomplish politically.

Nevertheless, any *state*-run system can become a prisoner of the left, which is not the case with a *private* system, as France has recently shown. The answer, therefore, is to allow all state schools to be bought out by private owners but run within a selective system laid down by the state and backed up by vouchers.

(g) *Defence*
A strong feature of the New Right has been its willingness to stand up to the threat of the CND and the Labour Party on defence issues, particularly nuclear weapons.

The left have increased their extra-parliamentary activity in this area over the past five years, and the New Right has responded to it,

[151]

as well as playing an invaluable role within the Conservative Party to strengthen anti-Soviet resolve.

Additionally, in my view, the New Right has been more committed to exposing Soviet society for what it is than have past generations of the old political right in Britain.

*   *   *

I think the reader can judge what progress has been made in each of these seven policies since 1975-76.

In some cases it has been quite good (as in trade union reform), in others woefully inadequate (in deregulation).

Those of us on the New Right know that an enthusiastic implementation of the principles outlined in this essay would create a more vibrant, prosperous and individually responsible, mature Britain than we have today.

In summary, the New Right has emerged because intelligent, committed young (and not so young) people were not prepared to stand by and let the left win the arguments and therefore power, and see Britain becoming a third-rate, stagnant, socialist slum, with all its accompanying loss of freedom and choice.

This degeneration of British life had gone on for a decade and a half, starting in the early 1960s. In 1975-76, a number of people decided simultaneously (and not by coincidence) that politically something had to be done. The New Right was with us; and it will be for many years to come.

MATTHEW LYNN

The third essay in this group presents the personal view of a Social Democrat.

Matthew Lynn was born in 1962, the son of a Professor of Psychology at the New University of Ulster and a lecturer in history at the Polytechnic of the South Bank.

He was educated at Willington Preparatory School, Putney, Emanuel (grammar) School, Battersea, and the Southwark College of Further Education. He graduated in Politics, Philosophy and Economics at Balliol College, Oxford, in 1984.

He works as a financial journalist.

His essay indicates his developing active interest in politics from Communism in 1978 to Bennite socialism and now to the SDP as 'a market-oriented social democrat' (which he interprets differently from the sense in which 'social democratic consensus' is used in earlier essays). His essay complements several others in discussing the influence of New Right thinking on the left.

The New Right is a reaction to the post-war dominance of left policies; it represents rejection of the revolutionary ultra-left by the gradualist view that 'nothing worthwhile can be built from broken fragments' and of the gradualist Labour notion that the lot of working people could be improved by collectivism.

The solution lies in the use of markets. The collectivist rejection of markets was based on lack of understanding. New Right policies — in education, health care, housing, pensions, etc. — could be given a 'left' slant and make for a consensus. The left could maintain its aims but abandon its discredited collectivist means: '. . . a basis can be laid for a political consensus built around market policies, just as the 1950s had a consensus built around collectivist policies'.

The New Right has made the running in ideas and policies 'more closely attuned to current realities and aspirations'. Disillusionment with the Conservatives' 'unradical attitude to many issues' opens the way to 'a more radical political force or party, perhaps the SDP, to carry out further market-oriented reforms'.

13

A SOCIAL DEMOCRAT'S APPROACH

MATTHEW LYNN

The progress made by the New Right in recent years has attracted considerable attention. Less noticed has been the increasing influence of New Right ideas on what may be loosely termed the left. Reaction on the left has been unduly slow and had consisted of either battening down the hatches and hoping for the best, as the right-wing of the Labour Party and sections of the S.D.P. have done, or seeing it as an excuse to move further to the left itself, as Tony Benn and his followers have chosen. Both responses are clearly inadequate.

Many of the ideas that have emerged on the New Right are a reaction to, and criticism of, the essentially left policies that have governed Britain for most of the post-war period. The undoubted power and appeal of those ideas stems from the failure of the left policies pursued in the 1960s and '70s. For the left to move on from that period will involve analysing, understanding, even accepting New Right ideas. Only by following this path can failure be overcome and progress be resumed.

My own position is that of a market-orientated social democrat, but I arrived at it from the far left. At the age of 16 or so I was active in the Young Communist League and later in the Bennite sections of the Labour Party. To a considerable extent that direction was set by the climate of the times. The mid-'70s were a good period for the ultra-left. A left-wing government in power that was both fairly right-wing and fairly ineffective set a poor example for the parliamentary road. At the same time a rising fascist movement suggested that strong resistance would be necessary, and high unemployment and industrial unrest suggested the revolutionary door might at last be opening. A naive view in retrospect, but one that attracted even some right-wing commentators at the time.

Revolution v. gradualism

For those on the left the crucial choice is between revolutionary and gradualist methods of social change. After that most other things are negotiable. The revolutionary abandons the requirement that he

[155]

thinks very carefully about the sort of society he will create by accepting the assumption that something new and better can be built from the rubble of the old. The gradualist, by accepting that nothing worthwhile can be built from broken fragments, is forced to think very carefully about the sort of society he is hoping to create if the steps and stages along the road are to be worked out. My own conversion to gradualism, therefore, determined the later development of my political opinions.

In contrast to the effect on the ultra-left, the mid-'70s were an exceptionally poor period for the gradualist social reformers who had dominated left thinking throughout the 20th century. The Labour tradition as represented by the Callaghan Government was not an appealing sight; neither was it seriously defensible. Its problems ran deeper than the economic troubles that there so apparent. The ideal itself seemed to have died. The idea that the lot of working people could be improved by collectivist state action, gradually, and without destroying the system itself, seemed to have collapsed, crushed by the very people it was supposed to have served. The trends were clear for anyone to see. The movement towards home-ownership, towards private provision of health and pensions, and away from trade unions were all signals of a general disillusion. Collectivist Government action, established in the post-war settlement, by the mid-'70s could no longer win general acceptance, let alone provide solutions to social or economic problems.

The politics of the late '70s and early '80s were clearly shaped by the demise of that Labour tradition. On the left there was a flight towards fundamentalist ultra-left solutions. On the right, which had been working within the essentially left post-war consensus, the New Right emerged with both a critique of the past and proposals for the future. Predictably politics polarised around those two points.

Choice between new left and new right

For a gradualist social reformer neither position is attractive. It was important to recognise that the old ways no longer worked, but perhaps not necessary to accept that the whole tradition had to be abandoned. The question that required facing was whether the reformist ideal been given enough rope and duly hanged itself, or had rather simply lost its way. Collectivism had clearly failed, but collectivism and gradualist social reform are not the same. True, they have been associated throughout most of the 20th century, and social reformers have argued for collectivist solutions. But was collectivism the ideal itself, or was it only a method? And if only a method could not the ends be rescued from the failure of the means?

The ends of social reformers have always been fairly simple — to eradicate poverty and to establish equality. Those at least are the basics. Looking back to the pre-war period it seems to me that the problems and their solutions were simpler than today. There were slums to be cleared. Children wanted both food and medicine if they were to have a chance of growing into a decent life. There were the old who wanted heat and housing if they were to have any reward for their lives of suffering and endurance. The solutions seemed straightforward. The slums should be cleared and new houses built, welfare benefits established, health care made free. It is unsurprising that social reformers who desired these ends should have looked to the state to bring them about. All that was required was an institution of sufficient size, power, and funds to put such reforms into operation.

Collapse of faith in the state

In that period therefore the use of the state to implement collectivist solutions may well have seemed appropriate. Today the conviction that the state through large-scale government programmes can be an active and successful agent of social change is less easy to sustain. The reasons are two-fold.

First, there is the increasing complexity of social problems. As absolute poverty was tackled it was replaced by relative poverty and deprivation. Council estates may be more comfortable and hygienic than slums but they are often ripped apart by vandalism and crime rife with unemployment, and are breeding grounds of depressive illness. The young may have free education but, if the state schools do not offer each child equal access to a full and rewarding life, large social problems remain. To pretend that significant inequalities of race, region, sex and class have not survived the establishment of the welfare state is to close your eyes to reality. Such inequalities persist to permeate and disfigure our national culture. But collectivist government action is a blunderbuss of a method to use against problems as subtle as these. Armies of social workers and the whole paraphernalia of quangos, committees and Royal Commission have all had little effect; they have served rather to bring reforming goverment into disrespect.

The second objection to collectivist government action, with its paternalistic character, is that it robs people of their individuality. By taking responsibility from them for their own destiny it diminishes them as human beings. But as affluence spreads these are the very qualities that people wish to develop. Hence the popular revolt against government that was so marked in the 1970s. Just as children eventually leave the influence of their parents, so paternalism is eventually rejected by those it was supposed to serve.

[157]

The question then is: can other methods be found to achieve social objectives? My own belief is that social reformers should look to market solutions, or at least market-oriented solutions. The market has traditionally been rejected out of hand by the left. Accepted thinking has it that the problems are caused by free markets and solved by collectivist government action. But this view is based on a lack of understanding of what markets can achieve. A market is, after all, in its most basic formulation, only a mechanism for bringing together the actions of many thousands of individuals and co-ordinating their decisions into a coherent result that is acceptable to all. The sort of results you get from a market system depends very much both on where you begin and on the sort of rules that are laid down for its operation. A totally free market is only one example of the species, and in the real world a very rare one. More common, and more desirable in most cases, are markets that are constrained, either by law or social convention or some other factor. By altering the constraints you alter the effects, and hence have the opportunity to produce a result that is more desirable socially or politically.

Making use of markets — in education . . .
The way in which the left can exploit the power of markets is best illustrated by example. The post-war reformers rightly established the principle of access to education for all. What they failed to do was establish the right to *equal* access for all. That some children should have a higher standard of preparation for life, and a larger amount of resources devoted to them, as in the private school system, is as clear-cut a case of social injustice as one could hope to find. But the approach of social reformers to the problem through the '60s and '70s neatly illuminates the bankruptcy of collectivist policies. By closing grammar and direct-grant schools they made the error of mistaking uniformity for equality. The outcome was not merely the creation of an even starker inequality between the state and private sectors. It also caused the widespread disillusion with state education that in part fuels the state/private inequality, because it robbed families of the involvement and commitment which the provision of choice and variety creates. The destruction of grammar and direct-grant schools was typical of the essentially bureaucratic and indeed authoritarian way governments tend to operate.

Those looking for reform in education have been lost for direction. The far left would have us push on ever more disastrously down the wrong road, by outlawing private education and placing all schools under the control of the state, a proposal that will always be dangerous and unacceptable to the public. The moderate left have had very little to contribute to the debate, seeing no way forward. But by looking to the market as a mechanism, progress and reform could

[158]

be made. A voucher system in education has long been proposed as a way of increasing choice, but its ability to overcome inequality has been largely overlooked. Most people are familiar with the essentials of the voucher scheme by now. Each child would have a voucher entitling their school to claim a certain amount from the government. Schools would then be presented with the discipline of parental choice.

Such a discipline would not only be more effective than the vagaries of council or state interference; it would also be more egalitarian. Under the class-divided system that handicaps Britain, middle-class and active parents are likely to have more influence with the school than working-class parents. With a market in operation, each voucher would command equal respect. But the system can be egalitarian in another way as well. Clearly, schools would have to work within a framework of law maintaining standards, and so on. Within that system it would be quite possible to prevent schools from receiving income from any source other than the voucher and so ensure that all children had an equal amount of resources devoted to them. Similarly, laws could limit the types of selection process schools could use — many people (including me) would favour banning selection on the grounds of *intelligence*. But no hint of authoritarianism is necessarily implied in this policy. We could ban selection by intelligence in the same way that we ban manufacturers from selling toys with dangerous spikes. But a market-based system has many advantages over the collectivist policy of comprehensivisation. It allows equality to be achieved without destroying freedom of choice. And it allows room for alteration without the major disruption that is inevitable once large-scale government bureaucracies have been created.

That is only one example of a market-based proposal for social reform. Its advantage is that it recognises the New Right critique of government-controlled programmes, and indeed accepts it as valid, but builds upon it to give it a left slant. By doing that the New Right proposal would cease to be confrontational and become instead the basis for a consensual approach to the issue of education. The example illustrates two effects. Left social reformers can indeed move away from collectivist policies whilst maintaining their aims intact. And, in doing so, a basis can be laid for a political consensus built around market policies, just as the 1950s had a consensus built around collectivist policies.

But could the left ever accept a completely market-orientated society? In the provision of health care and housing, and of certain welfare payments such as pensions, public opinion has clearly moved far ahead of political policy in seeking out market rather than state services. There is nothing in this shift of personal preferences which should necessarily worry egalitarians. Their real concern should be

[159]

the development of a deprived under-class, unable, through lack of income, to secure services in the market, and relying instead on government provision, probably under-funded and probably of poor quality. The use of vouchers overcomes this problem to some extent, although I think limited to 'merit goods' — there would be little point in providing people with vouchers for video-recorders or summer holidays. Considerable redistribution of income would therefore be necessary, but not the complex maze of taxes and benefits that characterised the collectivist era of social reform. Instead a simple system of positive and negative taxes to ensure a 'decent' income for all, and to prevent a distribution of income that generates poverty as an inevitable by-product, should be instituted. After that the market can be left to decide questions of production and distribution in the purely economic sphere.

The impotence of government

If social reformers are to lessen their expectations of what the state can achieve they must heighten their expectations of what people can achieve. That however is precisely what the most imaginative sections of the left have been doing. The feminist movement seems already to have recognised the impotence of government in the face of massive and inbuilt prejudice and has concentrated on building alternatives from the bottom upwards, rather than imposing change from the top downwards. Activists in ecological and community politics are trying to do much the same. Government can and should, of course, provide a sympathetic legal framework and funds for assistance. But it is a mistake to think that it can do the job itself. Instead feminist collectives, workers' co-operatives and alternative communities should be able to establish themselves within a free economy and society, and make themselves the vehicle for social change. As Mao would have said, let a thousand flowers bloom.

Even on the central issue of class division the market may prove to be a useful ally. The experience of the Soviet Union would suggest that common ownership does little to lessen the development of a class system. Quite plausibly this is because power divisions are the essential cause of class divisions. If so it is the breakdown of power divisions that will lead towards a classless society. Certainly a collectivist policy provides no way of doing that. But a market policy with its central concept of consumer sovereignty may be able, eventually, to do precisely that. If we can envisage everyone self-employed and working on a contract basis, we would, I think, be imagining a system far more egalitarian than the traditional smokestack society with its divisions between the employers and the employed. A society in which we have got rid of employment may seem like a distant prospect (although Chancellor Lawson is making good progress), but with the emerging technologies and work practices it may be practicable.

So far I have had more to say about the left than the right. The achievement of the New Right has been to expose the problems of collectivism and set out the advantages of a market structure as the core of the social and economic system. Its success in capturing both intellectual and political support has been clearly based on its ability to provide a clearly worked-out critique of past policies, and to provide proposals for the present. But total war between a free-market right and a collectivist left stretching endlessly into the future is a sterile prospect. The way out of that morass however is already emerging, as I have tried to illustrate, with the adoption on the left of what are essentially New Right ideas on free markets and their potential role. It is only in conditions of consensus and stability that true progress is made, and it is those conditions that we must establish.

A new consensus on means, not ends

The sort of consensus I see as possible — although by no means inevitable — is based not on bland attempts to agree, to split the difference, or to smother genuine conflict, but on agreement over method rather than aims. I would not expect people on the right to agree with what I have said about redistributing wealth or outlawing certain types of selection in education. All that is necessary is for them to accept *the way in which it is done*, for consensus to exist. In politics one cannot, and indeed should not, expect people to agree over ends. If they can agree about the means, that is sufficient.

It has been the New Right that has made the running in developing political and economic ideas more closely attuned to current realities and aspirations. The left has been thrown into an essentially conservative role of arguing for the preservation of the status quo. It is understandable that those who created the collectivist state should be unwilling to dismantle it, but nothing can be gained from developing into left-wing conservatives. Much of what is termed the New Right is anyway more liberal than conservative, and it is certainly a mistake to think that all their ideas are going to find a place in Conservative Party manifestoes. Already many people on the New Right are becoming disillusioned with the current Conservative Government's unradical attitude to many issues. It may be that a more genuinely radical political force or party, perhaps the SDP, will be necessary to carry out further market-orientated reforms. If so, within a few years, we may find dated the idea of placing market thinking on the right of the political spectrum.

[161]

PETER SAUNDERS

The fourth essay in this group is written from a critical Labour perspective. It argues that the New Right is half right and half wrong.

Peter Saunders was born in 1950, the son of a secondary school science teacher and a shorthand typist. He was educated at Duppas Primary and Selhurst Grammar School in Croydon. He graduated in sociology from the University of Kent in 1971 and won a doctorate at the University of London in 1975.

He has had academic posts at the University of Essex and at the University of Sussex where he has been Reader in Sociology and Urban Studies since 1984. He has held visiting posts at the University of Melbourne, the Australian National University, Canberra, and at the University of Canterbury, New Zealand. He recently began a two-year study of home ownership among the low-to-middle income groups.

He writes that 'capitalist crisis' has not enhanced the popularity of socialist solutions. Despite failure in unemployment, industry and welfare, a radical-right Government was re-elected in 1983 with nearly half the working-class vote. Socialist re-thinking has focussed on strategy but has not questioned the traditional commitment to collectivism. Yet, while market systems do not necessarily yield freedom, collectivist solutions necessarily repress it.

Nevertheless, socialist-humanist values of equality (of opportunity) and freedom (from want, etc.) should not be sacrificed in the march to the market. Its central weakness is that it generates inequalities. The inherent Marxist logic remains that capitalism tends to monopolisation of economic power. Marxism and New Right market philosophy are equally Utopian. It makes little difference in the modern period whether ownership of productive resources is vested in the state or in large private organisations. The problem is not capitalism (Marxism) or the state (New Right) but large-scale technology.

Faced with lack of control in the workplace, people try to establish a degree of individual autonomy in their everyday lives. Here the market is at its best — in home ownership, possibly also in private medicine and education, for, when such services are provided by the state, public sector producers assert their interests against those of consumers. Here libertarian principles are 'exciting and viable'.

14

THE NEW RIGHT IS HALF RIGHT

PETER SAUNDERS

> 'Economic liberalism gives rise to demands for state control,
> and ... state control provokes demands for liberalisation. The
> point, however, is not to choose one or the other; but to define
> the field in which both can be cogently put into effect.'
> Andre Gorz, *Farewell to the Working Class*, Pluto Press, 1982.

The socialist project in Britain is today in some disarray and
confusion. Old nostrums have proved wanting and new solutions have
failed to emerge. In journals such as *Marxism Today* and *New
Socialist*, left intellectuals now struggle to refashion and re-interpret
traditional socialist orthodoxies in an attempt to make them relevant
to the changed economic conditions and popular aspirations which
have become pressingly evident over the last few years. Everyone, it
seems, recognises the necessity of a fundamental re-appraisal of
policy, strategy and philosophy on the left, but no-one has yet
succeeded in breaking out of the theoretical strait-jacket which still
constrains and constricts much of the debate and argument.

The basic puzzle for socialist intellectuals and activists is that the
problems of British capitalism are now acute, yet the time-worn
socialist remedies are probably less popular and credible than at any
time in this century. Under a radical-right government, unemployment
has climbed to record post-war heights, the manufacturing base of the
economy has collapsed, the welfare services have been eroded,
political power has been centralised, large slices of public sector
industry have been sold off cheaply to private (mainly large
institutional) investors, and new investment capital has been flooding
overseas. Yet the long-awaited and often-predicted 'crisis of capitalism' has provoked not an intensification of working-class collective
solidarity and struggle but rather widespread popular indifference or
even acquiescence. The Thatcher Government has won two resound-
ing general election victories (on a minority of the popular vote) and
has carried with it nearly half of the manual working class and a large
proportion of trade unionists. And a succession of strikes, mainly in

the public sector and culminating in the long and tragic internecine miners' struggle of 1984-85, have been defeated or have collapsed in the face of government resolve and popular hostility.

Much of the rethinking on the left since 1979 has focussed on strategy rather than philosophy. What is notable in all of this is that the traditional commitment to collectivism, not simply as a means but as an end of socialism, has never seriously been questioned. Socialism in Britain remains fatally tied to a collectivistic ethos in which individualism and privatism are deeply distrusted. The humanistic vision of a socially just and free society, which drew many of its adherents to socialism in the first place, has increasingly been subordinated to an anti-humanistic, mechanistic programme in which equality and freedom are held to arise only out of collectivistically-organised social arrangements.

A personal re-appraisal: socialism flawed but . . .

Like many others before me, I have come to the conclusion that socialism as traditionally conceived is fundamentally flawed. The horrors of Stalin's Russia, Mao's China or Pol Pot's Kampuchea cannot be dismissed as historical aberrations, for there is something inherent in the collectivist project which tends to generate such regimes. Milton Friedman is in this sense right when he suggests, in *Capitalism and Freedom*, that there are only two ways of co-ordinating social and economic activity in a modern, complex society — state repression or the force of the market. And I would further agree with him that, while market systems do not necessarily produce political freedoms, collectivist solutions necessarily tend to repress such freedoms.

Similarly, I also find myself in agreement with the early 20th century sociologist and historian, Max Weber, who warned that to repress the rationality of the market place is simply to foster the intensification of the tendency in all modern societies towards uncontrollable and non-accountable bureaucratic domination through all areas of life. The market is, therefore, as 'the New Right' suggests, a sphere of autonomy and potential individual freedom which is counterposed to the monopoly, coercive power of the centralised, bureaucratic state.

Yet having recognised this truth, I then find myself holding back from unbridled support for and admiration of the market as the basic organising principle of social and economic life. Part of the reason for this reservation is undoubtedly that those old socialist-humanist values of egalitarianism (at least in the sense of equality of opportunity) and freedom (including freedom *from* want) seem to me still to be worthy values which should not lightly be dismissed in the

[164]

new hard-nosed climate of market orthodoxy and the minimal state. It may be true, as Hayek suggests, that the best of motives have often resulted in the worst of outcomes when people inspired by these values have attempted to put them into practice; but this objection does not convince me that the values themselves are not worth making some concessions and sacrifices to achieve.

A more substantial reason for hesitating in the face of 'New Right' advocacy of the free market is that markets tend to generate such inequalities over time that many people cannot in any meaningful sense be said to be in a position to participate in them at all, while some accumulate such a degree of economic muscle that they are able to control, influence and distort others' 'freedoms' to a point where most people's effective choices may become extremely narrow or may disappear altogether. Notwithstanding the 'New Right' rhetoric about breaking up monopolies and cartels, Marx was surely right when he argued that the inherent logic in capitalist market economies is towards increased concentration, centralisation and monopolisation of economic power.

For me, therefore, the 'New Right' faces a problem every bit as significant as that confronted by contemporary socialism. Socialists shy away from individualism and attempt to control or abolish market freedoms and inequalities, yet this policy necessarily leads to new forms of state compulsion and centralised, bureaucratic domination which undermine rather than enhance people's capacities to control their lives. The 'New Right', on the other hand, advocates a market system in the name of individual liberty when this liberty is increasingly and inexorably rendered mythical by the development of a capitalist world system in which massive industrial and financial conglomerates wield power certainly beyond any individual's control, often outside of individual government's control, and in practice responsive neither to individual shareholders nor to individual consumers. Most shareholding is itself concentrated in large financial institutions. And for consumers the experience of confronting a huge multi-national is little different from that of confronting a big government department; throughout much of the private sector there is in practice little more effective competition or consumer sovereignty than in the equivalent parts of the public sector.

Left and right equally utopian

Now, I draw a very fatalistic and gloomy conclusion from all of this. It seems to me that the futuristic prospects held out to us by Marxism (a society of associated producers in which aliented labour has been overcome and control is vested in the democratically-accountable delegates elected by the workers themselves) and by the 'New Right' (a society of competitive producers in which there is no obstacle to entry into the market and in which consumer preference prevails over producer control) are equally utopian.

Put another way, no matter which of Friedman's options we select, production in the modern world will continue to be experienced as a realm of social life which is beyond our control. Assuming that we do not wish to turn our backs on advanced technology, nor to sacrifice all concern with efficiency, I fear we are stuck with one area of our lives which will always be experienced as a realm of minimal autonomy and non-responsive constraint. The Marxist idea that we can be liberated through our labour and that work can be a realm of freedom if the means of production are socialised is for me no less nor more absurd than the belief among 'New Right' theorists that in privatising state monopolies we will somehow be able to reintroduce a free and competitive market in which individual entrepreneurship can have a chance to flourish. We live, as Max Weber suggested, in an 'iron cage' in which it really will not make very much difference whether legal ownership and control of the society's productive and administrative resources is vested in huge state agencies or in huge banks, finance companies and multi-national corporations.

I suspect that most people know this to be true through their everyday experiences. There are stories of how miners saw their hopes dashed when the mines were finally nationalised yet everything carried on very much as before. And I would be surprised if people's experience of newly-privatised industries and services, whether as workers or as consumers, has been very different in recent years. The problem, in other words, is not capitalism, as Marxists would have us believe, but nor it is the state, as the 'New Right' fervently argues. The problem is simply that the technology and scale of production and administration is now such that neither workers' control nor market competition can operate in the modern period, except possibly in small and generally backward sectors of the economy, in the interstices between state monopolies and multi-national oligopolies.

Most of us, whether we work in the private or public sectors, have long ago accommodated ourselves to this situation. Our response has been to seek to safeguard and extend our individual autonomy in consumption, the world of everyday life. And it is here, in relation to the issue of consumption, that the socialist project is at its weakest and that the writings and arguments of people like Hayek become, for me at least, most compelling.

Consumption: from housing to medicine, education . . .

As an academic, my specialist field is urban sociology and my main interest is in housing. From what I have read, seen and experienced, it seems clear to me that in Britain (though not necessarily elsewhere), ownership of a home is important for many people, not only economically (in terms of the capital gains which may accrue, the potential for transfers of wealth between generations which it creates, the opportunity to use personal labour to enhance the value of the property through DIY, and so on), but also culturally and socially. Ownership of a home brings with it some limited opportunity for autonomous control — over where you choose to live, how you choose to live, and so on. The popular and widespread desire to achieve owner-occupation can in my view mainly be explained in terms of a search for a realm of individual autonomy and freedom outside of the sphere of production.

It was over the issue of home ownership that I first became uneasy in my participation in the Labour Party. It is true that it has explicitly for at least twenty years accepted owner-occupation as a legimate housing tenure and that many (though by no means all) within the Party have today gone so far as to accept the right of council tenants to buy their homes. But all of this is grudging; it is certainly more due to a pragmatic acceptance of the electoral popularity of the ownership solution than it is to any principled and clearly-articulated commitment to the desirability of individuals being afforded such an opportunity.

The argument over home ownership was for me clear-cut. More problematic was the implication of what I was arguing for other consumption services supplied by the state. Gradually, and not without considerable discomfort, I came to realise that if it was right and desirable for people to participate in the market in order to accommodate themselves so too was it right and desirable for them to assume more control in other parts of their lives wherever possible in the sphere of consumption.

Slowly I became convinced of the 'New Right' case against state control and provision in services such as health care and schooling. I am certain that producer interests such as doctors and teachers (and university lecturers!) have been able to assert their own interests, even against the interests of their client populations, given the greater susceptibility of the state to organised producer interests as opposed to fragmented consumer interests. It is also the case that welfare services (and here I include the vast 'hidden' welfare state of subsidies and tax relief) have gone increasingly to people, such as the home-owning, highly-educated, middle-class who need them least. And there can be no doubt that people's experience as clients of welfare agencies has been one of powerlessness in the face of administrative indifference, professional self-interest and bureaucratic insensitivity.

[167]

Like thousands of other parents, I have recently gone through the ritual of 'choosing' a state secondary school for my children. Not only is there precious little choice on offer, for all the schools subscribe to the same sets of rules, norms and values. In practice moreover parents find that their preferences are often simply ignored and over-ridden by a local authority bureaucracy which allocates children to schools ultimately on its own administrative criteria of residence and availability. Every year demand exceeds supply for some schools yet falls far below it for others. Every year the same quotas are applied. Unpopular schools with poor resources, bad records and inexperienced teachers fill up on coerced pupils with very little effective pressure on them to improve. Popular schools, on the other hand, simply turn people away, for they have no incentive to expand.

Choosing a (state) school, or a doctor
Here surely there is a case for a transfer of power from producers and administrators to consumers? Yet such a transfer can only be effected through the introduction of a market-based system of allocation in which 'clients', the people who are forced to pay through their taxes and are obliged to accept what they are given, become 'customers' who choose to pay from their pockets for the type of service they prefer.

The same logic applies to the health services. Dr David Green's work on the history of the friendly societies shows that, even in the 19th century when real incomes were much lower than they are today, many workers were able to exert control over those who treated them by employing, often collectively but always voluntarily, doctors and pharmacists whose performance would regularly be monitored and scrutinised and whose contracts could be terminated in favour of cheaper or better competitors. In health, as in education, there is a compelling case for ending state compulsion, licensing and provision, and for returning control, choice, and responsibility to those who require the service.

Libertarian principles applied to the organisation of consumption provisions such as housing, schooling and health which are currently controlled or provided by the state are both exciting and viable. They are exciting because, for most people, these are precisely the central and most important aspects of everyday life. The home in which we live, the way in which our children (and we ourselves) are educated, the type and amount of health care we select — these together constitute the central concerns for many people today, and they are crucial to the determination of life chances. Just as importantly, it is in precisely this area that libertarian principles are also viable, for it is in the realm of consumption that personal autonomy and freedom may be cultivated.

[168]

For consumer control to be created, however, it must be possible for everyone to participate in this freedom. There is no point in ending the state ownership of housing if between a quarter and a third of households cannot afford to pay private-sector rents and lack the income to qualify for mortgage finance. The freedom to choose a school for a child is illusory if you do not have the capacity to pay the fees. And where is the freedom in a market system of health care if those at risk find they cannot get insured or cannot afford the medication they need?

In the 19th century it would certainly have been impossible for many ordinary people in Britain to cover their consumption wants out of household income. Today many people, especially in dual-earner households, can afford to buy a house, to take out medical insurance and even to cover part (nursery schooling, specialist tuition in music or swimming, etc.) or all of their children's education costs. Their number would obviously be much larger if the state withdrew from these services, for the tax burden on wages represented by the housing, health and education budgets is substantial. Nevertheless, there would remain a section of the population for whom private provision at any but the most rudimentary standards would simply not be possible. The problem, therefore, is how to ensure that the sick as well as the healthy, the elderly as well as the young, and so on, can achieve access.

Selective provision unnecessary

The response of the 'New Right', at least within the Conservative Party, is to residualise and stigmatise welfare provision to cater for those who cannot participate in the market. This solution in my view is unacceptable, undesirable and unnecessary. It is unacceptable because such essentially Benthamite solutions penalise the poor, set in motion a cycle of deprivation from which it is extremely difficult to escape, and exacerbate what are already deep cleavages within our society between people for whom life is tolerably comfortable and those for whom it is intolerable misery. It is undesirable because it perpetuates (albeit for a smaller number of people) the same experience of frustration and powerlessness within the state system of welfare which 'New Right' ideas are supposed to overcome. And it is unnecessary because a second-class welfare system coexisting with a flourishing private sector is not the only solution to the task of reconciling inherently high-cost services with low-income consumers. As Friedman has suggested, rather than making (inferior) provision in kind for people who cannot pay, it may make more sense to enhance their incomes by making provision in cash through a system of negative income tax, or perhaps through the introduction of voucher schemes, to be paid for out of the savings realised by withdrawal of the state from the direct allocation of these services.

Role of humanist egalitarianism

It is at this point that I feel the old humanistic-socialist value of egalitarianism must be brought back into the reckoning. I am *not* suggesting that we have to have equality of incomes to make effective choice possible in the sphere of consumption, but it is clear to me that any system of negative income tax would necessarily have to entail a fairly dramatic narrowing of the vast gap which still exists in Britain between the extremes of wealth and poverty if the libertarian ideal is to be made viable. The minimum household income would have to be set relatively high in order that everyone could, if they wished, enter into the market as an effective consumer. Equally, massive concentrations of inherited wealth would have to be reduced if they were not totally to distort that market by the weight of economic influence they could bring to bear upon it. In this respect, it is worth noting in passing that Hayek's defence of inherited and unearned wealth (in Chapter 8 of *The Constitution of Liberty*) is arguably the weakest part of his entire thesis, for his suggestion that the 'idle rich' perform an important function in modern society is likely to strain the credulity of even the most devout disciple of the new libertarianism. There is a good economic and social case for taxing inherited wealth, and it is an argument which in the past has been made from the right as well as from the left.

We arrive, therefore, at an apparent paradox. To make the libertarian ideal work in consumption, we must adopt some of the traditional socialist recipes for the redistribution of income and wealth. The popularity of the 'New Right' (as represented by 'Thatcherism') is in my view based on the acceptable and strong desire among many sections of the population to safeguard and extend the scope of personal freedom against the monopolistic power of the state and large private sector interests. But it is dishonest to pretend that this can effectively be achieved without also in-troducing radical and dramatic measures for redistributing income and wealth, just as it is facile to argue that this goal can be realised by transferring ownership of productive resources like the tele-communications system, the state airline or BL cars from a state monopoly to what are to all intents and purposes large private monopolies.

The libertarian project makes sense in the modern period only when applied to the organisation of consumption where, as in housing, health and education, individuals can potentially exercise effective autonomy and control and can enjoy real choices and freedoms. And to work there it has to entail 'interference' in the labour market so as to put enough money into people's pockets to enable them to enter the commodity market as effective consumers. What all this amounts to, as the quotation from Gorz suggests at the start of this chapter, is that we must draw on the methods of redistributive socialism in order to realise the ideals of the 'New Right'. And to do this we have to recognise the limited applicability of each to different spheres of life.

The problem at the moment is that neither tradition is prepared to take account of the other. I seriously doubt whether the modern Labour Party is willing or able to place these sorts of issues onto the agenda, but I have no intention of jumping from frying pan to fire by placing my hope in a radical right Tory party where any talk of income redistribution is anathema (and, incidentally, where libertarianism seems not to extend to many areas of policy such as civil liberties, freedom of information, personal morality, and so on).

Nor, let me hasten to add, does this lead me into the embrace of the Social Democratic Party, for while Dr Owen, with his talk of combining 'toughness' with 'tenderness', has certainly tried to bridge these two philosophies, he has done so in my opinion by combining the worst of each. He seeks to apply individualistic ideas of market competition to the organisation of the economy, where I have argued they cannot work, while adopting collectivistic remedies in the sphere of consumption, where I have suggested they are likely to be experienced as most constraining. In the penumbra of contemporary British party politics, therefore, I suspect I am homeless. I also suspect that many others are politically homeless too.

The challenge now facing us is to combine the truths and potentials of two traditions which have long been held to be incompatible. The basis for doing this is to recognise the inherent limits to individual freedom and control in the modern period and to develop a strategy in which this sphere of coercion is kept to a minimum and is as far as possible directed towards the fulfilment of the conditions necessary for freedom to flourish elsewhere in our everyday lives. It is in this sense that I would agree with the conclusion reached by Gorz:

> We know now that there is no 'good' government, 'good' state or 'good' form of power, and that society can never be 'good' in its own organisation but only by virtue of the space for self-organisation, autonomy, co-operation and voluntary exchange which that organisation offers to individuals.

The ideas of the 'New Right' take us a step towards this end, but the insights offered by its theorists are only partial. If this partiality is not recognised, and if the implications for income redistribution of the approach are not accepted, the freedoms which these writers offer us will prove no more than empty illusions serving to mystify and reproduce the continued domination of our lives by people or institutions we do nor understand and cannot control.

BRIAN MICKLETHWAIT

The small but growing body of mostly younger libertarians is not overtly represented by any of the four main Parties. This essay presents a libertarian diagnosis of our present discontents and their solutions.

Brian Micklethwait was born in 1947, the son of a Q.C. He is remotely related to the socialist Archbishop William Temple and to Labour-turned-SDP economist Nicholas Bosanquet, author of the optimistically titled After the New Right.

He was educated at Upton (primary) School, Windsor, Scaitcliffe (prep.) School in Surrey, and Marlborough. He studied architecture at Churchill College, Cambridge, and graduated in sociology from Essex University.

He is Assistant Manager of the Alternative Bookshop.

He edits the Libertarian Alliance Political Notes, *writes occasionally for periodicals including* Economic Affairs, *composes libertarian tracts and talks volubly on libertarianism to any who invite him.*

His political interest began as a socialist, but he was repelled by its dirigisme. He works with people in politics but is anti-political. He believes in maximum individual liberty, voluntary exchange, persuasion rather than coercion, and he wants to see the oppressive power of the state eliminated.

He receives most attention but not universal agreement from the 'New Right'. He argues for personal freedom in social as well as economic issues.

He has been influenced by Karl Popper, David Friedman, Hayek, Thomas Sowell, Murray Rothbard. He argues that belief in collectivism and socialism has collapsed, the Labour Party is in decline and becoming a quietist rump. Libertarian Conservatives are becoming impatient with status-quo Conservatives.

Libertarians exaggerate the importance of the political world. They should not present free-market solutions of problems that governments are solving (prevention of civil war) but deal with those they are not solving (world peace). The solution is a market in governments, so that people can escape from the worst and patronise the best.

15

THE CASE AGAINST POLITICS

BRIAN MICKLETHWAIT

When people ask me my political beliefs I sometimes describe myself as a 'libertarian' and sometimes not. It depends what picture I judge this word will conjure up in my listener's mind. When I use it I have in mind principles like (to quote the introductory leaflet of the Libertarian Alliance, *Our Enemy The State*) the following:

> The right of all persons to life, liberty and justly acquired property;
> the voluntary exchange of all goods and services;
> each individual's liberty to pursue his or her chosen life-style and to promote it by peaceful persuasion, but not to impose it forcibly on anyone else;
> elimination of coercive intervention by the state, the foremost violator of liberty.

New Right?

Are the above ideas 'right wing'? They are at the moment. I give talks about libertarianism to anyone who will listen; and I submit articles about libertarianism to anyone who will print them, and the response has been strongest from what definitely is the 'right wing'. But what of legalising dangerous drugs, and abolishing compulsory education and immigration controls? I nevertheless think 'New Right' is an accurate label for me. If words mean what people think they mean, 'New Right' it is.

Socialists oppose freedom not only in practice but in principle, and not solely in economic matters but to a remarkable degree on 'social' issues as well. Leftists now argue ever more vehemently for the censorship of opinions and eradication of attitudes that they disapprove of, such as what they regard as 'racist' opinions and 'sexist' attitudes. Even more fundamentally, and wickedly, leftists often argue that freedom is in some essential sense an illusion, that freedom isn't 'real' freedom, and that therefore to abolish whatever freedom people have is to abolish nothing of significance.

[175]

I'm 'right-wing', also, because I co-operate with other more conventionally right-wing folk, such as those in the Federation of Conservative Students, on such projects as the overthrow of the government of the USSR and the denationalisation of the British coal industry. I have a higher opinion of most Conservatives (in the UK) and Republicans (in the USA) than do many libertarians, which is not difficult.

Telling other people what to think

Some people hold opinions like mine simply because they do. I got there because I came to believe that freedom results in a better *system* than the other — socialist — system I had at first favoured. I went to schools where rich parents were the norm, and the rather puritanical attitudes of my parents towards indulgences like Jaguar cars and getting into debt caused me to disapprove of the more conspicuously consuming families of my school contemporaries. The Jaguar money should be taken from these vulgar plutocrats and given to the poor!

Perhaps if I had specialised in something other than maths at school, and in something other than architecture at Cambridge, I would have settled comfortably into another groove and forgotten all about telling other people how to live and what to think. But being bad at maths and worse at architecture I sought respite in paperbacks about Africa, Russia, poverty, history, philosophy and so forth, without ever being put off such subjects by being 'taught' them.

Eventually I went the whole way and did a sociology degree at Essex University. I didn't allow the teachers there to interrupt my ruminations upon the meaning of life either. I spent most of my time, when not reading, doing plays. Most of what is said in the right-wing press about the vices of sociology and of sociology departments is true. Sociology departments are dens of vice, the two main vices being Marxism and laziness. But suppose all sociology undergraduates had to work hard at the kind of sociology now offered at universities to get their degrees? Would that really be an improvement? It's surely a good thing that the taxpayer doesn't get as much sociology as he is paying for.

Many things caused me to abandon my socialist leanings.

Sociology isn't exactly the same as socialism, but this widespread popular confusion contains more truth than falsehood. Sociologists of the sort I encountered talked of vast but vague aggregations like 'class' and 'social structure'. They thought of themselves as doctors diagnosing 'social illnesses' for which they would one day supply cures of corresponding vastness and vagueness.

While studying architecture I learned that socialism and the so-

[176]

called 'modern movement' in architecture were different faces of the same *dirigiste* catastrophe. 'Modern architecture' is not the problem. The idea of using new materials like steel, concrete and plate glass to make buildings is here to stay. But the 'modern movement', with its hysterical manifestos and pictures of unbuildable dream cities, is no more the essence of modern architecture than a Soviet five-year plan is the essence of the Industrial Revolution. A major writing project of mine now is to help rescue the hated but healthy baby of architectural modernity from the befouled bathwater of the modern movement.

I came to see that the sorely-tried Vice Chancellor of Essex University, Albert Sloman, was right about his left-wing student tormentors, and the left-wing students and their Quislings within the faculties were wrong. The student protesters were Lenins with hair. Like Lenin, they said that you had to be either for the revolution or against it. Very slowly, I made my choice.

I recall a 'mass meeting' one evening at Essex. I attended it only because I had a small part in a play and had been given the night off from rehearsing at short notice. One of the left-wingers made what I thought was a particularly stupid speech, and I wanted to get up and say so. But then I thought, better not. The radical students might — just might — be provoked by my remarks into 'occupying' the theatre and demanding radical and relevant theatre about Chile and South Africa rather than the bourgeois stuff I and my friends indulged in. Then I thought, this is how Hitler got started. He and his pals used to stage *their* demonstrations, and people who didn't want their own enthusiasms smashed up didn't dare complain.

Karl Marx versus David Friedman

But it was books that really did it. Vignettes like the one in the previous paragraph served only to freeze in the memory certain principles that the books were forcing me to take note of. Unowned places quickly become unproductive, rubbish-strewn deserts. Hence the ghastly fate of all those 'public open spaces' the modernist architects had put between and underneath their skyscrapers. 'Planning' does *not* alleviate poverty. On the contrary, it leads directly to thuggery, because only by thuggish means can planning be made to work.

I decided that the parents of my school contemporaries should be allowed to keep their Jaguars, if that was what they wanted to buy. The process of confiscating the Jaguar money would be far more hurtful than the inequality of some having Jaguars while most didn't.

And were my own family's tastes really any less expensive than those of the Jaguar owners? We had — still have — a huge garden, compared to most people, and I have a mass of classical LPs. My

[177]

father's garden is to him a spiritual rather than merely material matter. To him it *means* a lot. Classical music likewise *means* things to me, while Jaguars are for me just flashy bits of mobile metal. But this is only a fancy way of saying that my father and I both prefer what we like to what we don't like.

I read Karl Popper on Plato, Hegel and Marx, and about the difference between pseudo-science and the real thing. I even read some Marx, and concluded that far from having been betrayed by his more monstrous followers, Marx was merely followed by them. *Das Kapital* is a spectacularly awful piece of writing: unscholarly, abusive, intellectually corrupt. The Marxist habit of using words to mean several different things at once — of using them up, so to speak — began with Marx himself. *The Communist Manifesto* at least breathes the clean fresh air of youthful folly. To read *Das Kapital* is to watch an older and wickeder man, advocating a system he no longer believes in but refuses to abandon.

And I read a peculiar American edition of something called *The Machinery of Freedom*, by David Friedman, whoever he was. This book was uncompromisingly in favour of capitalism, the free market, property, liberty and the pursuit of happiness. To believe in such things was not to endorse the boring status quo, said Friedman, quite the reverse. Capitalism was not to blame for traffic jams, whatever J. K. Galbraith or Vance Packard may have said. The problem was not the private ownership of cars and car factories; it was *public ownership of the roads*! Limited supply of road; zero price: result — traffic jams. But of course. I could still believe that everyone else was wrong, but now they were wrong for being *insufficiently* capitalist.

I later learned that David Friedman is the son of Milton Friedman, the noted Chicago economist. He is, I think, one of Milton Friedman's most impressive achievements, and I look forward to the day Milton Friedman will be best known for being David Friedman's father.

The arguments that convince me most were *comparisons* between different businesses and different countries. Look at only one business, such as British broadcasting, or only one country, such as Britain, and it is not at all clear exactly who may be properly praised to blamed for what. But when you *compare* the hi-fi trade with the health trade, or East with West Germany, North with South Korea, communist with capitalist China, the *contrasts* become irresistible.

The decline of socialism

The collapse of belief in collectivism in general and in socialism in particular is camouflaged only very temporarily by the large number of socialists that still remain and by the enormous din they still make. But the Blimps of the left are convincing only one another — and putting everyone else off, just as the Colonel Blimp imperialists of 50 years ago destroyed support for British imperialism by such devices as throwing homosexuals into fountains.

In Britain the Labour Party seethes with tactical disagreement about how to reverse its decline. Political entrepreneurs of the Ken Livingstone variety put together coalitions of 'minorities' whose support is to be bought with government money. Others say Labour should continue appealing to the dwindling but still substantial 'respectable' working class, who are now disloyally attracted by Mrs Thatcher's economically disappointing but morally uplifting style of government and rhetoric.

But the Labour Party problem is not whom they should talk to, but what they should say. Their problem is their unpersuasive *policies*, not the mere numerical strength of their potential support groups. It is the whole *idea* of sloshing out government money, not the mere details of who is to get it, that is now being questioned. Labour used to be a reasonably contented alliance between socialists and normal people, with no sharp distinction being made between the two. But now you have to be decidedly stupid and rather evil to be a full-blooded socialist, which has frightened a lot of normal people out of the Labour Party. Normal people aren't socialists at all. Labour may soon become a quietist rump.

A tiny but electorally repulsive minority of Labour activists are likely to resort to terrorism. The late 19th century terrorist problem occurred while socialism was a small but rising force, and was caused by socialist impatience. Now the socialist graph is sloping again — downwards — and terrorism now is the terrorism of despair. It's now or never, comrades. Think of the effect on Labour when a couple of Labour city councillors are discovered to be directly mixed up in a major terrorist incident.

The new Labour leader, Neil Kinnock, evidently *has* thought about this, and goes out of his way to humiliate the Labour hard left, and thus present himself to the electorate as a latter-day Stanley Baldwin — wholesome, middle-of-the-road, unprovocative and safe. But can the Labour Party cut its own idealogical roots away and still survive? If Labour is not sucked by its socialist inheritance into oblivion, will it have anywhere else to go?

Meanwhile the free-market rhetoric made popular by some Conservative leaders will increasingly be used to criticise the statist rigidities of Conservative government. Free-market populists will criticise the learned professions, farm subsidies to rich land-owners, and export credit guarantees to big, well-connected companies and their feckless foreign government customers, as libertarian writers have long done. Many 'libertarian Conservatives' will become impatient with statist and status-quo Conservatives who oppose the deregulation and tax cuts of which some of their leaders talk wistfully.

Most Conservatives realise that libertarianism and Conservatism are not the same, and recall that these positions were in opposition to each other a century ago. The first libertarian reforms of our own time have been introduced by the Conservatives, true. But the first socialist steps of the 19th century were also taken by the Conservatives, who always oppose the leading radicals of their day and collaborate with other radicals. Libertarianism is now replacing socialism as the major radical force for change, and socialists and Tory paternalists are now rebuilding the same anti-libertarian coalition that split up at the end of the 19th century. If you doubt this, ask (a) a True Blue Tory, and (b) a socialist, what they each think of MacDonald's hamburgers.

Much of the Conservative fear of the libertarian 'menace' in their midst is snobbery. A new generation of libertarian students is now coming of age, the successors of the grammar school pupils who formed the backbone of the Labour Party in its prime. Having nowhere else to go, these libertarians are now joining the Conservative Party. But this accidental alliance can only last for as long as socialism remains a plausible common enemy.

Perhaps these new libertarians will end up by taking over and liberalising the Labour Party.

Only the self-destruction of libertarianism can now reverse the socialist decline. A tiny step along this path would be for the tiny minority of rowdy 'libertarians' in the Federation of Conservative Students to continue smashing up peace camps and manipulating elections — in short, behaving like socialists. What such idiocy says is that mere ideas are unpersuasive. When I talk to such people, this is one of the things I say. Happily, the free market does not depend for its success on all those favouring it being nice people; and it makes nasty people nicer. (Socialism depends for its success on socialists being and remaining nice, but instead it makes them nasty.)

Libertarianism for fun and profit

I eventually decided to be a full-time political stirrer and pamphleteer, and came to London to make a start. I had no idea then how well libertarianism was doing, but was eager to help. I called in at the Institute of Economic Affairs. I'd read a lot of their output, and although hopelessly stuffy and gradualist it made as much sense as then seemed available. (The only true libertarians in the world at that time were David Friedman and me, so there wasn't much future in that.) The people at the IEA were buried in editorial detritus and far too grand and busy to talk to me, but I spotted on their foyer noticeboard an advert for the 'Alternative Bookshop'. 'Books on all aspects of freedom and the free market', 40 Floral Street, Covent Garden. When I got there I was home at last. There were other libertarians besides me and David Friedman! More than a dozen of them!

I now work at this Alternative Bookshop (now moved to 3 Langley Court, Covent Garden) spending my time selling books (including the stuffy and gradualist products of the IEA) and my spare time writing pieces like this one. During my university theatre days I designed lots of posters and tickets for plays, and became an expert in course graphics. I now apply the same tricks to producing book flyers and libertarian pamphlets, quite a few of which I have also written. Times have changed in this craft as in others. I had no computer at Essex, and no Canon photocopier/photo-reducer/photo-enlarger, both of which I have now bought with my inherited wealth, instead of buying a house. The price of the machine I want next is about £15,000, but falling fast. This will integrate the computer with the printer/copier, and with it I will be able to write, design and print an entire magazine — text, graphics and all — without once having to use scissors and paste, and in a fraction of the time it all takes now.

My longest publication to date is called *How To Be Successful*. I wrote this for self-instruction, but it has sold healthily in the Bookshop as a stapled A4 booklet.

The morality of freedom

Morality is the language of the general public because moral statements have general application, and are hence of general interest and say a lot very quickly. Economics tends to deal only with particulars. It thus has little general appeal, and is uneconomical in its use of words, and thus time.

In his recent Adam Smith Institute pamphlet *The Soul Politic*, David Hart says that 'Marxists, socialist and collectivist of all kinds have lost the economic debate'. But whereas the upper echelons accept that freedom makes better washing-machines, people in general remain anxious about about whether freedom is *good*. The moral debate for freedom has yet to be won.

Libertarianism is, among other things, an exercise in *popularisation*; it translates economics into morality, gobbledygook into English. A typical libertarian enterprise is to take an argument that free-market economists have already won in the privacy of their economics faculties and translate their victory into something shorter and more readable, with frequent references to why people should feel morally obliged, as opposed merely to academically inclined, to agree.

In the Alternative Bookshop we select and sell books on economics that already are in English and already contain moral generalisations. 'Austrian' economics has a built-in bias against mathematical elaboration, and thus sells better to our customers than 'main-stream' economics, including Chicago economics, despite being academically less prestigious than the Chicago stuff. (The great Chicago exception is Milton Friedman himself, who is a populariser of genius.)

In commenting upon an earlier draft of this piece, Arthur Seldon asked who I thought was the best *populariser* of Austrian economics, adding that the answer was not Frederick Hayek. I disagree. Hayek is not always easy to read, but at least it's Hayek you are reading, rather than some second-hander who is merely fluent. Hayek always *tries* to be understood, and so widely does he apply his ideas that his readership is now enormous and growing rapidly. As well as economics, Hayek has written about psychology, jurisprudence, political philosophy, the history of ideas (especially bad ideas), anthropology, and much else. He has a lot to say about architecture, without — I once asked him — even realising it. The test of a great thinker is the ability of lesser thinkers to see further when standing on his shoulders

Aside from Hayek and the Friedmans, I think that the writer who best combines being clear with being right is the black American economist Thomas Sowell. Hayek wrote a joyous review of Sowell's *Knowledge and Decision*, and perhaps wishes he could write as fluently as Sowell while retaining his own originality. Hayek has tamed ferocious jungles, and can be forgiven for wishing also to be an expert at ornamental gardening, as Sowell is.

The importance of libertarian 'extremism'

By libertarian popularising I don't mean merely expressing views that people already hold. You get nowhere as a persuader by trimming. Lots of good ideas make people angry, while many bad ideas are believed sound. The Libertarian Alliance would have no influence were it not prepared to take ideas to extremes, thereby to test their wisdom. You do not hammer out wise moral codes by conducting public opinion surveys.

One of the most interesting debates engaged in by the Libertarian Alliance has concerned the rights of children. Perhaps because children don't have votes, they are now usually discussed only as persons to whom things are done by others, and on whose alleged behalf choices are made by others. Adults now speak of children as if they owned them, which is not surprising given the present legal position.

I have yet to hear an argument against freedom for children that does not apply with equal lack of force to adults.

I think compulsory education should be abolished, as should the laws which stop children going to work. Children should be allowed to leave home, and parents should be allowed to chuck them out. Both education and family life should be *voluntary* activities for all concerned.

It is said that children are different from adults, and that if released from their prisons children would be even more troublesome than they are now. Who would look after them if not their parents or their teachers? Who would protect them from being swindled by adults who don't care about them? If not victimised by others, would they not become the victims of their own impetuosity and ignorance? Are children truly capable of choice at all?

Whether a child has in any particular case expressed a choice is a matter of evidence. A court may have to decide whether others should defer to a child's expressed choice, but the same principles should apply with children as with adults. If I forcibly restrain a drunk or mental defective from driving a car, no court would find against me. Nor would any court I had anything to do with (it would have to be a free-market court) punish parents for reclaiming a two-year-old who had sought ice-cream elsewhere. On the other hand if the two-year-old expressed a clear choice in a tug-of-love battle, that ought to settle it, in my opinion.

Parents who expel children knowing that the probable result would be death or severe injury would be in trouble, just as courts do not now encourage the sudden abandonment of crippled grandmothers.

The arguments for freedom for adults have never depended on anyone supposing that adults are equal to one another. There are some very ignorant and irresponsible adults in the world, some of whom make irrevocably ghastly blunders. Does that mean that all adults, prudent and foolish alike, should be stripped of their freedom?

Childhood as slavery

Many of the differences between children and adults are the result not of biology but of the way that children are now treated. Children are forcibly prevented from doing anything that others value, that is, from working. They are systematically cut off from what ought to be the natural rewards of working, such as money and status in the community. Is it any wonder that most of them become feckless, irresponsible drones, and that a growing minority of them are turning to crime to occupy their otherwise idle minds and hands?

Children now are in much the same position as negro slaves used to be in America. Slaves were allowed to excel only in physical strength, while children now are allowed to get ahead only if they have the knack of passing exams; and even that leads nowhere very obvious.

[183]

Slaves became permanently stunted people, and their owners sincerely believed that negroes were congenitally incapable of bearing the burdens of liberty. Adults contemplate children now, and believe in all sincerity that these intolerable parasites are inherently incapable of being free without catastrophe both to them and to everyone else.

Neither for adults nor for children does choice mean the obligation to invent and be in charge of the institutions or productive processes one is choosing to participate in. Children who chose to leave home would mostly be choosing another community (probably another family) which they considered preferable, not going off to live on their own. I'd be amazed if very many children did choose to leave their natural families.

Neither do I expect the majority of parents to expel their offspring as soon as the law allows them to, any more than parents now are in a hurry to expel teenagers.

By far the biggest step towards solving the appalling and increasingly serious problem of child abuse, sexual or merely violent, would be for children to have the right to make other living arrangements. Putting different adults in charge of children cannot be the answer to such problems, because invariably it is an adult in charge of the child who *is* the problem, and it is this adult's position of power that results in his child/victim having no escape. Giving social workers more and parents less power over children will merely mean that children will be brutalised and abused by vicious social workers instead of by vicious parents. A child should have the automatic right to avoid the company of any adult, including his or her own parent, and to do this *without having to explain.*

A hotel guest may check out of a hotel without having to embarrass everyone by explaining the decision, even if the insults or injuries to which the hotel guest was subjected were entirely imaginary. Suppose instead that you were being attacked or sexually molested by the staff of a hotel, but were obliged to convince the police of the truth of your accusations before you were allowed to leave, and were obliged to stay if you failed to convince the police. Suppose the police stripped you naked while searching for evidence of sexual or other injury, or that that you feared they might. Suppose that the police were in league with your tormentors, or that you feared they might be. That's the problem of child abuse.

Many fear that freedom for children would merely increase unemployment by several million and create a massive vagrancy problem. Whether you agree depends on what you think causes the unemployment we already have among adults. If 'freedom for children' means children being paid by the government to do nothing but taxed heavily as soon as they earn any money, then indeed youth

[184]

unemployment will be appalling, just as adult unemployment is already. Another way to boost child unemployment would be to make it hard for people to fire children once they'd taken the risk of hiring them. Laws forbidding adults from being prejudiced against children would boost unemployment among all age groups.

I believe that the economic benefits of freedom for children, provided it really is freedom, will be literally epoch-making, just as the economic benefits of freedom for adults already have been.

At present children are economically useless, and only the 'qualified' minority are considered even plausible bets to do anything useful without a long period of readjustment to the real world. Children spend years being 'prepared for life' and, when the school system finally spits them out and they become 'school-leavers', their utter incompetence at everything is considered not merely normal but inevitable.

Only leftists have so far tried to make any political stir with the issue of freedom for children. But the left-wing idea is to run the whole of society as schools are run now. How can they persuasively claim to believe in children's emancipation if they simultaneously urge the enslavement of adults?

If some of my Libertarian Alliance, and other, opponents in this debate are right about the results of freedom for children, that would change my mind about it, which also applies to my belief in libertarianism in general. I favour debates among libertarians about such things as freedom for children not only because I want to see children and adults getting along better now but also because such debates get libertarians into the habit of facing rather than funking difficult and unpopular questions.

For many libertarians freedom for children is a problem, not a solution or an opportunity. They don't believe in it, but find it hard to explain why not.

If libertarianism catches on in a big way, the world will be full of powerful people 'taking libertarianism too far', just as I and my relatively powerless friends already take it 'too far' in our arguments and publications. 'Extremist' debates like this one about freedom for children, or the one about legalising heroin, are indispensable preparation for the complexities of power.

Suppose that, instead of learning all they can about some of the difficulties and unpopularities their declared opinions may get them into, a generation of fanatics gets excited about libertarian ideas because the more scandalous and problematic implications of libertarianism have been concealed. This would be to imitate those socialists who privately knew that socialism would involve many unpopular actions if it caught on, but who preferred to keep this quiet. Remaining silent about the difficulties and unpopularities of a body of ideas whose strength is growing year by year would be far more irresponsible — far more immoral — than to anticipate such difficulties in a way that may cause some outrage. (Many argue that this disaster has *already* overtaken the 'libertarian' camp, in the form of the disappointments of Thatcherism.)

The economics of morality

It's a symptom of the moral commitment of the Libertarian Alliance that the willingness of its writers to challenge conventional moral judgements causes it to be labelled immoral. I understand why people think this, but of course I don't agree. Arguing that allowing people to be wicked is better than forcibly preventing them is not the same as being in favour of wickedness.

Young people are especially keen on learning about sound moral principles, and they recognise outrage as a by-product of intellectual seriousness. Some say this is because the hormones of the young have yet to settle down, but the true explanation is that young people face a world that stretches long into the future, while often being much less sure of what they'll be doing five year's hence. Moral arguments, which explore the rules that will bring long-run happiness, are thus of extreme interest to the young, the way they never can be to the elderly. J. M. Keynes' notorious crack about how 'in the long run we are all dead' omits the truth that some will be dead sooner than others.

Thus it is that the Libertarian Alliance has got its best response from university students, and in the faculties where lofty abstractions are the vogue rather than particular and marketable skills and qualifications. The case for freedom, in other words, is starting to trickle down the intellectual pyramid. Path-breaking intellectuals like Hayek and Friedman are being followed by a generation of libertarians young enough to apply their more plainly stated and more 'extreme' ideas to life outside the universities. This is the process by which socialism (and before that the now-despised idea of British imperialism) achieved its successes.

The libertarian writer Murray Rothbard is right when he says that the freedom idea will grow in strength because, fundamentally, it works. The world's peoples want to have better lives, both morally and materially. Collectivism will not satisfy these desires. Liberty will. So sooner or later these truths will become widely if not universally accepted.

Sell solutions, don't try to elect them

Libertarianism should not be thought of merely as an influence brought to bear upon elections. The idea is, after all, that decisions should be made by freely associating individuals, not by electorates. Part of libertarianism is the advocacy of deregulation, denationalisation and so on. But it is also a psychological attitude that enables you to do things for yourself, with what you yourself already control.

Libertarians can become too obsessed with laws, politicians, political parties and elections, and by hurling themselves at supposed legal prohibitions can lose sight of the real problems they are supposedly trying to solve. Self-help still works.

The *coherence* of government is exaggerated. 'The state' is a lot like 'the market'; it is a network of separate individuals rather than a single, fixed, superhuman entity. The relationship between state officials and state agencies is 'anarchic'. Can it really be said that the Prime Minister 'controls' the Government? She has at least as much control over the supposedly independent private sector as she does over her 'servants'. This same fallacy of the totally obedient state lay behind the expansion of the state in the first place.

Recently I was on LBC radio denouncing compulsory education, and while reading the subject up beforehand I found that British law gives a wide latitude to the local government officials concerned. If an education officer believes that compulsory education harms education he could end compulsory education on his patch right now, with no changes in the law. Getting rid of compulsory education means persuading people who could behave differently to do so.

World peace for sale

Consider the very popular problem of the nuclear arms race. Solving this problem is considered by all concerned to be an essentially 'political' problem. To get 'peace' you must first *become* a 'politician', and then try to badger all the other politicians to join with you in making this peace. I think this assumption *is* the problem.

The 'New Right' is not normally thought of as any kind of competition for the peace movement, but the lovely thing about freedom is that you never can tell what people will try to do with it next.

Suppose I think of 'peace' as a *commercial* problem, as the result of productive processes that I and my commercial partners might set in motion for ourselves. 'Peace' is a good example of what economists call a 'public good', which means something that many people benefit from a little, but from which no small number of people would gain enough to be willing to pay for the whole service and carry all the 'free riders' who cannot be made to pay by excluding them.

The business which specialises in extracting small sums of money from each of a very large number of people is called show business. I and my partners should therefore run our 'political' careers as if we were rock-and-roll stars. We could stick our whole effort onto world-wide television, raising as much ballyhoo and rumpus as the market will stand. There is, I believe, about to be a severe shortage of reasonably cheap TV footage to put on all these global satellite TV networks that are now getting started. Most 'politicians' — who only try to sell public goods to one small country — will be even more out of their depth on this kind of global TV than they already are on their national TV networks.

We'll also want to apply the age-old wisdoms of jurisprudence, for the process I have in mind is the free enterprise government of the planet from a televised, free enterprise court of law. Most people are puzzled by the idea of law being a commercially-provided service, but libertarians have become quite used to this notion. More precisely, what I'd like is a constellation of *competing* multinational corporations, or multinational 'protection agencies', as libertarian writers prefer to call such enterprises.

Critics of libertarianism say that libertarian notions about free-market defence often sound like Belfast or the Lebanon, and I agree. The libertarian mistake has been to propose alternative free-market answers to problems which national governments already solve comparatively well (such as the prevention of civil war), but not to deal with problems (like 'world peace') that national governments are bad at solving.

The difficulty with what is now called 'world government' would be to stop the process pillaging the planet to the point where people would prefer the resumption of the nuclear arms race. It's the old constitutional dilemma, of how to get the benefits of 'government' without the seemingly inevitable drawbacks. The way ahead is to see that there already is a 'market in government', in which people compete to 'make peace' just as they also compete to make lawn-mowers, computers and classical gramophone records. 'Protection agencies', known as 'states', *already* 'sell' government. The trick is for others to sell it better, by competing with one another to eradicate the worst excesses of those same states, and eventually to drive the states out of business altogether. If multinational protection agencies turn out *not* to be offering peace, but instead merely a differently administered and differently worded kind of war, they'll go out of business.

A competititve market in government

Aside from the practical difficulties of establishing such enterprises, might not this 'market in world government' itself stagnate into monopoly world government of the kind we're sadly familiar with nationally? Did not the feudal system begin as an impeccably contractual arrangement?

[188]

Maybe, but it would take several decades for a market in government to ossify into a feudalised mockery of a free society, and during those decades mankind will spread itself beyond this planet and learn to elude the worst that a monopoly world government might otherwise inflict upon it. As soon as self-supporting, self-replicating, mobile space-colonies become viable, the gateway to the stars will be open.

Whether sold or merely imposed, 'world government' will only be a passing phase. Mankind will probably come together in fellowship (or tyranny) for a few decades, any decade now, but will then fly off in all directions. A final end to war, arms races and so forth looks out of the question.

You have probably guessed that as well as books about such subjects as Austrian economics the Alternative Bookshop also sells science fiction.

An ideology takes wing when it becomes the vehicle of the imagination.

V

PERSONAL PERSPECTIVES

MARK A. SMITH

*Four essays are grouped as personal perspectives. The writers are a
British male undergraduate, a Canadian-British female undergraduate, an American second-generation immigrant, all of whom
regard themselves in the 'New Right', and an independent sociologist
writing a doctoral thesis on the influence, as he sees it, of the New
Right on thinking and policy in education itself.*

*Mark Smith was born in 1966. His father is Research Librarian
(and tracker of instant information) at the Institute of Economic
Affairs. His grandfathers were a brewery worker in South London and
a Post Office van driver in East London.*

*He was educated at state primary and comprehensive schools and at
Haywards Heath Sixth Form College, Sussex, where he studied history
and politics. He is now reading history at The Queen's University of
Belfast.*

*His interest in politics began early at age 10 when he visited the
House of Commons. At 16 he joined the Haywards Heath Young
Conservatives. He has been an officer of local regional and student
Conservative organisations and is now Treasurer for the Northern
Ireland Region of the Federation of Conservative Students.*

*His essay is a declaration of rejection of socialism and faith in the
Conservatives by a young man who until 10 years ago might have been
expected to turn left.*

*He contrasts the plethora of political exponents and popularisers of
left-wing thinking with the absence of political champions of the New
Right until the ascendancy of Mrs Margaret Thatcher.*

*He repudiates the association of coercion, racism and other 'nasty
isms' with the New Right.*

*Thatcherite Conservatives have to a degree adopted 19th century
liberalism, but the Conservative Party is flexible and has often changed
to reflect varying outlooks, as illustrated by the difference between the
Party when led by Lord Salisbury (1890s), Stanley Baldwin (1930s)
and Harold Macmillan (1950-60s).*

*In joining the New Right Conservatives he was influenced by
Hayek's* The Road to Serfdom, *and a visit to the Socialist Republic of
Romania in 1984.*

16

KEEPING THE ROAD TO FREEDOM WIDE OPEN

MARK A. SMITH

The New Right, Radical Right or even Neo-liberal Right — call it what you will — is a set of not yet precisely defined and uncertain beliefs that have come to the political and economic fore during the last decade. They are 'uncertain' simply because they are new and untried. The practical application of the theories are only just beginning to emerge in the 1980s.

The advent of the New Right (for want of a better name) to the point where Government sympathy for such a school of thought is now sometimes reflected in policy and tangible action has been a long process. It has still hardly begun. But the mainstream thinking that lies behind it is perhaps nearly half a century old. Some would argue that it is over a century old and that 'the New Right' is a mere re-hash of reincarnates like Richard Cobden, John Bright, Jeremy Bentham and other 19th century Liberals. There is some substance to this view, but on the whole it is over-worked.

The New Right, John Bright or no John Bright, has grown up during the past decade; and one of the most important contributory factors in its establishment as an acknowledged school of thought with influence on public affairs was the election of Margaret Thatcher to the leadership of the Conservative Party in 1975.

Many people would dispute this claim on the grounds that, given her position and Parliamentary majority, she and her Government have so far only tinkered with the application of New Right theory. This is true; nevertheless, her ascendancy within the Party was fundamental in the establishment of the New Right.

For many years the ideas of the left had been publicly aired by many politicians with power, in particular Mr Tony Benn and others of like mind. Such views as he holds have become not so much accepted as 'acknowledged'. People knew his brand of socialism; trade union leaders, especially those on the left, had a national platform upon which to declaim their so-called 'Democratic Socialism' (the label is a misnomer). The New Right has the theorists, the most eminent among many being Professors F. A. Hayek and Milton Friedman. They have written and spoken over many years but not popularly to mass rallies (except occasionally to unknown numbers on television). The followers of these two academic economists had no politically active Tony Benn to popularise their teachings. Although socially lethal, the leftward view was getting across and influencing politicians. Since the New Right had no figurehead, its views and ideas were essentially confined to political and economic journals — until the beginning of the 1970s and the rise of Mrs Thatcher and like-minded people in the Conservative Party. The emergence of people thinking along Hayekian and Friedmanite lines was a breakthrough for the New Right, and marked an end to the post-war political-economic consensus which had stifled its teachings.

Conservative or liberal?

Some in their ignorance will attack the New Right and condemn it as the *far* right. Many jump on the word 'right' without thinking. Collectivism, coercion, racism and many other nasty 'isms' have no place in the New Right. But why 'New'? Does this mean that there is an Old Right? In answer to my own question: essentially, no. 'New Right' is not the best of terms; but nor is neo-liberal, radical right, even rational right. None of these labels is appropriate because not one is itself correct.

The former Secretary of State for Defence, Sir John Nott, said in *The Guardian* in September 1982: 'I am a nineteenth-century Liberal; so is Mrs Thatcher'. Milton Friedman in *The Observer*, also in September 1982, said of the Prime Minister: 'She is a nineteenth-century liberal'. Both Sir John and Professor Friedman have put modern Conservative thinking into a pigeon-hole that is tinted with 19th century liberalism. They are not totally wrong, but neither are they totally right. Many of the principles held by Liberals during the last century, especially laissez-faire, have percolated through to the 20th century and have been adopted in varying forms by many Conservatives. The ideas are the same, but the title changes. Neo-Liberalism sums up more about the new thinking and its emphasis on the individual: free trade, equal opportunity, personal freedom; yet all these ideas come under the one umbrella of modern Conservatism.

The Conservative Party, from its fundamental leg-up by Disraeli in 1868, has always been pragmatic; within its walls are many views, of which one was the ascendant and mainstream thinking. At the beginning of this century the Party of the Marquis of Salisbury had a different outlook from that of the Party of the 1930s under Stanley Baldwin. The Baldwin Party was different again from that of Mr Macmillan in the 1950s. And so on. the Conservative party is fluid and ever changing. Today what is termed the thinking of the New Right or

[194]

neo-liberalism has some of its roots in the past, but also an outlook to the future and a name that has been good since 1868 — Conservative. At the present time Conservatism combines many strands of thought. Here the ideas of Adam Smith, Hayek and Friedman are on top. It can still be termed New Right or neo-liberal, but it is in essence modern Conservative thinking. 19th century liberalism perhaps, but more accurately late 20th century Conservatism.

In terms of economics the New Right's policies for Britain are based on a belief that money does not grow on trees, nor come from Heaven, but from an over-taxed people. Government might have all the money in the world, but it still cannot create jobs — only the conditions in which jobs can grow. In a well-worked garden that is over-watered, nothing will grow, and what has already established itself will weaken or die. Money is the root of all evil, so they say, but carefully and prudently managed it can be the root of all good.

Liberty and efficiency

Economic freedom is not only a fundamental prop of New Right conservatism but an essential part in the revival of the British economy. You cannot believe in personal freedom and at the same time not believe in economic freedom. Regulations and restrictions will not benefit those in jobs or who buy the products these jobs make. Statutes and practices that hamper job creation and prohibit lower prices have to be swept away. If they are not, competition founders or becomes non-existent, and job creation falters because, for example, of restrictive practices employed by unions. It is a sad truth that unproductiveness does no one any good: it loses customers, which furthers the precariousness of jobs, since they can be won and kept only by merit and not by right. As unproductiveness is bad for business, so is over-manning. No one likes putting men and women out of work, but it has to be done and new jobs found. It is a hard and unpopular thing to say, and a view that the Labour Party and others are cowards not to accept: over-manning is a serious ill. If because of it Britain loses orders abroad, it is not only bad for a factory but harsh on a community and hard on the nation. Mrs Thatcher has said: 'Do you really think we can compel the rest of the world to buy our goods?' Compelling anyone to do anything is difficult enough, especially in the tough world of international trade. We cannot demand that people buy our wares. They must be persuaded by attractive prices, the best of quality and promptness of delivery. All of this goes to make up the market.

The 'market' is not a dirty word, as socialists would have us believe; and New Right Conservatives believe it is not. The United States, for example, has created more prosperity and well-being for millions inside and outside its frontiers by its free-market economy than any Eastern European socialist country has through political organisation and the suppression of freedom.

There are many services in which the presence of government is unnecessary; they could be performed just as well or better by individuals trading among themselves in the private sector. Restrictive regulations on wages which artificially predetermine the size of the market and the strong (but thankfully weakening) hold of the trade unions, for example, are often a hindrance rather than a help. Trade union restrictive practices have lost many customers and many jobs, especially in the building industry and in the fading dockyards. The main objection to unions are that they are restrictive and infringe the freedom of the individual. If they are so very good, why does it have to be made compulsory to join them?

Freedom throughout is the distinguishing feature of the New Right modern Conservative. Economic freedom through free trade, and political freedom, freedom of the individual and freedom from the auspices and overbearing constraints the state may impose. It is important that the nation and people inter-react together as harmoniously as possible. Nevertheless, as a 'One Nation' pamphlet of 1950 says, the state 'must not burden the individual so that he loses his initiative and enterprise'. Stifling incentive and opportunity gets us nowhere. Even so, this does not mean the state does nothing; it has a subservient role to play, with the people as master, not as servant.

Social welfare

The provision for social welfare by the state is now entrenched in daily life. At present the emphasis is on the state to care. This view is right, but should be realised at a minimum so that people can provide for themselves. This approach leaves the state to care for those who *cannot* look after themselves. Today there is no reason that people should be totally beholden to the state for health care when there are numerous private and semi-public services and schemes on the market. Competition in health can save lives as well as money. It will take money to pay for, but the cost can be cushioned by private health insurance. It is a long-exploded fallacy to believe, as the left has taught, that welfare services are free. Health costs money either publicly or privately, and the cheaper the better. It might seem callous to equate health with the workings of the market, but here competition keeps down the reliance on the state, which is static: choice is all-important in all aspects of life.

Democracy is a natural right and one of many freedoms the New Right holds dear. It is a right for all regardless of how lowly or how wealthy you are. Nevertheless it must not be taken for granted. The ideas of the New Right, which is influencing and is part of modern Conservatism, are founded on real freedoms: the freedoms of speech, thought, religious worship and toleration, for example. Such freedoms are now established in our unwritten constitution but are frequently under attack by what is termed the 'New Left'. Their views, dominated and preoccupied by the ideals of socialism and the class struggle, leave little room for reality to creep in. Professor Hayek's *The Road to Serfdom*, now just over 40 years old and still being reprinted, makes it clear that socialism is an ideology that aims at regulating life from the centre and will ultimately lead down the road to control, regulation and constraint — economically, politically and socially. Professor Hayek believed in his message so strongly he dedicated his book to 'the socialists of all parties'. This is a man who has witnessed exactly what he had laid down on paper: the rise of Adolf Hitler and the totalitarian Third Reich (to fall only 988 years short of its full duration) and previously the aspirations of Lenin and Trotsky in their revolution. And Hayek wrote about the follies of both total and partial collectivism.

The new left and its breed of socialism can only lead to totalitarianism. As Elie Halevy once said, 'the Socialists believe in two things which are absolutely different and perhaps contradictory: freedom and organisation'. The New Right must advance itself in the face of socialism which encompasses aspects that are in themselves disturbing: the concepts of 'Democratic Socialism' and 'People's Democracy'. Why 'Democratic' and 'People's'? We normally assume that an ideology is either democratic or undemocratic and that a freedom, like democracy, is for the people. Both go without saying; so why tell us that they are? The only conclusion one must draw is that the two concepts are not all they appear to be; wolves in sheep's clothing, a misnomer like the 'Peoples' Democratic Republic of This, That and T'Other' — not for, by or with the people.

Freedom is the mainstay of New Right Conservatism. Freedom and its cause is one of the world's greatest; we should value it and resist steps which encroach upon it. Such a commodity is precious and should not be taken for granted since one day it might be taken away. We should not be deceived by socialist 'freedom' through organisation and economic planning: which does no one any good, anywhere. This is the New Right's strongest challenge — that of keeping socialism at bay through reasoned argument.

The politics of an undergraduate

Since I have not yet completed my first year at Queens, Belfast, I have not had a lifetime upon which to base my political beliefs. Having said that, I am not a Tory simply because my parents are. I am one because I believe in what it means, and my thoughts have leant towards the New Right brand of Conservative political thinking. All of this coincided with Mrs Thatcher's election as Conservative leader when I was only eight years old and cared little for ideologies (but loved my green racing car).

The 1979 General Election saw me well out of my racing car by quite a few years and taking more of an interest in politics. I was politically-minded in my tender years, thinking for myself, without being influenced by others, and spurred on by the coverage the General Election was getting on the news. But the time the 1983 General Election came round I was still unable to vote for what I believed in, but campaigned vigorously with the Young Conservatives for our local and neighbouring Members of Parliament. It was here my beliefs were brought together, since it would have been difficult to discuss and argue topics with the voters while canvassing if you didn't know what you were talking about.

I read Hayek's *Road to Serfdom*, which had a strong effect, especially on my determination to uphold and respect freedom and condemn all forms of restrictive practices and ideologies which placed the state above the individual. Such thinking led me to consider myself a part of what was being called the New Right. These views were compounded when in April 1984 I visited the Socialist Republic of Romania. The restriction and lack of freedom in this socialist nation was ever-present. The State and the Party was everything, even in this 'mild' Communist country. When I asked our official guide the name of his President because I had difficulty in pronouncing it, he would not reply — in case, he told me, someone thought we were talking politics! That incident had a profound effect on me; nothing is better than freedom, and nothing worse than a false pseudonym for utopia — Socialist Democracy.

Very personal events in my life have shaped my thinking. It is because I rejected socialism that led me to the way I think. In many respects the New Right is a reaction to stagnant socialism. Socialist policies, it seems to me, would reshape our own society and create a New Order for Britain. Many people value the traditions and the essence of the British way of life too much to warrant change for the sake of change. New Right Conservative thinking is full of change but it is rational and progressive: change which can benefit all, unlike the left's, which is emotional as well as retrogressive and would lead to a new feudalism: with the state first and people second.

We should cry out against injustice and the forces that disregard people and treat them as sheep. A nation with no independence of human spirit is no nation at all. The people make up the nation. Their fulfilment is the nation's fulfilment, which emerges by giving help only where it is needed and letting individuals be simply people who

[198]

want nothing more than to get on with their own lives. The road to serfdom must never be opened and the road to freedom never closed.

JANET PARRETT

The second undergraduate was born in 1967. Her father was a Professor of Chemistry at the Royal Military College of Canada and is now an industrial/chemical consultant. Her mother is an artist.

She was educated in Canada and at comprehensive schools in Greenwich. She began a graduate course in October 1985 at the London School of Economics.

She was active in Conservative politics from the age of 15, and has been National Vice-Chairman of Women and Families for Defence. She recently founded and directs the Student Economist Research Foundation.

She describes herself as a 'new liberal' because the ideas she supports originated in 19th century classical liberalism.

The state is being seen as the foe rather than the friend of the individual. It endangers freedom because it has grown too big into 'mega-government'. Constitutional reform will not suffice to remove the dangers. Democratic government now compromises between the claims of competing interest groups: it no longer represents the interests of individuals in society at large.

Ownership by the state does not carry ownership by the people. 'Public' ownership does not create private property rights that the individual owner can sell. Little wonder that privatisation is popular.

State welfare has discouraged the growth of private welfare. Government is out of control, and individuals are escaping from employment to self-employment. Individuals must be enabled to better their condition if society is to advance.

17

RESURRECTION OF THE LIBERAL

JANET PARRETT

Big government undermines individual liberty

There is no universally accepted answer to the question of the origins and purpose of mankind. It is generally thought, however, that man should seek to make 'the best of life' and aim to ensure maximum happiness. But what is happiness? The task facing human society is to answer this question. In Britain and in other countries there has been a tendency to forget that happiness is a subjective term meaning different things to different people. It cannot be legislated for by governments.

The premise for my political philosophy is that the individual is best qualified to determine the criteria for his happiness and, left to his own devices, he will pursue it. A society that maximises individual freedom will enjoy a higher degree of general contentment than one in which the requirements of the individual are prescribed by governments and other collective bodies. I would call such a freedom-maximising society 'liberal'.

The political map

I am a neo-liberal in the sense that the ideas I support originate predominantly from thinkers of the 19th century and are re-emerging in the late 20th century as the most dynamic challenge to socialist thought. The liberal will aim to ensure: that individual freedom is maintained at a level which does not conflict with one person's freedom harming another's; that power, particularly the power of the state, is dispersed; and that economic exchange occurs voluntarily in the market place rather than through the coercion of government.

The label 'New Right' has emerged in an attempt to illustrate where the resurgent liberal can be placed on the political map. I reject the notion that liberalism warrants such a label. The conventional political 'spectrum', with the extremes of left at one end and right at the other, is outmoded and was never a useful guide. Left and right occupy the same extreme ground, the subjection of the individual's requirements to those of the state. Liberalism is largely antithetical to this position. But I am not an anarcho-capitalist. I do not see liberty as an absolute value *and* deny the logical admissibility of government to undertake some functions it now performs. I therefore cannot place myself, like the anarchist, diametrically opposed to the state. Adam Smith in *The Wealth of Nations* indicates three functions of government consistent with a 'system of natural liberty'. The first two duties Smith prescribed for government are straightforward enough: national defence and law, order and 'an exact administration of justice'. The third duty of

> erecting and maintaining certain public works and certain public institutions which it can never be in the interest of any individual, or small group of individuals, to erect and maintain,

has been erroneously used to justify much unnecessary government intervention. Smith's application was more limited — to the maintenance of certain kinds of infrastructure like roads and environmental health. The functions Smith prescribed for government are, characteristically, the provision of public goods: those which cannot be provided by the market since the benefits derived from them cannot be excluded from people who cannot be made to pay. There is an additional function government should adopt. Once it has established minimum standards in health and education, government should seek to maintain a minimum amount of income so that all have the purchasing power for freedom of choice. Although it is argued that maintaining minimum income is compatible with free institutions, because 'minimum income does not preclude individual effort to rise above the minimum' (Arthur Seldon, *Wither the Welfare State*), it would inevitably involve some redistribution of income from rich to poor. Redistribution is traditionally a socialist or 'left wing' policy. I cannot deduce, from my views on the functions of the state, any reason that my politics should be considered any more to the right than to the left.

Liberal and conservative

The 'New Right' is not a term with which I would like my liberal views associated lest I be confused with the extreme 'conservatives' who have also attracted the label. I find their views repugnant because the state is more important to them than individual liberty. They resist change for the better, because they consider change in itself a bad omen for the stability and survival of the state. They are intolerant of diversity in human nature. They profess overt nationalism, racism and intolerance of other cultures to the extent that they consider

[202]

themselves justified in forcing their own 'superior' culture and lifestyle on others. Colonialism was a consequence of this attitude. This is not to say that the liberal is not patriotic and without sensibility towards his own country, nor that he would not like to see undesirable behaviour altered. It is to say that a liberal is tolerant towards modes of existence other than his own and that, if he wishes to change the behaviour of others, it is through persuasion and example rather than coercion.

How liberals and conservatives approach the formulation of their attitudes towards the European Economic Community, for instance, is an illustration of their different philosophies. The conservative will oppose outright moves towards increased European integration because he sees it as a threat to British institutions and culture. The liberal will formulate his attitude by assessing whether European integration will enhance liberty and prosperity — whether there would be more potential for economic exchange. The liberal will encourage the alteration of British institutions if he believes that, in the late 20th and 21st century, they will offer no benefit in their existing form. Additionally, the liberal will see culture as an evolutionary process. The interaction of culture in free societies is inevitable and desirable. Cultural uniformity would be very dull. It is the preoccupation of the conservative to confuse accepting cultural evolution with burning history books. In a free society a sense of history is ever-present.

The emphasis upon persuasion and example rather than coercion is very evident in the liberal view of the formulation of morality and acceptable social behaviour. Many liberal writers have professed that society will act as a natural constraint on undesirable social behaviour. John Stuart Mill in his essay *On Liberty* argued that, as long as the constituted rights of other individuals are not violated by a person's bad behaviour, 'the offender may be duly punished by opinion, though not by law'. Mill goes on to argue that there are limited instances where government may be justified in intervening.

> As soon as any person's conduct affects prejudicially the interest of others, society has jurisdiction over it, and the question whether the general welfare will or will not be promoted by interfering with it becomes open to discussion.

It is on questions of social behaviour that my position is distinguished from that of the 'libertarian'. I tend to establish sooner the point at which I believe certain forms of social behaviour 'affect prejudicially the interest of others'. Prostitution and taking heroin are harmful to society at large. Libertarians believe such activities should not be subject to legal control as those who engage in them are not restricting 'the constituted rights of others'. On the whole, I rarely advocate legislation to prevent kinds of behaviour I disapprove of, although I would hope the attitudes of society at large would encourage a public morality I thought acceptable.

Government — friend or foe?

What led a Marxist commentator like Andrew Gamble to assert in *Marxism Today*, July 1983, that,

> 'the New Right has won the battle to shape the new consensus on how to respond to the recession. The new agenda of public policy will reflect their priorities, and the opposition parties will be pulled along in their wake'?

The shift in the political debate that Gamble magnanimously indicates can be attributed to increasing recognition of the constitutional and economic crises resulting from the growth of government induced by socialism and socialist notions of 'equality'. The 'New Right' or liberal resurrection has sprung from the realisation that recent economic stagnation has been due to the stifling of individual initiative through overt and unnecessary state intervention: the state has become so powerful as a consequence that individual liberty cannot be upheld against it by any constitutional arrangement.

In *Free to Choose* Milton Friedman argues that there is a problem in ensuring 'that coercive powers granted to government in order to preserve freedom are limited to that function and are kept from becoming a threat to freedom'. The British constitution is based on conventions which in theory are presumed to ensure that the interests of the individual are protected; that government will use its power in the manner intended by society. A 'sovereign' Parliament is elected. The state must act within the law and is liable in the courts for a breach of the law. The judiciary is independent of the other arms of government.

The growth of government seriously threatens the reliable operation of a liberal constitution based on the existence of these principles. Rather than power be dispersed, 'mega-government' has concentrated power increasingly in the executive (the Cabinet and the bureaucracy) arm of government, which now takes the bulk of decisions and has assumed judicial functions. The position of the individual relative to the state has been progressively weakened over a century. It is a folly to presume the individual is adequately protected by existing constitutional arrangements.

Government takes over 40 per cent of the National Income each year and spends it. The sheer size of this task makes it impossible for Parliament to scrutinise every penny of expenditure. The bulk of legislation passing through Parliament is 'delegated legislation' which gives law-making powers to Ministers, officials and administrative authorities. The ability of Parliament or the courts to review the exercise of such powers is very limited. The doctrine of ministerial responsibility, which is intended to make Ministers accountable for the actions of their civil servants, is inoperable. Of the work undertaken by any department of government, the Minister will know of and supervise only 5 per cent. Sir Thomas Dugdale's resignation in 1954 over the Critchel Down affair was the last instance where a Minister resigned as a result of actions by his civil servants, although he was not aware of their undertakings. Additionally, it is evident that the bureaucratic machine will use the power it possesses to achieve its own 'departmental aims' rather than the political objectives of the Minister. The Civil Service is accused of being 'secret government' because of its ability to control and organise the political heads of departments — it controls the information a Minister will see, prepares policy options, uses its numeric superiority and its 'expertise'. A recent example of this kind of power being utilised against a Minister's political aims is the rejection by Sir Keith Joseph of a voucher scheme for education because his civil servants had convinced him that it was administratively unfeasible. The bureaucracy has evidently acquired unaccountable powers, and this development is not tolerable in a free society.

In the 1950s the political commentator Robert Mackenzie deduced that the UK was moving closer to 'Prime Ministerial Government'. As a consequence of massive government functions, more decisions have to be taken and the Cabinet, meeting collectively, cannot undertake this task. Thus a system of Cabinet sub-committees, chaired and co-ordinated by the Prime Minister, has developed. Of all Cabinet Ministers the Prime Minister is the most informed, and has the most influence over decision-making.

Big government — compromise between interests or representative of society?

The Burkean perception that the prime duty of the Member of Parliament was to exercise his own judgement has been replaced by overt loyalty to the Party which took him to Westminster, to the Prime Minister whose powers of patronage control his career prospects, and to powerful interest groups, trade unions and professional bodies. The pluralistic model of government as a compromise between powerful competing interests has replaced democratic government representing the interests of society at large and ensured by the independence of the MP's judgement.

The ability of the citizen to ensure government adherence to the law is in doubt. The case of Gouriet v. the Union of Post Office Workers, 1977, illustrates this proposition. The Attorney General's decision to prevent court action was challenged by Gouriet in the Court of Appeal which ruled that unlawfulness might be inferred if the Attorney General failed to state the reason for his decision. The House of Lords then backed up the Attorney General, declaring that the Appeal Court had no right to review the Attorney General's decision as 'public rights' can be asserted only by him. The executive had used a judicial function which it possesses to prevent an individual from seeking the redress of a grievance in the courts. In the face of the government's power to assert 'public rights', the position of the judiciary in upholding individual rights seems weak.

The executive can also use the protection of the Official Secrets Act and various Royal Prerogatives (over national security), to prevent the courts from questioning its decisions. All government papers are automatically classified as secret whether their contents would be harmless or useful to public knowledge. It was not until 1982 that the Government decided that the public had a right to see the reports of HM's Inspectors on schools. It baffles me to imagine why vast quantities of harmless classified information vegetate in government offices. Leaks from officials have often revealed the excessive and unnecessary nature of government secrecy. In the 1984 Clive Ponting trial it was revealed that information had been withheld from the public not in the interests of national security but for the morally suspect motive of avoiding the embarrassment of confession to an administrative blunder. In addition to secrecy in administration, the individual's position is weakened by the inadequate process for seeking redress for administrative error or unfairness. Administrative tribunals can be criticised for their insufficient independence from the executive. Appeals against the decision of a tribunal involving the Department of Health and Social Security go directly to the Minister. Additionally, where consultation with the public is required to take place by statute before a decision is made, it is often evident that the consultation is a façade and the decision has already been taken.

Whether the constitution is codified in one document or based on conventions, statutes and judicial statements is not the crux of the problem. It is the growth of government, which has led to a massive multiplication of the individual's encounters with the state, that threatens his liberty. The priority for reversing the decline of liberty is to revert to the kind of limited government advocated by the liberals of the so-called 'New Right'. 'Mega-government' is inconsistent with individual liberty no matter what kind of constitution you devise for its preservation.

[206]

The mixed economy — the so-called balancer of community and private interests — has failed to live up to the public expectations of enhanced prosperity. It has failed the test of time. The state-controlled side of the equation has grown at the expense of the private sector. The 'New Right' has responded to the disillusionment by reasserting faith in the free market as the best provider of goods and services. Government intervention reduces the potential growth in output and thus consumer satisfaction.

Economic ailments of state intervention
A 'market' is where buyers and sellers meet to determine price, which will reflect the quantity of goods the sellers are willing and able to supply and the quantity buyers wish to purchase. The price mechanism becomes the mode of communication between consumers (buyers) and producers (sellers). An increased demand for a good or service will raise its price. The expectations of bigger profits as a result of the increased price will encourage producers to supply more of the good or service until the increased demand is satisfied. The price mechanism is remarkable. Through fluctuation in price, millions of individual decisions or events which affect changes in the conditions of supply or demand are co-ordinated. In this way the price or market system will allocate resources in a manner responsive to human desires.

Attempts by the state to undertake the production of goods and the provision of services can never be as efficient as the market. The state becomes the powerful third party which forces its arbitrary assessment of the requirements of society on producers and consumers. The rejection of the market means that no automatic mechanism exists to alert the state to changes in individual tastes and requirements.

The socialist justification for 'public' (state) ownership of production is that 'ownership means control'. A 1975 Conservative Party pamphlet summed up the reality well: 'ownership by the state does not mean ownership by the people'. State ownership has been increasingly recognised as a burden on the people rather than something they share or own. A dividend is not received at the end of each year, but only demands for ever higher taxation to help finance the losses of the nationalised industries. To rub salt into the wound, the people cannot even sell their 'share' as they now can with British Telecom, Jaguar and other private shares. It is no wonder that the privatisation programme of the Thatcher Government has been so popular.

The harmful effects of nationalisation have been more recognisable over a long period of time. In the same way as the interaction of supply and demand will determine the price and output of a particular good, so will it ease the transition between the production of different

[207]

types of goods and services. The exclusion of the nationalised industries from the realities of the market place means that vast quantities of capital and labour have become tied up in the production of goods and services for which demand is declining. The decisions on pricing and output in these industries have been perverted by short-term political considerations. Decisions to reduce over-manning and over-capacity in declining or contracting industries, such as mining, railways, teaching and farming, have been neglected or postponed by subsidy. Over a long period the cost of nationalised production is not only the sum of the losses they have made from trading but also the 'opportunity cost' — the production forgone by preventing scarce resources from being used in profitable enterprises in the private sector. Subsidising inefficiency in decaying industries has denied resources for investment in the new high-technology industries.

The state has also adopted the provision of welfare services under the assumption that only it can provide welfare in a manner which is 'just'. After nearly half a century of the 'welfare state', the consensus which brought it into existence has broken down. People who require assistance claim that its provisions are inadequate, and those whose taxes pay for it claim that it is astonomically expensive. Increased expenditure in the welfare state by consecutive Governments seems to have gone on financing its administration, rather than raising its standards of provisions.

A consequence of the welfare state is that it has acted as a disincentive to private provision — private health and employment insurance, pension schemes and schooling. Instead of providing a 'safety net', the welfare state has instituted an equality ceiling. In trying to enforce equality and uniformity, it has denied society at large the benefit of general improvements in standards which can only be achieved if some are allowed to rise above the minimum. In *Wither the Welfare State* Arthur Seldon sums up the present situation:

> The purpose of the welfare state in day-to-day reality has changed from the prevention of inadequacy to the pretence of equality. And since the effort to create equality — however unsuccessful — requires the suppression of differences, the welfare state has come into conflict with the free society.

There is no reason that welfare, including health and education, cannot be provided by the market. Instead of providing universal welfare which imposes a maximum standard, minimum standards should be formulated and government should top up the incomes of the poorer members of society enabling them also to be free to choose in the market place.

One of the most horrific areas of government intervention in the economy has been in 'preventing unemployment'. Governments were prompted in their actions by the economic theories of John Maynard Keynes, who maintained that unemployment could be prevented if government used fiscal policy (adjusting taxation and government expenditure) to maintain aggregate demand in the economy consistent with output which ensures 'full employment' of labour. This task involved government statisticians in calculating how much government would have to increase expenditure. It also involved them in calculating 'full employment' (the politicians seemed the quickest judge of this figure). Apart from the difficulty of making such calculations, there are serious deficiencies in this kind of policy.

The essential fault in Keynesian theory is that it assumes that the demand for commodities is equal to the demand for labour. The production of commodities involves the combination of other factors of production besides labour, which will be combined in different ratios according to their relative prices and efficiency. Keynesian theory also failed to recognise the consequences of its fiscal measures. Increased government expenditures to maintain employment resulted in higher expenditure on state welfare and in the nationalised industries, thus enhancing all the problems. Moreover, deficit expenditure was financed by increased government borrowing or by printing money, which creates inflation and raises interest rates thus discouraging private firms from borrowing to finance new investment.

Keynesian demand-management served to fuel the growth in state expenditure, nationalised industries and the welfare state and to accelerate inflation at the expense of the private sector and the individual. But did this policy prevent unemployment? The answer is no: it helped to create it. Inflation made British goods uncompetitive. Orders from abroad would be lost, as would jobs in the production of exports.

The situation exploded beyond tolerance in the 1970s and gave the strongest impetus to the rise of liberalism in the 1980s. Until the breakdown of the system of fixed exchange rates in 1971, which had pegged the value of the pound in relation to the dollar, governments had to exercise some restraint on expenditure to avoid balance of payments crises. Thus a discipline on expenditure was removed and governments took advantage of their new-found freedom to spend and inflate.

Government out of control

In the later 1970s the Labour Government began to realise that Keynesian demand-management would perpetuate both inflation and unemployment. This was not the only factor that had to be recognised. The 1970s witnessed the adverse effects that trade-union privilege and consequent power have on production. Their actions, including violent picketing and intimidation, repelled even their own members. It was not surprising that a third of trade unionists voted in 1979 for the Conservative Party, which had pledged to reduce trade union privileges in law and give the ordinary member more say in running his union.

The liberal takeover of the Conservative Party by Margaret Thatcher and the subsequent 1979 election and 1983 re-election of her Party into office is evidence of the public recognition that government had got out of control. The wealth-creation process, which originates from the individual's desire to better his own and his family's condition, was under threat. Taxation and over-regulation had encouraged individuals, rather than take risks with starting their own businesses, to seek employment with someone else — the state or a large firm. Government had grown so large that there existed no incentive to step out on your own.

In 1960 in *The Constitution of Liberty* Professor Hayek, one of the foremost creators of the resurrection of liberal ideas, wrote

> It may indeed prove to be the most difficult task of all to persuade the employed masses that in the general interests of their society, and therefore in their own long-term interest, they should . . . enable a few to reach positions which to them appear unobtainable or not worth the effort or risk.

Over twenty years later, the concern with equality has rightly become outmoded. There has been at least a verbal recognition that conditions which encourage individuals to secure their own betterment are essential if society at large is to advance. The concern now must be to sustain the momentum of liberal ideas. A huge intellectual effort reversed the tide. The energy of that effort must be continued.

MARILYN DALJORD

The third essay in this group, by a libertarian (the second author with Russian ancestry), argues that the New Right embodies old virtues, essentially the spirit of individualist pride, self-help and emulation as against dependence and resignation in a 'welfare' environment.

Marilyn Daljord was born in New York City, the granddaughter of once-wealthy Russian immigrants whose fortunes fell: her grandfather worked as a train conductor, tailor and marketstall trader.

She was educated at Brooklyn College, and holds a BA Summa cum laude in theatre and classics and a Master's degree in Performing Arts Management from the City University of New York. She is completing a doctoral study of theatre history, and plans to read Land Economy at Queen's College, Cambridge, in 1986.

She has written for American periodicals, edited Performance Management Newsletter, *and worked in theatre as stage manager, actress, administrator and researcher. (A member of American Actors' Equity, Screen Actors' Guild and the American Federation of TV and Radio Artists.)*

She has lived in England since 1979 and is a member of the (British) Libertarian Alliance.

Her essay, well written in good English, draws on her family's experience to illustrate her libertarian argument: the family was a 'private army'. And she analyses American experience — of good intentions that have produced bad results — which forms a warning for Britain.

18

THE NEW RIGHT REASSERTS OLD VIRTUES

MARILYN DALJORD

'Eat the rich', read the exhortation on the wall. The writer of that statement could not have been a libertarian, for if a libertarian had lost his respect for private property sufficiently to scrawl graffiti on a wall, he would have written '*Be* the rich'. And that goal is what spurred on countless immigrants to achievement in their new homelands.

I write as a second-generation American. I find nothing new about the tenets of the so-called 'New Right', for what I believe as a libertarian, my grandparents believed as immigrants, and my parents believed, too. I must first cavil at the use of the terms 'right' and 'left' in their political senses; use of either often produces an unthinking, knee-jerk response in many people. The 'Right' has been equated with authoritarianism and entrenched, complacent conservatism, both of which, as a libertarian, I reject entirely.

There had been a fall in fortune for my maternal grandparents by the time they arrived in New York from Russia, via Canada. I remember my grandmother telling me of her carriage and horses, her household staff, her jewelry, and the magnificent samovar she brought with her from Russia. My grandfather had become a well-off builder while they lived in Toronto, until a client went bankrupt and took my grandfather down with him. Grandmother and Grandfather then came to New York. There was no welfare state to provide its dubious help and definite hindrance; to live, they had to work — and they did. My grandfather became a train conductor and sometime tailor, and my grandmother (the daughter of the Grand Rabbi of Kiev, so family history goes) ran a fruit and vegetable stall. They were poor, in real terms, not merely in comparison with their former state. My mother still remembers wearing shoes which weren't a matched pair because they were all her father could afford to buy — and any shoes were better than no shoes.

Pride and self-help
What they never lost was pride; yes, my grandmother bitterly re-

[213]

sented her changed circumstances but she did work hard, running the stall and raising the five children which survived beyond infancy. My grandparents had been brought up to believe in the 'mitzvah' (the good deed, the blessing) of giving to charity; no matter how little they had, there were always those worse off than themselves. It was not, to their minds, the responsibility of the state to help the less fortunate, but a personal obligation to be discharged. The word 'mitzvah' was derived from the Hebrew word 'tzvah' or 'tsivah', meaning 'command-ment'; one was *commanded* by God to do good deeds. But my grandparents were horrified at the thought of being recipients of charity and refused it outright from others; charity was for people in desperate straits, in which my grandparents did not believe themselves to be.

They had the will to survive, and more — to raise themselves and their children to a better life. They would work even harder, if need be, to reach that goal, without relying on the charity of others, relying only on their own efforts. They did not regain their former wealth, but by the time 1940 rolled around, they were home-owners.

This narrative is not intended as a glorification of my grand-parents; they were, in many ways, petty, small-minded, superstitious, ill-educated. But their stubbornness and pride, their refusal to give up, their acceptance that their lives would be what they themselves made of them: these were valuable qualities which have my respect.

My mother inherited those qualities, and from an early age was no stranger to hard work. My father had been out in the streets from the age of nine, selling newspapers and shining shoes. My parents were, and continue to be, a major source of strength in my life. They were determined that my brother and I would have better childhoods than they had, and that our futures and theirs would continue to improve.

The hard work, the struggle to keep their heads above water, went on. Every financial debt was honoured, each creditor paid a small sum every week until the full debt was discharged. The butcher, grocer, baker, doctor: they all trusted my parents; there were no written contracts — just a handshake and one's given word. Failure to honour that word meant shame and loss of the claim to integrity and self-respect. These were far stronger sanctions than that of the threat of punishment by law. Honour was not, as someone of my acquaintance once said to me, 'a fine, intellectual concept'; it was a way of living one's life.

My brother and I didn't have stylish clothes or family holidays or summers in camp, as many of our contemporaries did. There was no family car. A day's outing was a three-mile walk each way to Coney Island, where the four of us would share one hot dog at Nathan's Famous, one orange drink, and have a ride on the carousel. On special occasions our parents would buy us, at our importunings, one excruciatingly pink mass of cotton candy to share. There was no meanness at work here, only a lack of money; but there was that goal to make our dreams reality.

Mom and Dad lived from one loan to the next, paying off every penny steadily. My father worked at two jobs (I remember once seeing him fall asleep from exhaustion as he stood in a doorway); my mother not only looked after us and her mother, but had an outside job, did typing homework and volunteer charity work. A wonderful house of our own and financial security for all of us were the goals.

Family: the private army

Although I sometimes longed for fashionable clothes, especially when puberty struck with its unsubtle hand and left me deeply self-conscious and shy, I don't recall feeling a sense of deprivation. We had books, a second-hand piano, and a battered record-player. There was also a television; my Uncle Harry worked with R.C.A. and got one cheaply for us. These were all nice things to have, but they were nothing compared with the sense of *family* we shared. There was never any question in our minds that we were loved, and that we were worthy of love. My family and I have always considered ourselves to be our own private army, there to support, encourage, protect. Self-esteem and an acceptance of responsibility for our actions were firmly established early on, and continually reinforced.

Thinking back over my early childhood, I must always have been a natural libertarian. 'Myself', I said emphatically; I was less than two years old and my uncle was attempting to spoon-feed me. Even then, my instinct was to reach for control of that spoon and feed myself, without an intermediary. Then there was the occasion when a foolhardy aunt ordered me to bed, to leave behind an adult gathering whose conversation seemed fascinating to me. Unconcerned and unaware that my aunt's action was a usurpation of my parents' position, I only cared that my dignity and individual liberty were being attacked. Spluttering with offended outrage, I declared: 'You ... you ... you can't tell me what to do'. Even unto this day, say my loving parents, no-one can. It is true that I would bow to the imperative of a loaded gun aimed at my head, but that would be an act of expediency, for survival, and not an acceptance of the gunman's right to dispose of my life as he chooses.

The regard for the tradition of the 'mitzvah' had been passed on to us. Added to that was a natural inclination in me towards generosity and spontaneous expressions of affection (qualities now somewhat tempered by growing up and becoming aware that not everyone feels benign toward me, even those who, by any intelligent reasoning, ought to). I used to give away my toys to the other children in our

[215]

neighbourhood who, understandably in retrospect, backed off from me as if I were crazy — by their lights, perhaps I was.

It is difficult to pinpoint the intellectual genesis of my libertarianism, the keystones of which are the beliefs in free will and personal freedom I've had from childhood. My philosophy of life (which is to say, my libertarianism) did not come from reading — it was *reinforced* by reading Ayn Rand, Nathaniel Branden, Professor Hayek. I believed (*still* believe) in compassionate feeling and action, but almost instinctively knew that anything done out of a sense of false guilt could only damage both giver and receiver. I rejected the idea of collective guilt espoused by American 'liberals'. It was not *just*; individuals were responsible for their own actions, for good or evil. Unless it could be proven to me that, rather like an ant colony, whole nations, races, or 'classes' thought and acted with one mind, these were still only groups of individuals, not single entities. Nazi Germany was an abhorrent reality, but not all Germans were Nazis.

The values of the immigrant before the welfare state

This is not meant to be my autobiography. By relating family history, I wish to show that the values of what is called the 'New Right' are, in no small measure, a return to what I'd call the values of the immigrant: the freedom to work hard, with neither expectation of nor demand for aid from the state; the will to achieve a betterment of life, without denigration of 'materialism'; belief in a free market economy, people trading goods and services by voluntarily made contracts, without coercive state intervention; a belief in and respect for oneself, a knowledge that one's life, to make or break, is one's own, and not owed to, or owned by, society or state.

People emigrated to America from all over the world and, before the welfare state was ever established, struggled and achieved and contributed not only to the success of themselves and their families but also to the prosperity of all America. The Pakistanis and Hindus, among other immigrants in Britain, show the same pattern of industriousness, working long hours, seven days a week, often in family-run businesses. I asked an Indian why his was the only shop open late on Sunday in the shopping area. He said: 'I am not English-born. And I want to be a millionaire before I am forty. If I must work all day every day to do that, I *will* do that'. This drive, this pattern of self-help, along with a very strong family life and a shared sense of *community* self-help, have certainly enabled these immigrants to achieve a better integration into the economic (if not the cultural) life of the larger society. It was no different for all the Poles, Russians, Germans, and others who emigrated from their native homelands to America. Immigrant culture was an enterprise culture. The subsidy culture came with the dawning of the welfare state.

[216]

Participation in politics, to my parents (and to me when I came of age), meant no more than being registered Democrats, members of what was seen as the working- and middle-class party. The Republican party, on the other hand — the 'right' — was seen as representing solely the rich and powerful, the vested interests in America. Libertarianism, as an 'ism', was not known by us.

We had grown up extending the idea of the act of 'mitzvah' to a world vision; the Democratic party came to power and began to legislate 'compassion'. The poor and needy would never again go hungry or have to worry about having roofs over their heads. And yet, as time went by, we became conscious of something going wrong. All those altruistic, compassionate bits of Democratic legislation raising our taxes ever higher were not producing a better environment, particularly for people in poverty, but were creating more squalor, and an onslaught of mindless violence on a scale we could not have envisaged. What had gone wrong?

As often happens when the state enters the arena of moral issues, in which, by its very nature, it has no credibility, it can create worse havoc and deterioration in many cases than if it had done nothing. It was supposedly to help the unfortunate that the welfare state was instituted; it was also a lucrative boondoggle, with the vast mass of state subsidy never reaching the truly deserving recipient, and with large sums disappearing into administrative costs. It took the healthy, the hard workers, the creators and producers in society and taxed them higher and higher the more they achieved, stealing, in no uncertain terms, the fruits of their labours.

A new Robin Hood

A new Robin Hood rode the land, only he wasn't robbing the rich to help the poor now; his victims were the middle class, most of whom had struggled up from the poverty of their immigrant beginnings in the hopes of making sure that their children would never have to suffer as they had. And now they saw all their hard-won attainments being forcibly redistributed by governmental order. It was all very Marxist: 'From each according to his abilities, to each according to his needs'. And needs, now that the other fellow was paying for them and the government had sanctified them, proliferated. No longer was it the starving poor, the honest person temporarily on the skids, who asked for and received help. Now 'help' — support from cradle to grave — was demanded as a right. A 'Them and Us' dichotomy, however usual in any society, was exacerbated by a now-legal right to behave badly and be rewarded for it, to be paid for by others simply for being alive.

With no residency requirements for receipt of welfare, New York City, birthplace and home of my family and myself, became a dumping ground by other states for all those of their citizenry considered by them to be their 'wretched refuse'. Some states reputedly offered their unwanted the bus fare to go to the big city and get onto the welfare rolls. Some people with honourable hopes of a fresh start, and others looking for a ride on the gravy train, came on their own, flooding the city. There weren't enough jobs to handle this influx; many young, able-bodied people were left idle in the street. As there was no 'workfare' program, they were given weekly salaries simply because they were here. Many of the unskilled and uneducated refused, with false pride, to take jobs they considered to be menial, even when the work was all they were equipped to do at the time. It was an odd sort of pride, as it did not seem to be offended by living off the taxes of people who worked.

Coercive legislation causes racial friction

Then came bussing; children of minority groups (although who in America is not?) were transferred every day by bus from their own communities to attend school in what must be described as alien territory. Someone, somewhere, must have thought that this intrusive exercise would result in more racial harmony through propinquity. The truth is that there is not, and never was, a 'Melting Pot' America. Like prefers to be with like, whether the commonality of experience is that of race, religion, or education and intelligence. That is neither a bad nor a good thing; it is truth. People want to maintain not only a sense of personal identity, but a sense of belonging to a like-minded group, with shared experiences, visions, and expectations of life. This is separatism, but not evil in itself. Setting the races against each other is evil. That is precisely what coercive legislation has done.

Immigrants and minority groups were led to believe that all their problems could and should be remedied by governmental action. Their supposed oppressors were subjected to further legislation to force them to adapt themselves to the newcomers. Bending over backwards to redress old inequities led to reverse discrimination. To be white was to be wrong. Some of racist persuasion might deem that fate poetic justice, but justice did not enter into it. Throughout history, at one time or another, one group has oppressed, abused, or feared another. All immigrants, all minorities, have suffered disadvantages simply because they are outsiders, not yet integral parts of the surrounding society. That integration must involve adaptation, to some extent, by people wishing to partake to the fullest in that society.

Instead, the instantly easy life, without expenditure of individual energies to earn it, continued to be expected as a right. Demands were made for open entry into higher education, for members of minorities, regardless of past academic performance. Classrooms became overcrowded, freshmen were enrolled who lacked the ability to cope with the curriculum, and a deterioration ensued in the quality of education. The pursuit of the sort of knowledge which a university is best able to give became secondary to political, sexist and racist ideologies now glorified as 'Studies' degree programs. Educational authorities, afraid of being labelled racists, awarded BAs to students whose work would have failed formerly. Students who fomented militant disruptions on campus were allowed free rein, so that these troublemakers would not shout the feared epithet. The BA was considerably devalued during this period; now nearly everyone could have that piece of paper. It no longer guaranteed to prospective employers that a standard of achievement, of excellence, had been attained by the holder. The 'Open Entry' idea had backfired with a vengeance.

Follies increased. Unmarried mothers on welfare went on irresponsibly producing large broods of children. Why take contraceptive precautions when the welfare program would give you an additional allowance for each child? Taxes went on rising, and many young middle-class couples postponed having families, not to pursue careers in many cases, but because, despite both partners working, they couldn't afford to have children. An unmarried welfare mother who had produced ten children defiantly said in a television interview: 'You gonna tell me how many children I can have?' Many long-suffering taxpayers must have silently cried, 'Yes, I will, as long as I'm the one who has to pay for them'. Large numbers of these children grew up in the streets, without parental supervision. There were the memorable occasions when welfare recipients rallied to demand an annual allowance of $100 each so that they could buy Christmas presents, and several hundred dollars annually for new clothes for each child and adult, which was more than most of the working-class families could afford to spend on themselves. There appeared cases of up to four generations of the same family still on welfare. For them, welfarism as a way of life had produced a hereditary disease. In giving up dominion over their own lives, they were enslaved.

Pseudo-intellectuals' collective guilt

For a while, some of the middle-class and the pseudo-intellectuals, in a delusion of collective guilt, wallowed in masochistic behaviour. The cry of the liberal was 'Mea culpa, mea culpa, mea maxima culpa'. A new fashion for the misguided wealthy appeared — 'Radical Chic'. It was considered quite a coup to have a Black Panther (a member of a

[219]

highly militant racist organisation) come to a cocktail party to sneer at and loftily harangue all present with their supposed history of crimes against his people. He might, nonetheless, graciously permit them to expiate their sins partially by opening their cheque-books and writing hefty donations for The Cause. Incredible as it may seem, some people were sufficiently bamboozled to nearly fall over one another in their haste to pay.

In Manhattan in particular, the 'haves' and 'have-nots' are crowded into one small bit of geography. They often live in separate areas — except for welfare families who were put up in such elegant hotels as the Waldorf-Astoria because no other accommodation was judged as suitable and available for them at that time; the taxpayer who couldn't afford a meal at the Waldorf was paying for someone else to live in a suite there — but they share the streets, constantly exacerbating the fear and loathing between them. In that constant proximity, something had to give. It did — violent, random crime increased to a devastating degree. Used to demanding and receiving money from the government, who took it from the taxpayers, it was not a huge leap to view the *individual* taxpayer as a lamb for slaughter, without waiting for the state to act as intermediary. From accosting people in the street with 'Gimme a quarter, man', came the escalation to rampant disrespect for the lives and property of others. If someone had more than you or had something you wanted, you had a right to take it from them. They *owed* you. This attitude was a direct result of the welfare state.

Welfare dependence produces cripples

Welfare is supposed to mean a faring well, for both the individual and society, but the opposite was created. The time to teach a man to swim is not when he is drowning. But to withhold from him the knowledge of how to swim, then throw him in the water, and when he's going down for the third time, rescue him and expect his heartfelt gratitude, is unreasonable. People would learn to swim, would learn to build rafts, if government did not destroy initiative through welfare and taxation. No one is done a favour by being made dependent on others permanently; only cripples can be produced by that method. Many abdicate responsibility for their own lives because the state ruins their ability to take care of themselves. On either end of the spectrum, people are damaged — the producers in society through heavy taxation, the non-producers by being kept that way through the expectation that someone will *have* to take care of them. When people feel they have no control over their lives, some will sink into passivity, their outlook and existence increasingly dull and narrow. Others feel that, if they have no control over their lives, they cannot be held

[220]

responsible for their actions. Whatever they may do, it isn't their fault, it is society's. This view provides a justification for violence against others. Whether the response to womb-to-tomb subsidy is passive or violent, neither can produce a healthy society; in concert, they are deadly.

The state creates incompetence

The state treats people like children, not as responsible, intelligent adults, with the result that many people believe themselves to be helpless and uncomprehending. Nanny knows best. If you tell a child often enough that he is stupid and incompetent, you frequently end up with a stupid, incompetent child. Social workers interfere in the sovereignty of the family, acting without a display of doubt that they always know what is best. They, like bureaucrats and politicians, somehow forget (or would like us to forget) that they also are only human and subject to error. We all know the horrors the mistakes of these 'experts' have caused. The way to Hell is surely paved with good intentions, but also with the will to power over others, and power once held is never easily relinquished. I note the words Shakespeare gives to Cassius in *Julius Caesar*: 'I cannot tell what you and other men think of this life, but for my single self I had as lief not be as live to be in awe of such a thing as I myself'. We can learn, if permitted to do so, from our mistakes, and can then become the best judges of our own interests. Protect fools from their folly and you only fill the world with fools.

The welfare state, that is, socialism, is a major cause of violent crime, the devaluation of higher education, the destruction of morale and moral values, the weakening of the family, and is the curse of the working and middle classes. Perhaps London can learn from the mistakes of another once-great city, 3,400 miles across the Atlantic. Look at all the people sleeping in cardboard boxes or under the railway bridge by Embankment tube; look at all the homeless while council-owned buildings in the thousands are kept empty and locked; look at the impoverished elderly; look at the rising crime rate and the rate of taxation. Socialism has not worked; it will not work, here or anywhere else. It has failed as a means of advancing prosperity and improving living conditions wherever it has been tried, whether that be the Soviet Union, or South America, or the so-called Third World countries. On the contrary, it has caused the collapse of productivity and a deterioration of the economy.

A return to the feeling that one's destiny is in one's own hands will breed a new sense of self-respect and responsibility. Collectivist state planning has led to the loss of individual freedom. In doing so, it has also severely damaged the individual's belief in himself. Bureaucratic interference and destructive taxation must be abolished if the entrepreneurial spirit is to be revived in Britain. The complacency and despondency, the inertia and inefficiency that plague so many aspects of life in this country need not permanently remain to sap her strength.

A free market can produce wealth not necessarily only for the few, but for the many. The more people allowed to participate in an entrepreneurial revival, the stronger the prospects for success. At present, successful entrepreneurs are viewed with mistrust and suspicion; there is envy of these achievers and little desire or even belief in the possibility of emulating such success. The anti-Americanism of some in Britain, delivered as if from a height of moral superiority, is ultimately grounded in that base feeling — jealousy.

Socialists have promoted the view that capitalism causes poverty for the many, fosters materialism, and lacks compassion. But the world stage shows it is socialism that produces poverty. There is nothing wrong with pursuing material growth. Growth and compassion are not necessarily mutually exclusive. In any event, we need only examine the methods and results of socialism to discover that it is based on coercion and is morally bankrupt. There is no 'compassion' when a person or the state or any other body forces someone else to pay for what he or it feels should be supported. Compassion, like love, can be felt and given only voluntarily, not ordered by legislation. 'I believe this to be a good thing, therefore *you*, not I, must pay for it' — so ordains the socialist.

There is nothing inherently evil about money. People who possess it are not automatically going to burn in Hell when they die. People who have little or no money are not made virtuous by pecuniary lack. I have never known a 'have-not' who did not want to become a 'have'. Do the virtuous, noble, down-trodden poor suddenly become wicked oppressors if their lot in life improves?

These are the words of a man born poor, who valued hard work and education:

> You cannot bring about prosperity by discouraging thrift;
> You cannot strengthen the weak by weakening the strong;
> You cannot help the wage-earner by pulling down the wage-payer;
> You cannot further the brotherhood of man by encouraging class hatred;
> You cannot help the poor by destroying the rich;
> You cannot keep out of trouble by spending more than you earn;
> You cannot build character and courage by taking away a man's initiative and independence;

> You cannot help men permanently by doing for them
> what they could and should do for themselves.

These words repudiate all that socialism stands for. They were written 120 years ago by Abraham Lincoln, a libertarian in spirit.

Forget a return to 'Victorian' values; that term only conjures up visions of the workhouse and repressed sexuality. The New Right re-asserts instead the values of the immigrants. There lies the key to a restoration of this nation's prosperity and the recovery of her courage, determination, and dignity.

CHRISTOPHER KNIGHT

The last essay in this group is an assessment by an academic analyst of the influence, if any, of the New Right on one major sphere of public policy, economic activity and human experience — education. The author properly does not exhibit his personal judgement for or against the New Right.

Christopher Knight was born in 1949 of working-class parents in Tunbridge Wells. His father was a telephone operator, later supervisor, in Sevenoaks; his mother was a waitress, school cook and paper factory worker.

He was educated at Wildernesse Secondary School, Sevenoaks, West Kent College of Further Education, and London University, at which he graduated as Bachelor of Education in 1972. A dissertation on school accountability (to parents) and performance appraisal (of teachers) earned an MA in Educational Administration in 1982. Since 1984 he has been researching into 'The Sociology of Educational Conservatism' for a doctorate at the Polytechnic of the South Bank.

He has written on educational management for the learned and technical journals.

His essay records his impressions so far in the first of his three-year doctoral course. He reviews the strands of New Right thought, the reasons why the New Right emerged in education thought and policy, whether the school of thought is new, and its influence.

He says the New Right has emerged as a reaction against collectivism. Its central doctrine, that the individual generally manages his affairs better than governments, appeals especially to the lower-middle and working classes.

Two central ideas — parental influence with state schools and parental power to escape if dissatisfied — comprise a populist appeal combining Tory themes of family, standards, etc. with aggressive neo-liberalism.

New Right radicalism would dramatically change the state system to competitive private autonomy with school income dependent on the number of pupils attracted.

19

THE NEW RIGHT AND EDUCATION

CHRISTOPHER KNIGHT

> Before he [Heath] finally settled on the policies and the team
> with which he was to fight the 1970 general election . . . he
> experimented with a great many ideas, and with a number of
> people . . . he gave full rein to the burgeoning radical wing of
> the party, and . . . a position and a base within the Party which
> they were never to lose, and which left them with consider-
> able power and influence in 1974. . . .
> Patrick Cosgrave, *Margaret Thatcher, Prime Minister*, 1979.

> The breakdown in consensus politics in some Western
> democracies has led to the rise of a New Right which has no
> hesitation in attempting to shape society according to its own
> cherished image. The current battle of ideas is, in part, a
> battle between visions of the future: a clash of utopias.
> Geoffrey Hodgson, *The Democratic Economy*, 1984.

The burgeoning of the New Right in British politics has attracted the
attention of the left as well as the right: economists, social and
political theorists and sociologists of education.

In this personal assessment of the New Right and education I shall
suggest, from the perspective of a school teacher and student of
educational administration, some of the implications for education
policy of recent moves from the right to encourage consumerism and
the application of market pressures to the control and organisation of
state schooling. How, during the last 15 years, has 'conservative'
educational rhetoric and argument influenced the pursuit by the 1979
and 1983 Governments of initiatives to extend choice in education
and to raise standards in state schools?

Ideas, and four questions

What are the various strands of thought of the New Right? Why and
when did the New Right in education emerge in Britain? Is it entirely

[225]

a 'new' school of thought? What has been its impact on the formation of education policy?

The two strands commonly identified within the New Right, neo-liberalism and ' authoritarianism' (the advocacy of government based on an established system of authority, rather than on explicit or tacit consent) are seen by critics as complementary rather than contradictory. A characteristic of both is the confident assertion of the nature of the Good Society. This is significant because between 1970 and 1985 'education' has been defined relatively in terms of 'discipline', 'standards', 'examinations' and 'parental choice'. But such relative definitions are intrinsically arbitrary. They have largely emanated from the 'New Conservative' rhetoric (the minimal state, the open market, the responsible family) which has dominated the political arena of the 1970s and 1980s. In these terms the New Right has been a reaction to collectivism. Its central doctrine, that the individual generally manages his or her affairs better than governments can for them, and that efficiency is to be found more often in privately-run enterprises than in bureaucracies, struck a new mood in the country.

For many people — especially the lower-middle and working classes — such a belief was a personal rediscovery, for it made life in some way newly tolerable. No longer could 'officialdom' disguise its weaknesses. People would no longer so readily accept the 'wisdom' of the 'professionals'. The conspiracy of the 'bureaucracy' against the common man was exposed.

While the expression 'the New Right' is used to denote the recent resurgence of Conservative and anti-socialist thought in the UK, USA and France, it is sometimes more often applied to describe individuals and groups who are sceptical of the 'blanket welfare state'. Indeed, the foundations of the philosophy of the New Right (as espoused by a range of people from academically-minded liberals like Professor Jack Wiseman and Arthur Seldon to Neo-Conservative politicians led by Sir Keith Joseph and Margaret Thatcher) is a radicalism of practical Manchester Liberal descent. Here the New Right have resurrected many of the ideas and approaches of 19th century liberalism, sharing a resolute individualism and a commitment to the supreme virtues of personal ownership, consumer choice in markets and minimal government described as laissez-faire. Pervading everything is the Victorian watchword 'economy'.

It has been against this background that what I shall term the New Right 'intelligentsia' — represented by, amongst others, varying institutions like the Institute of Economic Affairs (IEA), the Centre for Policy Studies (CPS), the Adam Smith Institute (ASI), the Social Affairs Unit (SAU), the Conservative Philosophy Group, the Salisbury Group, the Freedom Association and specifically in education the

[226]

Friends of the Education Voucher (FEVER) — has made appeal to the very large 'centre group' in Britain of people who have strong views on law and order, morality, personal enterprise and responsibility, educational standards, discipline and national pride. And certainly since the late 1960s an increasing number of intellectual and political figures have proposed setting off firmly in a 'new' direction, on a new programme of action to constitute a post-socialist society, a trumpet-call for the Good Society which would restore free choice, individualism and standards of excellence to their rightful place as central values in the life of the people.

Thesis and antithesis

Professor G. H. Bantock, one of the most prolific defenders of the traditionalist approach to education, has argued in his recent *Studies in the History of Educational Theory* (1984) that 'educational discourse takes its colour from the priorities and concerns of its time'. I suggest that the gestation period for the ascendancy of the educational ideas of the New Right can be found in the period of Conservative opposition (1964 — 1970), which culminated in the first education Black Paper (1969). In this and subsequent Black Papers on the internal deficiencies of state education one can see the desire to preserve the traditional curriculum against aggressive mediocratisation. In these years books and pamphlets were published asserting the threat to educational standards from the egalitarian and social-engineering aims of the left's education programme. Significant amongst these writings were Angus Maude's *Good Learning* (1964) and Dr Rhodes Boyson's collection *Right Turn* (1970). Both are important since they are early examples of work which challenged the consensus of so-called 'progressive thinking' that was seen as controlling much of the thought of the country since the war and weakening both the nation's enterprise and sense of unity.

The New Right's educational agenda

The theme of the educational atavism of the New Right has been a defence of education as a creative force in society, a stress on the role of professional educators and their specialist studies in preserving 'excellence' and 'standards', in expressing and transmitting the achievements of the past, in defending and protecting the child from ignorance and exploitation, in warding off a collapse into barbarism. Such arguments are currently being refurbished by Sir Keith Joseph. Briefly, people are naturally unequal. All known societies have hierarchies with stratification by function and status, but it need not lead to class antagonisms. So, rather than seek an unnatural and

[227]

forced equality, we should arrange diverse educational channels whereby each individual may achieve 'functional excellence' in his own sphere.

There is controversy on both left and right whether we are witnessing a radically new departure in educational practice in Britain. Although the New Right has strongly supported the reform of the state education system, its central strands do not indicate a 'unitary model', and it would be wrong to give the impression that the spokesmen of the New Right speak with a single voice. There has been considerable disagreement, for example, on how the currency of education, in the sense of curriculum balance and school-leaving certification, is to be restored. I suggest that the promotion by the New Right of policies which one might broadly term 'educational conservatism' (the formulation of initiatives which have sought radical changes in LEA control and in school and teacher autonomy over the curriculum) has been marked by a gradual realisation that they can be made only if applied universally and not left to local experiment.

The principal items of the educational agenda of the New Right include:

— the restoration of the currency of educational credentials (the New Right has been keen to stem the inflationary tide of credentials/qualifications);

— the return to traditional values in education by the removal of curriculum 'clutter';

— the raising of school standards, partly to be achieved by improving teacher quality, the removal of incompetent school staffs and the reform of 16-plus examinations;

— the retrieval of education from its 'capture' by LEA bureaucracies, schools and teacher unions;

— the creation of real parental choice and participation in education;

— the creation of a 'market' in education to allow parents to choose the school they want and to escape from those they don't (FEVER's campaign for a school voucher); and

— the reform of the school curriculum to give more emphasis to the requirements of industry.

Behind such radical changes lies the central argument of its promoters: that in contrast to the popular notion that 'public' education would serve the 'public interest', the disagreeable evidence is that it creates wide scope for political distortion, bureaucratic empire-building and teacher trade union self-interest at the expense of the public — the taxpayer, elector and parent; and that a hundred years of growing state education has created much failure — of schools, of little reward for the taxpayer's pound, and of children's chances in employment.

The New Right in education therefore seeks, amongst other aims, a progressive reduction in taxpayer financing of education.

Surrounding the calls for the education voucher and more parental influence on school governing bodies (two central though, to date, not unifying themes of the New Right in education) is a populist appeal which combines the resonant themes of Toryism (nation, family, duty, authority, standards, traditionalism) with the aggressive themes of a revived neo-liberalism (self-interest, competitive individualism, anti-statism). Both the 'education voucher' and 'parental influence at school' lobbies display a strong emphasis on a more traditional ideology: namely, a concern for the virtues of the market, competition, elitism, individual initiative and the inequities of state intervention and bureaucracy.

This New Right populism in education has made a particular appeal to people (the technocrats, the 'new model' bourgeoisie and the salariat) defined by their education and their occupational role as the gearbox of an increasingly technical society. Many such people have themselves risen out of the working class; they have been attracted by the ideas of self-help and have sought to rise out of their social origins.

The ascendancy of the New Right in education

Since 1945 some of the main ideas of the left, especially egalitarianism, have been under heavy intellectual challenge. This challenge has come largely from libertarian philosophers like F. A. Hayek and Michael Oakeshott, many of them with personal experience of European socialism and the fascist reaction to it. In its call for 'liberation from socialism' the New Right has attacked fashionable collectivist doctrine and appealed to all those (teachers, academics, economists, and people in the church and industry) who have failed to understand the strength of the moral case for a free society. This appeal is of crucial importance if the New Right is to be seen almost as a religious crusade akin to the 'moral majority' in America.

In education the New Right's resurgence is partly explained by the reaction against the 'permissiveness' of the 1960s, where the youth culture, though promoted as a way of liberation, was increasingly perceived by the middle-aged and middle classes as servitude to sin and sociology, and by a sharp change in public attitudes to schooling, which increasingly saw 'child-centredness', 'free-expression' and 'mixed-ability' teaching as harmful to many children and partly to blame for rising pupil illiteracy as well as for the pitiful performance of British industry through the 1970s and into the 1980s. Such perceptions as these were the soil in which New Right ideas on education could grow.

But the shift to the right in education is not too easily located. This is because here in Britain the 'new' intellectual right is neither a 'school' nor a conspiracy, whereas in the USA the New Right is well-financed and organised. Rather, its spokesmen are part of a 'loose nexus' of individuals and bodies that associate with one another on an *ad hoc* basis and who sometimes contribute writings to one another's journals, although they may also differ on fundamental issues as do, for example, the liberals of the IEA and the conservatives of the Salisbury Group.

The strands of the New Right in education may therefore be traced in the emergence of such publications as early 1960s IEA Hobart Papers, Research Reports and books; the *Swinton Journal* (Swinton College Group, 1967 to 1973) carrying early essays by Angus Maude and Rhodes Boyson; the books published under the banner of the Constitutional Book Club (Churchill Press) between 1970 and 1975, perhaps the most influential being Dr Boyson's collection of essays *Education: Threatened Standards* (1972) and Caroline Cox's and John Marks' *The Rape of Reason* (1975); pamphlets from the National Council for Educational Standards (NCES) (1970 onwards); the writings of the Education Study Group of the CPS since 1980, the most important of which has been *The Right to Learn* (1982); as well as the more recent 'free-market' publications of the SAU and the ASI.

Mapping the route of the right

The impact of such groups on education policy has been variable. In law the IEA is an 'educational and research trust' and its activity is to publish papers on the workings of markets. It is very much committed therefore to the arena of political economy. The IEA has been influential to the extent that it has been instrumental in pushing 'economics' into 'new' areas. Indeed, it has produced original, seminal elements in the 'New Right' approach. Here it has contributed an analysis of three aspects of markets: the principle of freedom of choice, state monopolies and private monopolies. But while politicians are 'receivers' of information, the IEA itself is non-political: it does not accept contract research nor receive taxpayers' money. A major achievement has been to research public opinion on welfare services; the IEA was the first group to do this (Harris and Seldon, 1963 to 1978), and it supplied the strongest evidence (based on questions that were *priced*) of popular preferences for market welfare. The IEA feels it is close to the opinions of the 'silent majority', and through its journal, *Economic Affairs*, it has continued to promote debate on

[230]

state monopolies (including education and medicine) and carried arguments that employees in public activity should push for the removal of state domination of their employment. An interesting example is the article by Andrew Melnyk (1985) on teachers and the harmful consequences *on them* of state control.

On education policy one must cite the deep influence of Professor E. G. West's *Education And The State* (IEA, 1965), which re-examined the history of education since the 1870 Education Act, on Dr Boyson's views on education vouchers and loans in the first *Black Paper* (1969) and the later *Battle Lines for Education* (1973). The influence of the IEA in debating 'choice' in education may be seen in at least three IEA tracts — Professor Alan Peacock's and Professor Jack Wiseman's *Education for Democrats* (1964), which opened the contemporary British debate on vouchers and loans, Professor Harry Ferns' *Towards an Independent University* (1969), which precursed the development of the independent University at Buckingham, and Professor S. R. Dennison's *Choice in Education* (1984), a remarkably astringent analysis of the political economy of state and private education. In their individual ways these and other IEA papers point to the perils of state monopoly in education, where the major danger is that it will pursue objectives which are politically determined, removed from the wishes of the consumers who are forced to pay for it. The IEA has been less involved with the internal issues of educational standards, a debate carried forward fervently by the CPS, the SAU, and the ASI.

Whereas the market economists of the IEA have argued for *exits* from state education where it is unacceptable, perhaps it has been in the publications from the CPS Education Study Group, together with Dr Digby Anderson's Social Affairs Unit that the New Right's thrust to open out to teachers, parents and politicians the intellectual debate on standards within state education has been most effectively achieved.

Unlike the CPS Education Study Group and the SAU, the Adam Smith Institute has made direct policy proposals to government. Its Omega Report, *Education Policy*, contains a series of initiatives which its authors (including Dr Anderson, Baroness Cox, Professor Antony Flew, Professor David Marsland and Lawrence Norcross) offer as a 'route map' of the future for the Conservative government. Indeed, the report suggests the largest and possibly most innovative policy programme in education ever devised, even though it is in part a somewhat derivative rehearsal of the argument as earlier formulated by other New Right authors.

In total the arguments of the New Right comprise a radicalism which, if implemented, would dramatically change the administration of the schooling system, and point the way to competitive, deregulated educational provision, with a much increased degree of

[231]

individual parental freedom and responsibility. It includes both tax changes to allow more choice in education and to encourage exit from the state sector and proposals which would give more power to boards of elected parent governors, and would make school funding dependent upon the numbers of pupils attracted. The government of education would be radically reformed, with a consistent and continual extension of a rolling programme on privatisation in education.

Present and future trends

A number of the manifold changes to the schooling system proposed over the past 15 years have been, and continue to be, made under the strong influence of the ideas of the New Right. But this is not necessarily a marked departure from earlier periods. Although some aspects of policy can be interpreted as expressing the latest doctrines of New Right political economists (like vouchers and tax rebates), other aspects (like matching the curriculum more closely to the requirements of industry) display strong continuities with the practice of previous governments. What we now see are more precise changes being made in action by central government. It is resources which now dominate the education debate. Certainly since 1979, a more interventionist Government has been seen to nudge LEAs and schools towards a more utilitarian view of schooling. Moreover, some of Sir Keith Joseph's utterances during the 1984-1985 teachers' pay dispute indicate that if firmer (not to say rigid) controls emerge, they are more likely to do so through a resource-based route (books and staffing allocation) rather than as a direct result of concerns with curricula.

The emerging utilitarianism of the right, represented by Sir Keith Joseph at the DES, is now plainly in the ascendancy. The principles and structure of the 'progressive' mode in education have been successfully challenged. In their place has been restored a technicist approach. The New Right in education now has confidence and panache. Geoffrey Hodgson's remark that 'The philosophers of the New Right now walk the corridors of power' may suggest that, if events until May 1985 are anything to go by, the educational world is likely to face continuing calls from the New Right for schools to be directed by the forces of the market. Yet there are a number of obstacles to this happening. First, and most importantly, the various right interest groups organised to achieve drastic reductions in the state monopoly of education are not monolithic: they do not all agree over the same priorities for reform (the SAU, for example, does not favour a return to grammar schools). Second, almost every 'idea' (vouchers, loans, wider parental choice, access to private education) championed by the New Right since 1970 has inevitably been obstructed by the administrator's fear of a loss of control and the teacher's fear of uncertainty of employment.

What seems likely is that the impact of the New Right on education will increasingly take the form of 'alliances'. Educational change transpires when there is a strong alliance between interest groups (including consumers), the educational press and senior civil servants. This tripartite linkage is most important for the successful evolution and implementation of any educational innovation. Some recent casualties, notably the education voucher (whose temporary demise was announced in 1983) and increasing the parent membership of school governing bodies (strongly opposed by the teacher unions in 1984), have each indicated that when the linkage is broken the political 'death' of an educational reform is almost assured. The linkage may be broken because participants fear ideas involving immediate, massive and uncertain modifications to school organisation and finance.

If this is true I suggest that we should not let the issue of the voucher dominate the discussion by the New Right of educational reform. Rather we should all recognise that, while political reasons often prevail (the voucher might, for example, come to be seen by teachers as a lesser evil than central government control of curricula), it is ultimately the consumer that counts as the arbiter of change.

VI

THE BURGEONING NEW RIGHT

CHRIS R. TAME

The final essay argues the widening range of thought that has reacted against the intellectual dominance of statism — from economics and political philosophy through sociology and psychology to ethics and aesthetics, novels and science fiction.

Chris Tame was born in 1949 in Enfield, Middlesex, of working-class parents. His father was a process engraver and a Father of the Chapel (shop steward) of his trade union.

He was educated at a state primary and secondary schools, and graduated in American Studies from the University of Hull.

He has worked at the IEA, as Manager of the Alternative Bookshop and for ITV Channel 4's Diverse Reports.

He is the founder of the Libertarian Alliance and Secretary of the Adam Smith Club, writes for numerous periodicals, and has appeared on radio and TV to present the libertarian case.

In his reflective, philosophic essay Chris Tame says the New Right should be rechristened the New Enlightenment because it echoes the English and Scottish Enlightenment of the 18th century. He reviews the main elements in the New Enlightenment and its main thinkers.

He explains why the liberal counter-revolution was delayed until after the second world war, why the Chicago school of liberal economists, who tested the results of government intervention by quantitative studies, attracted more attention than the American liberals (Mises, Kirzner, Rothbard), whose doubts about mathematical methods are increasingly being vindicated by a growing number of younger 'Austrian' economists in Britain and the USA.

The libertarian advance is being reflected in and sustained by popular culture, with a new emphasis on individuality against authority. Socialist writing has degenerated from confident certainty in inexorable victory to doom-mongering, conservative conservationism, and opposition to change.

The 18th century Enlightenment and the New Enlightenment are linked by the common inspiration of progress, science and optimism. Scientists, social and natural, promote truth and progress. Politicians, bureaucrats and interest groups are retrogressive: they inhibit change to preserve their power.

20

THE NEW ENLIGHTENMENT

CHRIS R. TAME

Since the end of World War II there has emerged in almost every academic discipline or realm of thought a growing tide of opinion which we might categorise for the moment under the label — suggested by Edward Pearce — of the 'non-left'. Whether in economics or political philosophy, ethics or aesthetics, sociology or psychology, and even in artistic endeavour, there have arisen powerful challenges to the intellectual hegemony long held by collectivist, statist and anti-capitalist thinking.

Left and right: the unhelpful dichotomy

I used Edward Pearce's phrase hesitantly, since the language of 'left' and 'right' is profoundly unhelpful. Not only have the terms reversed their meaning (pro-free market, liberal ideas were originally categorised as 'left'), this language also conceals a massive and fraudulent conceptual package deal. Thus, a group of collectivist and anti-individualist doctrines — national socialism, fascist corporatism, racial collectivism, and anti-semitism — are lumped together as 'right-wing' with their polar opposites — liberalism, individualism, and capitalism. This has indeed proved a most useful weapon for Marxist and socialist opponents of liberalism, who seem well aware of Lenin's old dictum that 'once you have labelled something you don't have to argue with it'. Liberalism and liberals are constantly being smeared as somehow 'reactionary', and linked with unpleasant and inhumane doctrines.

Indeed, every few years the term 'the New Right' also gets dusted off and applied to some school of thought that socialist writers or journalists have suddenly deigned to notice. In my lifetime I have thus seen it applied to:

- advocates of *real* Burkean conservatism like the American Russell Kirk;
- the half-liberal, half-authoritarian conservatism of William F. Buckley;

[237]

- the religious fundamentalism and social authoritarianism of the 'Moral Majority';
- the free-market economics of Milton Friedman and the Institute of Economic Affairs;
- the National Socialism of the National Front in Britain;
- the ex-Marxist French New Philosophers;
- the rabidly anti-immigrant Front National of J. M. Le Pen in France;
- the Europe-wide quasi-Nietzschean organisation GRECE;
- contemporary libertarianism and anarcho-capitalism;
- sociobiologists;
- researchers into genetics or intelligence (many of whom are socialists!);
- advocates of racism;
- those disillusioned former American welfare statists (inaccurately) termed 'neo-conservatives' like Irving Kristol;
- the High Toryism of Roger Scruton and other *Salisbury Review* writers . . ..

It should be amply clear why the whole language of left and right should be disposed of *in toto*.

The new enlightenment

A far more informative label for the post-war liberal revival would be 'the new liberalism' or the now widely used neologism 'libertarianism'. A phrase I find particularly suggestive, however, is "The New Enlightenment". Liberalism was born in the Enlightenment of the 18th century. The concepts of individual liberty, individualism, the free market, and rationalism crystallised in the intellectual systems of Adam Smith and the Scottish Enlightenment, the rationalism of David Hume, and the natural-rights political philosophy of John Locke. The myriad views I shall discuss resemble nothing so much as a new statement of the ideals and aspirations of the original Enlightenment.

The fall and rise of liberalism

The concept of the New Enlightenment is also particularly fruitful in drawing attention to the question of *why* classical liberalism declined, *why* it was deposed by Marxism and various forms of socialism in the 20th century, and *why* the hopes and promises of the original Enlightenment were not fulfilled. The answer, as I argued in my essay

[238]

'The Revolution of Reason', lay within the very ambiguities of Enlightenment liberalism itself, its inconsistencies and inner contradictions. Moreover, the contemporary revival of liberalism can very much be seen as the belated attempt to resolve those ambiguities and to restate systematic liberalism without any of its fateful errors; in the words of Michael Polanyi, in *Knowing and Being*:

> to restate the great work of the Enlightenment without danger of the traps that have so disastrously ensnared its progress in the present century

Science and freedom

Perhaps one of the most fatal ambiguities of classical liberalism lay in its concept of science. It justly celebrated the achievements of science, the liberation to be found in man's mastery over nature. But unfortunately the ethos of *science* became transformed into the ethos of *scientism*, in reality a profoundly *unscientific* attempt to transfer the methodology of one scientific discipline to another, ignoring the crucial and distinctive attributes of their respective subjects. In the study of man and society, rational consciousness and free will hence became ruled out virtually *a priori*. The liberal ideal of the autonomous individual was subverted in various ways by the predominance of social sciences that ruled out of court the validity of introspection, and were characterised by a militant reductionism* and determinism,* by methodoligical collectivism* and holism,* and by historicism.* This vision of science was embodied not merely in Marxism's claim to be 'scientific socialism', a science of society, but the idea that science endorsed or implied the concept of a 'scientifically' controlled society. (Words asterisked are explained in the Glossary, page 247.)

One of the major roots of the New Enlightenment and the new liberalism has thus been a sustained critique of scientism by Michael Polanyi and Karl Popper. Polanyi, a noted physical scientist before he turned his attention to the philosophy of science and to the humane sciences, explored in a number of seminal works 'an alternative ideal of knowledge, quite generally' (as he put it in his *Personal Knowledge*). His task of 'conceptual reform' rejected not merely the 'scourge of physicalism' in psychology and the life sciences — the idea that human beings are irrevocably determined by internal or external forces — but a reassessment of the very 'conception of knowing' and its reconstruction upon the basis of 'knowing as an active comprehension of the things known' and 'the *personal participation* of the knower in all acts understanding'. His philosophy constituted not merely an answer to the materialistic,* determinist* and scepticist*

[239]

positions which had resulted in the 'moral inversions' of nihilism* and totalitarian doctrines (whether National Socialist or Marxist international socialist). He also drew out the mistaken conception of science that undergirded the concepts of the 'scientific' planning of society and economy, by his view of 'tacit knowledge' — knowledge that cannot be formally written down, or can only be expressed in the terms of action. It was this epistemological* approach which thus led to his critique of various forms of alleged planning, whether the democratic variety of Britain (a muddle) or the Soviet form (tyranny). I use the word 'alleged' since, as he demonstrated in his seminal studies — *The Contempt of Freedom* and *The Logic of Liberty* — of what occurs in the Soviet system, such planning is a myth, an impossibility. The sort of knowledge necessary to make such planning possible is outside the reach of the would-be planners.

A similar, but arguably even more impressive and systematic, philosophy was to emanate from another refugee to Britain, Sir Karl Popper. Again, the failings of much of the mainstream of European philosophic and scientific thought provided the stimulus, in the words of John Gray in his essay 'The Liberalism of Karl Popper', to 'a defence of liberalism . . . which gains much of its power from the fact that . . . it is embedded in a comprehensive philosophical perspective on the nature of human knowledge, rationality and freedom of thought and action'. Revolutionary ideologies like Marxism and fascism were based, in Popper's view, on pre-scientific and irrational modes of thought (although disguised by the mantle of science) that he designated as holism* and historicism.* His case against holistic 'social engineering' stems directly from his case against holistic methodology in social science. Just as holistic methodology ignores the inevitable selectivity of observation and attempts the logically impossible task of studying social wholes, holistic social engineering attempts to centralise knowledge. This attempt is both epistemologically impossible, but also inherently coercive and systematically self-defeating, since it walls itself off from real information and the corrective process of criticism. Popper's 'falsificationist' and 'error elimination' approach sees knowledge as an evolutionary process. It is a view remarkably analogous to the functioning of the free market process.

The autonomous individual

Since, as Ellen M. Wood has put it in *The Mind and Politics*, 'a conscious or unconscious conception of human nature underlies every choice of social or political values', it is not surprising that the success of particular political doctrines has been intimately associated with the success of related ideas in psychology and social theory. Both Polanyi and Popper rejected the deterministic or reductionist view of

[240]

man, the idea that man's behaviour is overwhelmingly dictated by forces beyond his control, whether biological, racial, psychological, social, historical or economic. Their colleague Arthur Koestler similarly carried on a sustained critique of determinism within psychology and the life sciences and a vindication of human creativity and free will.

At the same time there also arose a broad movement in reaction against what Koestler called the 'ratomorphic' image of man. Under the banner of 'humanistic psychology' there arose a myriad school of thinkers and therapists who rejected determinism. The most distinguished figure in this movement was undoubtedly Abraham Maslow who outlined a new 'psychology of being' that did not deny our introspective experience of free will and, moreoever, built upon the pyschology of the healthy individual, the 'self actualising' individual, as an ideal. This temper ran through many schools, too numerous to mention here. Although all possess their fair share of weaknesses and errors, they all embodied a common liberatory and voluntarist image of man.

Although many of the humanistic psychologists and therapists had no political orientation, or even an anti-liberal one, many were well aware, as Maslow put it, their 'new world view' implicitly contained 'a new image of society and of all its institutions'. Maslow moved from an early socialism to an almost completely libertarian position by the time of his death. His disciple and biographer, Frank G. Goble, was an outright libertarian, while a growing number of explicit libertarians have also added their weight to the ranks of humanistic psychology and have integrated and extended its insights into the broader framework of libertarianism. Here one would cite the work of New York University's Dr Thomas Szasz, or Dr Nathaniel Branden, and Dr Peter R. Breggin.

The anomalies of statism

Why did not these counter-collectivist, counter-statist revivals occur until after World War II? If liberalism declined essentially because of its own inherent weaknesses, why didn't liberals correct them earlier?

Liberalism did not entirely disappear before the War. Friedrich Hayek, Ludwig von Mises, Lionel Robbins, Wilhelm Röpke, Frank H. Knight and other economists wrote the bulk of their major work in that period, but gained mass followings and substantial influence only after it. The reason is largely that any intellectual system needs some sort of fair intellectual crack of the whip, so to speak, before it strengths and weaknesses can be fully assessed. Before we can properly refute any conjecture (to use Popper's terminology), it must be boldly conjectured.

Here we might find Professor Thomas Kuhn's concept of the paradigm particularly useful. Kuhn, a distinguished historian and philosopher of science (also influenced by Popper), argued in *The Structure of Scientific Revolutions* that science does not progress in the way most people assume. All scientific work takes place within what he called a paradigm, a fundamental conceptual world view. Scientific research is a working-out and application or extension of the fundamental assumptions of the paradigm. Since any scientific paradigm is more or less related to objective reality, 'anomalies' will occur, 'violations of expectations', facts that cannot satisfactorily be explained by the accepted paradigm. Eventually a new paradigm, arising out of the anomalies of its predecessor will become accepted (usually by a new generation of scholars).

Collectivism and statism, in their many and varied forms, have had their fair crack of the whip — usually more than metaphorically. National Socialism, the fascist corporate state, racial collectivism (both black and white), communist central planning, Conservative interventionism, Keynesianism, the mixed economy, the welfare state — every conceivable form of collectivism has been elaborated (often to a tedious degree) and put into practice. And the results, according to whatever variety has been adopted, have been mass exterminations, repression, famine, poverty, inflation and economic decline. In other words, collectivist *theories* have been given plenty of time to be put to the tests of reason, while collectivist *practices* have generated more and more 'anomalies', effects which are simply not explicable in terms of his own conceptual theory.

It is particularly notable that the American Chicago School developed its vindication of neo-classical economics from a background of highly detailed empirical studies of government intervention. As one leading Chicagoan, Yale Brozen, the author of many such studies, put it in his 1965 essay, 'The Revival of Classical Liberalism':

> Now that we have lived so long with government intervention in our economy, a few professional economists have begun to examine the results of that intervention. Some findings from these examinations are beginning to appear and affect, at least, the attitudes of an increasing number of scholars. If any resurgence of liberalism is occurring, this is the primary place it is apparent to me.

Chicago scholars and their intellectual comrades at the Institute of Economic Affairs in Britain have thus built up a massive library of evidence on the effects of minimum wages and rent controls, the nature and effects of regulatory agencies, prices and wages control and virtually every form of intervention and regulation. In Milton

[242]

Friedman's theoretical and historical analyses of the supply of money and its attempted regulation — by both Keynesians and pre-Keynesians — we have an impressive vindication of the quantity theory of money (monetarism as it is frequently, and unhelpfully, called). Black libertarian economists and sociologists like Thomas Sowell and Walter Williams have demolished the statist analysis of ethnic minorities and its disastrous policy proscriptions. The so-called 'public choice' or 'economics of politics' school, which grew out of the Chicago School, has taken the war into the enemy camp. Its analysis of the real nature and workings of the governmental, political and bureaucratic process further demonstrates the failings of the political process just as its forebears demonstrate the mythical nature of the much-touted 'market failure'.

It is probably this rootedness in empirical research which explains why it has been the Chicago School rather than the Austrian School which has received the most attention. The Austrian School, especially as manifest in such figures as the late Ludwig von Mises, in Israel Kirzner and Murray Rothbard, possesses a methodological approach at such variance with the predominant philosophical paradigm that it has really only started to gain a wider audience *after* the 'crisis period' of statism has become so apparent. The Austrian School is being increasingly considered as individuals seek a radical alternative to the established macro-economic and positivist* paradigm.

The crisis period of statism

That we are now deeply in the crisis period of statism is apparent from the fact that the exposers of its anomalies by no means come to their work with a prior commitment to libertarian values. Thus Professor Martin Anderson, who wrote a devastating and influential critique of America's urban renewal programme, started that study as a 'liberal' (in the American sense that is, an interventionist). It was precisely that objective study that generated his opposition, turned him into a libertarian and a career as one of the Republican Party's most influential policy experts.

A whole school of intellectuals emerged. Many of them had been involved in the creation or administration of statist policies, recognised their failure and subsequently called for a re-orientation in social policy toward the market mechanism. They have been confusingly and inaccurately called the 'neo-conservatives'. Writers like Irving Kristol, Nathan Glazer, Daniel P. Moynihan, (the Assistant Secretary of Labour under Presidents Kennedy and Johnson), Norman Podhoretz, and others frequently associated with the journals *Commentary* and *The Public Interest* are among the most notable figures in this group. If the 'neo-conservatives' rebelled against aspects of statism from the very centre of the statist paradigm and policy elite, the 'New Left' in America of the 1960s also largely arose as a reaction against statism and what it termed 'corporate liberalism' (the technocratic, paternalist corporate state). The failure of the New Left to resolve its own internal contradictions, however, led to its dissolution, to a decline in some cases simply back into old-style Marxism, into total disillusionment, or indeed to an incorporation into free market libertarianism.

Ayn Rand and the New Libertarian paradigm

One of the major figures of the New Enlightenment was the Russian-born American novelist and philosopher, Ayn Rand. In some respects she stands in relation to the rest of the New Enlightenment as Locke did to the original Enlightenment. In both her philosophic novels and in a large number of non-fiction essays she attempted to create a broad philosophic system following a consistent path from meta-physics, through epistemology to ethnics and politics, and not forgetting aesthetics. In essence her approach was neo-Aristotelian* (but attempting to correct the errors she perceived in its earlier forms). What made such an impact was her bold moral defence of capitalism. Rejecting the consequentialist,* utilitarian or Christian approaches manifested by writers like Hayek, Henry Hazlit or Paul Johnson, she defended what she saw as a scientific morality, an ethical egoism — the 'virtue of selfishness' as she termed it in the title of one book. Individuals have a right to exist for their own sake, the pursuit of their own happiness, and not for the sake of any alleged 'social good', or some fictitious collective or entity, whether the people, the nation, the race, the fatherland, or God.

Although initially Ayn Rand's approach was treated with scorn or contemptuous silence in academic circles, all her works were best-sellers and had an enormous impact among young people. Indeed, they have probably had numerically the biggest impact in converting young people to libertarian ideas. And there are now a substantial number of young professional academic philosophers, like Tibor Machan, Eric Mack, David Kelley, Douglas Den Uyl, Douglas Rasmussen and Leonard Peikoff, explaining and developing her approach. Even Robert Nozick, whose *Anarchy, State and Utopia* has so far proved to be the libertarian work which has received the most academic attention, while rejecting the basis of the Randian moral argument had to devote a serious critical analysis to it in his discussion 'On the Randian Argument'.

'Bliss It Was' . . . Some personal reflections

I have attempted to sketch some of the principal forces at work in the revival of libertarian ideas. My own experience is very much a micro version of the macro intellectual forces outlined. My own personal background was what is called 'working class', and I note with interest that many of my political colleagues share this socio-economic origin. Our *personal* experience of socialism and the welfare state undoubtedly enabled us to see through their bogus claims — and the ethos of social determinism.

It is difficult to convey the excitement I and many of my friends experienced as we discovered the diverse streams of libertarian thought which emerged in our lifetime. In his influential textbook, *Economics*, Paul Samuelson quoted Wordworth's famous lines about the French Revolution:

Bliss was it in that dawn to be alive
But to be young was very heaven.

For Samuelson these lines summed up his excitement in discovering Keynesian ideas. But Keynes' fallacious and feeble dilettantism pales into insignificance besides the synthesis emerging from the post-war New Enlightenment. Here were the clear explanations for the world we experienced, its successes and its many tragic failures and problems. Moreover, these were not barren unfalsifiable dogmatisms but a continuing 'research programme', in which a plenitude of different discoveries were unmistakenly pointing in the same direction and to the same conclusions. In a phrase, we were observing the emergence of a libertarian paradigm clearly destined to replace the statist paradigm.

The recovery of nerve

But this does not, perhaps, tell the full story. Why does not everyone perceive the same truth? There are undoubtedly some interesting psychological factors at work here (and some libertarians, like Andre Spies, are exploring this issue). A further aspect of interest is undoubtedly the infuence of 'popular culture', which, while despised by the statist intelligentsia, constitutes the real cultural 'alternative' or 'underground' of the 20th century.

The cultural mainstream for this century has been as much dominated by anti-libertarian ideas as the politico-economic mainstream. It has been characterised by the ethos of an 'Age of Defeat', as Colin Wilson has put it in one perceptive book of that title, of 'the unheroic hypothesis' or the 'discussion of triviality'. Doctrines of naturalism or realism echo collectivism's social determinism. The traditional novel of manners evokes mainly boredom. Literary and stylistic experimentation seem devoted to little but 'disillusionment, cynicism, disgust and gnawing envy' or in 'making delicate picture-puzzles out of the butt-ends of life', as the American literary critic Henry A. Murray has put it. A large part of literary and cultural enterprise has also been characterised, in the words of John Weightman in 'The Concept of the Avant-Garde', by 'the flight from reason' — a 'disgust . . . with the idea of science', evocations of perceptual and epistemological chaos, and embodiments of crackpot philosophies and cults.

In many of the young libertarians I meet as Secretary of the Libertarian Alliance and the Adam Smith Club I have found an enormous alienation from the products of 'establishment' or 'mainstream' or 'high' culture (whatever we chose to call it), or, to be more accurate, from its 20th century manifestations. As Ayn Rand put it in her essay 'The New Enemies of the Untouchables', 'When a culture is dominated by an irrational philosophy, a major symptom of its decadence is the inversion of all values'. Rational moral values, a life-affirming sense of life, a voluntaristic image of man, have been preserved in what Rand calls the 'bootleg' forms of romanticism, in the adventure, detective, thriller and science-fiction genres. It is no accident that the Frankfurt School Marxist Max Horkheimer con-temptuously referred to the 'rhetoric of individuality' within popular culture. It is no mere rhetoric. There are no social determinist apologies for crime in the 'Dirty Harry' films, only a love of justice and sympathy for the victim. Individual integrity, honour, justice: these are the core values in so much popular culture, from the Italian westerns to films on the Eastern martial arts. It is particularly in science fiction, however, that we find those specific values that Professor Peter Gay, in his definitive *The Enlightenment: An Interpretation*, attributed to the original Enlightenment, 'the recovery of nerve' in humanity's potential and destiny, 'the celebration of industry', science, and technology.

It is notable that for countless libertarians like me it has been popular culture, and especially science-fiction, that have influenced and emotionally sustained us. Leading science-fiction authors like Robert Heinlein, Poul Anderson, Jerry Pournelle, Larry Niven, and F. Paul Wilson, among many others, consistently dramatise themes relating to the issues of rationalism versus superstition, progress versus reaction, freedom and individualism versus socialism and authoritarianism.

It is also significant that socialism, having failed to deliver the goods, is increasingly abandoning the mantle of science. Its predominant tone is now one of doom-mongering, of hysterical prophecies of environmental disaster and the limits to growth, of rabid technophobia* and opposition to progress and science. Indeed,

[246]

some like Robert Heilbroner explicitly call for a return to a neo-feudal, no-growth system in which a superstitious populace are manipulated — for their own good and that of 'nature', of course — by a new priestly class of ecologists. The original Enlightenment identified itself 'with sound method, progress, success, the future', declared Professor Gay. The inspiration many libertarians find in science-fiction and their enthusiastic commitment to the vision and role of science makes the name of 'the New Enlightenment' even more opposite.

The Future

What are the prospects for this New Enlightenment? There is no inevitability in history. And while scientific paradigms generally move in the direction of increasing credibility and truth, the broader socio-political community is somewhat different from the scientific community. The scientific community has characteristics which provide an impetus to the discovery of the truth. The socio-political community, unfortunately, has characteristics which, to say the least, are not especially amenable to change. Special interest groups, the 'tax eaters' who use the political means of state power to exploit their fellows, are going to be less than objective in examining either the justice or the consequences of their mode of existence, as John Burton has shown so illuminatingly in his recent essay 'The Instability of the Middle Way'.

Nevertheless, there is a power to truth. We have a powerful emergent libertarian synthesis — the beginnings of a 'science of liberty' — that explains the anomalies of statism and offers a research programme of enormous promise. But it is entirely on us as individuals, on our dedication and commitment to political and intellectual struggle, that the prospects for ideological victory depend.

Glossary: short definitions

Reductionism
Doctrines or analysis that attempt to reduce one type of phenomenon to a more basic one: in this context, doctrines which deny the reality or importance of human consciousness and explain human behaviour in allegedly more basic biological, physiological or chemical terms.

Determinism
Any doctrine which denies human free will and claims that human behaviour is determined by external or internal forces — such as society or specific social institutions, the economy, racial character, etc.

Historicism
That variant of determinism which attempts to explain human history by

[247]

unalterable historical laws, and predicts future developments on the basis of these alleged laws.

Naturalism
In this context that school of the novel characterised by its adherence to a pessimistic materialistic determinism.

Realism
In this context the literary viewpoint which holds that literature (or art in general) should reflect reality — conceived in pessimistic terms.

Voluntaristic
Philosophic approaches which, contrary to determinism, stress human free will and automony.

Methodological Collectivism and Holism
The approach in social science that treats 'wholes' (like society, the economy, capitalism, class, the nation, the race) as entities in themselves, understandable without reference to their real constituent parts (individuals).

Epistemology
The branch of philosophy which studies the basis of human knowledge.

Metaphysics
The branch of philosophy which studies the nature of reality.

Aesthetics
The branch of philosophy which studies the nature of art and the artistic experience.

Materialistic
In this context the doctrines which deny human consciousness and posit the reality only of material entities.

Scepticism
The philosophic view which denies the possibility of real knowledge.

Nihilism
The denial of ethical values.

Utilitarian
In this context the classic view that morality should be based upon the 'greatest good for the greatest number'.

Consequentialist
The view that actions should be judged morally by their immediate consequences.

Positivism
The general term for philosophical and methodological positions that stress the 'factual' aspects of knowledge, its basis in immediate sensation or observation.

Neo-Aristotelian
A revised version of the philosophical approach of Aristotle.

Technophobia
The extreme fear of, and aversion to, technology and technological civilisation.

Appendix

WHAT TO READ

CHRIS R. TAME

Such is the vigour of the libertarian revival that, as in my essay, this sketch covers only the broad outlines of its literature. I have had to omit major writers and subjects (for example, the important rediscovery and extension of classical liberal class analysis and exploitation theory). Nevertheless, this bibliographical essay gives some taste of the scope and abundance of the new libertarianism.

It will, I think, prove useful to new and young adherents of libertarianism. It would perhaps be sanguine to hope that it might prompt some of the journalistic, political and academic opponents to read these works. For far too long there has been an absence of real political debate. The socialist and Marxist intellectual establishment still seems overwhelmingly content to either ignore its opponents, or to engage in abusive caricatures of the 'right' (including libellous fabrications intended to portray libertarians as covert racists, etc.).

On 'Left' and 'Right'

The best discussion of the origins and ambiguity of the left/right spectrum are in Murray N. Rothbard, 'Left and Right: The Prospects For Liberty', *Left and Right: A Journal of Libertarian Thought*, Spring 1965; Samuel Brittan, *Left or Right: The Bogus Dilemma*, Secker and Warburg, London, 1968; *idem*, 'Further Thoughts on Left and Right', in *Capitalism and the Permissive Society*, Macmillan, London, 1973; and the perceptive comments by Elie Kedourie, 'The History of Ideas and Guilt By Association', in *The Crossman Confessions and Other Essays in Politics, History and Religion*, Mansell Publishing, London, 1985.

To confuse things further it was indicative of the 20th century decline of liberal ideas and values that in the United States the very word liberalism reversed its meaning. Originally it designated an ideology of individualism and anti-statism but became expropriated by the 1920s by advocates of collectivism and statism. Ironically, the term 'conservative', which originally designated an anti-rationalist and anti-individualist philosophy which glorified 'communal' values, tradition, authority or the nation, became applied to libertarians (much to their justifiable horror). The Conservative Party in Britain has eventually come to include some libertarians as well as real conservatives.

The Enlightenment, Old and New

The best general study of the Enlightenment remains Peter Gay's *The Enlightenment: An Interpretation*, 2 vols., Weidenfeld and Nicolson, London, 1967, 1970. My essay, 'The Revolution of Reason: Peter Gay, The Enlightenment, and the Ambiguities of Classical Liberalism', *The Journal of Libertarian Studies*, Vol. 1, No. 3, Summer, 1977, explores the libertarian significance of the period.

'The New Enlightenment' has also been chosen by David Graham as the title for the six-part television series about the liberal revival being made by his company, Diverse Productions, for Channel 4 in Britain, probably on an American educational TV channel and for worldwide distribution. It was also independently conceived and employed in Jerome Tuccille's penetrating *Who's Afraid of 1984?*, Arlington House, New Rochelle, New York, 1975, pp. 209-215.

On Michael Polanyi

A good overview of Polanyi's philosophy can be found in *Meaning*, with Harry Prosch as co-author, University of Chicago Press, 1975. Another useful general work is Richard Gelwick, *The Way of Discovery: An Introduction to the Thought of Michael Polanyi*, Oxford University Press, 1977. Polanyi's major philosophical works are *Personal Knowledge: Towards a Post-Critical Philosophy*, Routledge, London, 2nd edn., 1962, and *Knowing and Being* (edited by Marjorie Grene), Routledge and Kegan Paul, London, 1969.

The economic insights of his *The Logic of Liberty* and *The Contempt of Freedom: The Russian Experiment and After*, Watts, London, 1940, were further extended and integrated with the Austrian School view on economic calculation by Paul Craig Roberts in *Alienation and the Soviet Economy*, New Mexico University Press, Albuqueque, New Mexico, 1971. Other scholars were influenced by Polanyi in philosophy and the life sciences, as shown in Marjorie Grene (ed.), *The Anatomy of Knowledge*, Routledge, London, 1969; *Toward a Unity of Knowledge*, International Universities Press, New York, 1969; *Interpretations of Life and Mind*, Routledge, London, 1971.

[253]

The Scientistic Fallacy

Two representative examples of the scientistic, social self-regulation position are Wesley Clair Mitchell, 'Intelligence and the Guidance of Economic Evolution', in Mitchell *et al., Authority and the Individual,* Harvard University Press, 1937; H. Levy, *The Universe of Science,* Watts, London, 1932, p. v. For of brevity my essay did not discuss Friedrich Hayek's critique of scientism in his *The Counter-Revolution of Science,* Allen and Unwin, London, 1952, nor the fruitful personal and intellectual relationships between Hayek, Popper and Polanyi.

Murray Rothbard's 'The Mantle of Science', in H. Schoeck and J. W. Wiggins (eds.), *Scientism and Values,* Van Nostrand, Princeton, New Jersey, 1960, provides an incisive critique of the pseudo-scientific nature of 'scientism' and of the conformity of libertarianism with the premises and nature of real science. A forthcoming work by Don Lavoie develops this analysis in more detail. The concept of libertarianism as 'the science of freedom' can be found in Murray Rothbard, *Egalitarianism As A Revolt Against Nature,* Libertarian Review Press, Washington, D.C., 1974, p. x. Interestingly, the phrase is also used by Peter Gay as the subtitle for the second volume of his study of the original Enlightenment.

On Sir Karl Popper

Popper's classic work on the theory of knowledge and the philosophy of science remains *The Logic of Scientific Discovery,* Hutchinson, London, 1959, but readers are also referred to his *Conjectures and Refutations,* Routledge, London, 1963, and *Objective Knowledge,* Clarendon Press, Oxford, 1972. More directly addressing political issues are *The Open Society and Its Enemies,* 2 vols., Routledge, London, 1945 and *The Poverty of Historicism,* Routledge, London, 1944, P. A. Schilpp (ed.), *The Philosophy of Karl Popper,* 2 vols., Open Court, La Salle, Illinois, 1974, contains a collection of papers about Popper's work, as well as his own 'Replies to my Critics' and an 'Intellectual Autobiography'. John Gray, 'The Liberalism of Karl Popper', *Government and Opposition,* Vol. 11, No. 3, Summer 1976, p. 339 (reprinted as *Scientific Notes,* No. 2, Libertarian Alliance, London, 1985) provides an interesting account of the unity of Popper's philosophical and political approaches. A fascinating comparison of the similarity between the Popperian concept of science and the market process can be found in Bill Stoddard, 'The Scientific Method as an Application of Economics', *Scientific Notes,* No. 1, Libertarian Alliance, London, 1985.

On Arthur Koestler

Koestler's anti-reductionism is elaborated in 'Of Dogs and Men', 'Of Geese and Men', 'Of Apes and Men', and 'The Poverty of Psychology' in *Drinkers of Infinity: Essays, 1955-1967*, Hutchinson, London, 1968, and A. Koestler and J. R. Smythies (eds.), *Beyond Reductionism: New Perspectives in the Life Sciences*, Hutchinson, London, 1969. A good overview of his work can be found in Koestler's *Janus: A Summing Up*, Hutchinson, London, 1978. In spite of his rejection of Marxism and his penetrating remarks on the 'delusionary streak' in human behaviour that leads to self-identification with mythical collectivities, Koestler remained politically naive: Stephen Toulmin, 'Arthur Koestler's Theodicy: On Sin, Science and Politics', *Encounter*, February, 1979.

On Humanistic Psychology

Major works in humanistic psychology and therapy include: Abraham Maslow, *Motivation and Personality*, Harper and Row, New York, 1954 and *Toward A Psychology of Being*, Van Nostrand, Princeton, New Jersey, 2nd edn., 1968; Carl Rogers, *On Becoming A Person*, Houghton Mifflin, Boston, 1961, and *Client-Centred Therapy*, Houghton Mifflin, Boston, 1951; Sigmund Koch, 'Psychological Science Versus The Science-Humanism Antinomy: Intimations of a Significant Science of Man', *American Psychologist*, Vol. 16, No. 10, October, 1961, 'Reflections on the State of Psychology', *Social Research*, Vol. 38, No. 4, Winter, 1971; Sidney M. Jourard, *The Transparent Self*, Van Nostrand, Princeton, New Jersey, 1964; Joen Fagan and Irma Lee Shepherd (eds.), *Gestalt Therapy Now*, Penguin Books, Harmondsworth, Middlesex, 1972; William Glasser, *Reality Therapy*, Harper and Row, New York, 1965; Albert Ellis, *Reason and Emotion in Psychotherapy*, Lyle Stuart, New York, 1962; Viktor Frankl, *The Will To Meaning*, Souvenir Press, London, 1971; Robert Assagioli, *Psychosynthesis*, Turnstile Press, Wellinborough, Northants, 1975.

Viktor Frankl, in *Man's Search For Meaning: An Introduction to Logotherapy*, Beacon Press, Boston, 1959, pp. 136-7, sums up the temper of the humanistic movement:

> Man is ultimately self determining. . . . What he becomes — within the limits of endowment and environment — he has made out of himself. In the concentration camps, for example, in this living laboratory and on this testing ground we watched and witnessed some of our comrades behave like swine while others behaved like saints. Man has both potentialities within himself; which one is actualized depends on decisions but not on conditions.

The Libertarian Psychologists

Frank G. Goble, *The Third Force*, Grossman, New York, 1970; Peter Breggin, *The Psychology of Freedom: Liberty and Love as a Way of Life*, Prometheus Books, Buffalo, New York, 1980. Nathaniel Branden, *The Psychology of Self-Esteem*, Bantam Books, New York, 1971, *Breaking Free*, Bantam Books, New York, 1972, *The Disowned Self*, Bantam Books, New York, 1973, *The Psychology of Romantic Love*, J. P. Tarcher, Los Angeles, 1980, *Honoring the Self: Personal Integrity and the Heroic Potentials of Human Nature*, J. P. Tarcher, Los Angeles, 1983.

Thomas Szasz's works are so voluminous that it is invidious to have to select the major ones: *The Myth of Mental Illness*, Paladin Books, London, 1972, *Ideology and Insanity*, Calder and Boyars, London, 1973, *The Ethics of Psychoanalysis*, Routledge, London, 1973.

On the Concept of the Paradigm

Thomas Kuhn, *The Structure of Scientific Revolutions*, Chicago University Press, 2nd edn., 1970. His concept of the paradigm has been put to fruitful libertarian use by Murray Rothbard in 'Ludwig von Mises and the Paradigm For Our Age', in *idem, Egalitarianism as a Revolt Against Nature*, Libertarian Review Press, Washington, D.C., 1974, and by Roy Childs in 'Liberty and the Paradigm of Statism', in Tibor Machan (ed.), *The Libertarian Alternative*, Nelson-Hall, Chicago, 1974.

On the Chicago School of Economics

Yale Brozen, 'The Revival of Traditional Liberalism', *New Individualist Review*, Spring, 1965, p. 6, surveys the early empirical Chicagoite work. Brozen has also edited a valuable anthology of Chicago scholarship, *The Competitive Economy*, General Learning Press, Morristown, New Jersey, 1975.

My 'The Chicago School: Lessons From the Thirties For The Eighties', *Economic Affairs*, Vol. 4, No. 1, October, 1983, might be helpful in understanding the nature of Chicagoism.

Milton Friedman's work is wide-ranging. Classic examples can be found in Milton Friedman and Anna J. Schwartz, *A Monetary History of the United States, 1867-1970*, Princeton University Press, 1963; *Essays in Positive Economics*, University of Chicago Press, 1953 and *Capitalism and Freedom*, University of Chicago Press, 1962.

There is a huge body of confirmatory scholarship on 'monetarism' by English and American economists.

Thomas Sowell, *Race and Economics*, Longman, London, 1975, and

The Economics and Politics of Race, William Morrow, New York 1983; and Walter Williams, *The State Against Blacks,* McGraw Hill, New York, 1982, are examples of the Chicago approach applied to this issue.

Both *The Journal of Political Economy* and *The Journal of Law and Economics* are indispensible sources of Chicago analysis, as are the publications of the Institute of Economic Affairs and the journal *Economic Affairs* in Britain.

The Public Choice School

The literature of the 'public choice' or 'economics of politics' extension of the Chicago School is now becoming as numerous as that of its intellectual progenitor: for example, D. C. Mueller, *Public Choice,* Cambridge University Press, 1979; Gordon Tullock, (ed.), *Politics of Bureaucracy,* Public Affairs Press, Washington, D.C., 1964; *idem, The Vote Motive,* Institute of Economic Affairs, London, 1976; Gordon Tullock and Robert D. Tollison (eds.), *The Theory of Public Choice: Political Applications of Economics,* Michigan University Press, 1972. Introductions can be found in Arthur Seldon, *The New Economics,* Study Guide No. 2, Libertarian Alliance, London, 1985 and Charles Rowley and Arthur Seldon, *A Primer in Public Choice,* Basil Blackwell, Oxford, forthcoming.

The public choice school is in turn part of a broader phenomenon of 'economic imperialism', the vindication of the relevance of economics to the analysis of all aspects of human and social existence: Richard B. McKenzie and Gordon Tullock, *The New World of Economics: Explorations into the Human Experience,* Richard D. Irwin, Homewood, Illinois, 2nd edn., 1978.

The Austrian School of Economics

The great representatives of the Austrian School in the 20th century are Ludwig von Mises and Frederick Hayek. As with most of the Austrians both men were polymaths, political and social philosphers as much as economists. Representative works by them are von Mises, *Human Action,* 3rd rev. edn., Henry Regnery, Chicago, 1966, and *Liberalism,* Sheed Andrews and McMeel, Kansas City, 1978; Hayek, *Individualism and Economic Order,* Routledge and Kegan Paul, London, 1949; *The Constitution of Liberty,* Routledge and Kegan Paul, London, 1960. His three-volume *The Fatal Conceit,* Routledge and Kegan Paul, is awaited.

Recent restatements of the Austrian School approach are E. G. Dolan (ed.), *The Foundations of Modern Austrian Economics,* Sheed and Ward, Kansas City, 1976; L. M. Spadaro (ed.), *New Directions in*

[257]

Austrian Economics, Sheed, Andrews and McMeel, Kansas City, 1978; M. J. Rizzo (ed.), *Time, Uncertainty, and Disequilibrium: Exploration of Austrian Themes,* Lexington Books/D. C. Heath, Lexington, Mass., 1979; L. S. Moss (ed.), *The Economics of Ludwig von Mises: Toward A Critical Reappraisal,* Sheed, Andrews and McMeel, Kansas City, 1976; G. P. O'Driscoll, Jr., *Economics as a Coordination Problem: The Contributions of F. A. von Hayek,* Sheed, Andrews and McMeel, Kansas City, 1977; Alex Shand, *The Capitalist Alternative: An Introduction To Neo-Austrian Economics,* Harvester Press, Brighton, 1984; W. Duncan Reekie, *Markets, Entrepreneurs and Liberty: An Austrian View of Capitalism,* Harvester Press, Brighton, 1984.

Learning the Lessons of Experience

Martin Anderson, *The Federal Bulldozer,* M.I.T. Press, Cambridge, Mass., 1964, was the classic case of the American 'liberal' learning from reality. Anderson's conversion to libertarianism is discussed in Beatrice Hessen, 'Review of *The Federal Bulldozer',* *The Objectivist,* April 1966, pp. 11-12.

On the so-called neo-conservatives, see Nigel Ashford, 'The Neo-Conservatives', *Government and Opposition,* Vol. 13, No. 3, Summer, 1981; also Norman Podhoretz, *Breaking Ranks: A Political Memoir,* Harper and Row, New York, 1979; Irving Kristol, *Two Cheers For Liberalism,* Basic Books, New York, 1978; Daniel P. Moynihan, 'Where Liberals Went Wrong', in Melvin Laird (ed.), *The Republican Papers,* Doubleday, Garden City, New York, 1968. In my view this trend would be better characterised by a label like 'revisionist liberalism' or 'chastened liberalism'. The growth of a new realism about the effects and potential of state power was manifest in the work of many who were not necessarily perceived as neo-conservatives: for example, Professor Jay Forrester at the Massachusetts Institute of Technology. Forrester described what he called 'the counter-intuitive behaviour of social systems' that 'should make us cautious about rushing into programs on the basis of short-term humanitarian impulses. The eventual result can be anti-humanitarian. . . . At times government programs cause exactly the reverse of the desired result' — in 'The Counterintuitive Behaviour of Social Systems', *Reason,* Vol. 3, Nos. 4 and 5, July and August 1971; also Charles Murray, *Losing Ground: American Social Policy, 1950-1980,* Basic Books, New York, 1984.

Other works on the crisis in American 'liberalism' were Theodore J. Lowi, *The Politics of Disorder,* Basic Books, New York, 1971; Milton Mayer, *Man v. The State,* Center for the Study of Democratic Institutions, Santa Barbara, California, 1970; Matthew P. Dumont, 'Down the Bureaucracy!', *Trans-Action,* Vol. 7, No. 12, October, 1970;

William Pfaff, *Condemned to Freedom*, Random House, New York, 1971. In my monograph 'In Defense of the City: The Rise of Urban Revisionism', *Study Guide* No. 3, Libertarian Alliance, London, 1985, I discuss similar developments — like the work of Jane Jacobs — in urban studies.

The New Left and Liberty

On the libertarian aspects of the American New Left, see Ronald Hamowy, 'Left and Right Meet', *New Republic*, 12 March 1966. An example of such quasi-libertarianism can be found in Hal Draper, 'Neo-Corporatism and Neo-Reformers', *New Politics*, Fall, 1961, and 'The Two Souls of Socialism', *Our Generation*, January 1969. The most detailed examination of this subject can be found in my *Contemporary American Radicalism: The Left, The Right, and the State*, B. A. Dissertation, Department of American Studies, The University of Hull, 1969 (unpublished).

Ayn Rand and Objectivism

Ayn Rand called her distinctive philosophy 'Objectivism'. Her major novels are *The Fountainhead*, Panther Books, London, 1961 and *Atlas Shrugged*, New American Library, New York, 1957. Amongst her major non-fiction works are *The Virtue of Selfishness*, New American Library, New York, 1964, and *Capitalism: The Unknown Ideal*, New American Library, New York, 1967; *The New Left: The Anti-Industrial Revolution*, New American Library, New York, 1971; *Philosophy: Who Needs It?*, Bobbs Merrill, New York, 1982. A major biographical study, *The Passion of Ayn Rand*, by Barbara Branden is forthcoming. I provide a brief introduction in 'The Moral Case For Private Enterprise', in Cecil Turner (ed.), *The Case For Private Enterprise*, Bachman and Turner, London, 1979.

Virtually the only exception to the academic philosophical establishment's haughty attitude to Rand was the head of the University of Southern California's School of Philosophy, Dr John Hospers. He discussed her ideas in his popular philosophy textbook, *An Introduction to Philosophical Analysis*, Routledge, London, 2nd edn., 1967. He also wrote an excellent introduction to libertarianism, *Libertarianism: A Political Philosophy For Tomorrow*, Nash Publishing, Los Angeles, 1971. Among the younger professional philosophers influenced by Rand are Tibor Machan, *Human Rights and Human Liberties*, Nelson Hall, Chicago, 1975, Douglas J. Den Uyl and Douglas B. Rasmussen (eds.), *The Philosophic Thought of Ayn Rand*, University of Illinois Press, Urbana, Illinois, 1984; David Kelley,

The Evidence of the Senses, Louisiana University Press, forthcoming; Leonard Piekoff, *The Ominous Parallels: The End of Freedom in America*, Stein and Day, New York, 1982.

On Robert Nozick

His *Anarchy, State and Utopia*, Basil Blackwell, Oxford, 1975, is indispensible. His essay, 'On the Randian Argument', is reprinted, together with a reply by Den Uyl and Rasmussen, in Jeffrey Paul (ed.), *Reading Nozick*, Basil Blackwell, Oxford, 1983.

Major Works in Contemporary Libertarianism

The anarcho-capitalist school of libertarianism can be found expounded from an Austrian approach (combined with a natural rights philosophy) in Murray Rothbard, *For A New Liberty*, Collier-Macmillan, New York, 2nd edn., 1973, and *The Ethics of Liberty*, Humanities Press, Atlantic Highlands, New Jersey, 1982; from a Chicago (and largely utilitarian) approach in David Friedman, *The Machinery of Freedom*, Arlington House, New Rochelle, 1978. Other major works include M. and L. Tannehill and J. Wollstein, *Society without Government*, Arno Press, New York, 1972; Jerome Tuccille, *Radical Libertarianism: A New Political Alternative*, Harper and Row, New York, 2nd edn., 1971; Harry Browne, *How I Found Freedom In An Unfree World*, Macmillan, New York, 1973; Tibor Machan (ed.), *The Libertarian Alternative*, Nelson-Hall, Chicago, 1974, and *The Libertarian Reader*, Rowan and Littlefield, Totowa, New Jersey, 1982; David Osterfeld, *Freedom, Society and the State*, University Press of America, New York, 1983. Henri Lepage in *Tomorrow, Capitalism*, Open Court, La Salle, Illinois, 1982 and Geoffrey Sampson, *An End To Allegiance: Individual Freedom and the New Politics*, Maurice Temple Smith, London, 1984, also provide useful introductions.

The Cultural and Literary Dismensions

Colin Wilson's *The Age of Defeat*, Gollancz, London, 1959, and *The Strength To Dream*, Gollancz, London, 1962, have provided telling criticisms of the prevailing negativity of 'establishment' culture. Robert Conquest has penned dissenting essays on literary and aesthetic matters, many gathered in *The Abomination of Moab*, Maurice Temple Smith, London, 1979.

Tom Wolfe, a vigorous libertarian conservative, has extended his witty and caustic cultural portraits (of such social phenomena as 'radical chic') to more systematic criticism in *The Painted Word*,

Farrer Straus Giroux, New York, 1975 and *From Bauhaus to Our House*, Jonathan Cape, London, 1982.

The most influential work has been Ayn Rand's *The Romantic Manifesto*, New American Library, New York, 1971. Much of the critical and literary work stimulated by her writing has so far appeared only in fugitive publications. The most distinguished is currently *Aristos: The Journal of Aesthetics* (P.O. Box 1105, Radio City Station, New York, New York, 10101, USA).

On Progress and Science

The literature of doom-mongering and statist 'ecology' is enormous. Heilbroner's *The Human Prospect*, Norton, New York, 1974, is representative. I offer a detailed critique of Heilbroner's significance, in *Environmentalism and Totalitarianism: An Obituary For Modern 'Liberalism'*, Libertarian Alliance, London, 1985.

Libertarians have produced a voluminous literature outlining the fallacies of hysterical environmentalist, 'no growth' and anti-nuclear movements. My essay on Heilbroner provides a bibliography of this literature. Given the hysteria and ignorance on the subject, I feel constrained to recommend Professor Peter Beckmann's *The Health Hazards of Not Going Nuclear*, Golem Press, Boulder, Colorado, 1976.

Some Useful Addresses

The major sources of free-market analysis and policy proscription are, respectively, The Institute of Economic Affairs, 2 Lord North Street, Westminster, London, SW1, and the Adam Smith Institute, 50 Westminster Mansions, Little Smith Street, London, SW1. The world's largest selection of libertarian books is at The Alternative Bookshop, 3 Langley Court, Covent Garden, London, WC2. The major libertarian group in Europe is The Libertarian Alliance, c/o 3 Langley Court, Covent Garden, London, WC2. The Alliance produces a stream of Political Notes, Economic Notes, Philosophical Notes, Cultural Notes, Sociological Notes, Study Guides, etc., as well as other pamphlets and *Free Life* magazine. It also holds regular meetings, seminars and conferences.

Readers interested can explore the literature of individual liberty further in my *A Bibliography of Freedom*, Centre For Policy Studies, London, 2nd edn., 1980.

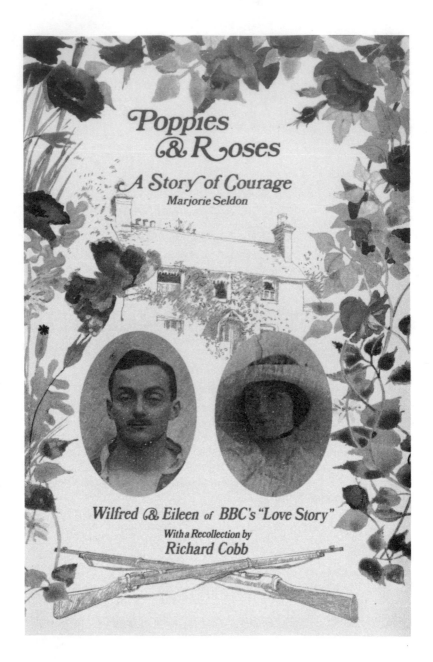

Poppies & Roses

A Story of Courage

Marjorie Seldon

Wilfred & Eileen of BBC's "Love Story"

With a Recollection by
Richard Cobb

E & L Books'

First Title

Poppies & Roses

A Story of Courage by Marjorie Seldon

'A vivid and haunting picture of English village life in the 20's and 30's through the eyes of a child.' *T.V. (South)*

'. . . a book of great charm.' *Sunday Telegraph*

'. . . village life charmingly recalled.' *Daily Mail*

'The true portrait of a casualty of the war to end wars.' *The Listener*

'Frank, fluent and highly readable.' *County*

'. . . Her portrait of life in the village of Matfield is valuable in itself . . . the real interest lies in Wilfred's conversion to Socialism . . .' *New Society*

'. . . The author captures the soft Southern countryside.' *Yorkshire Post*

'Mrs Seldon's observant eye and occasionally caustic tongue recall at times Mrs Gaskell's CRANFORD.' *Bygone Kent*

'One of those memoirs which outdo most novels as works of insight . . .' *Alexander Baron, novelist and television dramatist* (Jane Eyre, Oliver Twist, etc.)

— and many more broadcasts and press reviews.